Architectures

New Interventions in Art History

Series editor: Dana Arnold, *University of Southampton*

New Interventions in Art History is a series of textbook mini-companions – published in connection with the Association of Art Historians – that aims to provide innovative approaches to, and new perspectives on, the study of art history. Each volume focuses on a specific area of the discipline of art history – here used in the broadest sense to include painting, sculpture, architecture, graphic arts, and film – and aims to identify the key factors that have shaped the artistic phenomenon under scrutiny. Particular attention is paid to the social and political context and the historiography of the artistic cultures or movements under review. In this way, the essays that comprise each volume cohere around the central theme while providing insights into the broader problematics of a given historical moment.

Art and Thought
  edited by *Dana Arnold and Margaret Iversen* (published)

Art and its Publics: Museum Studies at the Millennium
  edited by *Andrew McClellan* (published)

Architectures: Modernism and After
  edited by *Andrew Ballantyne* (published)

After Criticism: New Responses to Art and Performance
  edited by *Gavin Butt* (forthcoming)

Envisioning the Past: Archaeology and the Image
  edited by *Sam Smiles and Stephanie Moser* (forthcoming)

Architectures
Modernism and After

Edited by Andrew Ballantyne

© 2004 by Blackwell Publishing Ltd

350 Main Street, Malden, MA 02148-5020, USA
108 Cowley Road, Oxford OX4 1JF, UK
550 Swanston Street, Carlton, Victoria 3053, Australia

The right of Andrew Ballantyne to be identified as the Author of the Editorial
Material in this Work has been asserted in accordance with the UK Copyright,
Designs, and Patents Act 1988.

First published 2004 by Blackwell Publishing Ltd

Library of Congress Cataloging-in-Publication Data

Architectures : modernism and after / edited by Andrew Ballantyne.
     p. cm. — (New interventions in art history ; 3)
  Includes bibliographical references and index.
    ISBN 0-631-22943-4 (hardcover: alk. paper) — ISBN 0-631-22944-2 (pbk. :
alk. paper)
    1. Architecture, Modern—19th century. 2. Architecture, Modern—20th
century. I. Ballantyne, Andrew. II. Series.
    NA62 .A733 2004
    724′.5—dc21

                         2003008642

A catalogue record for this title is available from the British Library.

Set in 10.5/13 pt Minion
by Graphicraft Limited, Hong Kong
Printed and bound in the United Kingdom
by MPG Books Ltd, Bodmin, Cornwall

For further information on
Blackwell Publishing, visit our website:
http://www.blackwellpublishing.com

Contents

List of Illustrations

Notes on Contributors

Andrew Ballantyne is Professor of Architecture at the University of Newcastle upon Tyne. He has held research and teaching posts at the universities of Sheffield and Bath, and is now Director of the Centre for Tectonic Cultures at Newcastle. His previous books include *Architecture, Landscape and Liberty* (1997), *What is Architecture?* (2002), and *Architecture: A Very Short Introduction* (2002). He is currently working on *Architecture as Experience* (forthcoming, 2004).

Elizabeth Cromley is an architectural historian with a special interest in the vernacular landscape. She teaches in the Architecture Department at Northeastern University in Boston, Massachusetts. In addition to her book on New York apartments (*Alone Together*, 1990), she has published on the resorts of the Catskill Mountains; practices of home renovation; the history of Riverside Park in New York City; and the use of Native American motifs in decorative arts. She was American editor for the history of design handbook, *The Elements of Style* (1996), edited by Stephen Calloway, and has co-edited two volumes in the series "Perspectives in Vernacular Architecture" with Carter Hudgins. Her most recent work is a co-authored book with Thomas Carter, *Invitation to Vernacular Architecture* (forthcoming, 2004).

Andrew Law is a PhD candidate in the Department of Geography at the University of Newcastle upon Tyne. He is currently completing his doctoral thesis on conservation of the built environment in Britain, and is looking at groups such as the Society for the Protection of Ancient Buildings, the Georgian Group, the Victorian Society, and the Civic Trust. He is centrally interested in Englishness and with related issues of social class, landscape, heritage, and identity. He is currently writing an article on "The Revival of the Arts and Crafts in Landscapes of Class and Englishness."

Gerard Loughlin is Senior Lecturer in Religious Studies at the University of Newcastle upon Tyne. He has teaching and research interests in religion and film and is the author of *Alien Sex: The Body and Desire in Cinema and Theology* (forthcoming, 2004).

Sarah Menin is Lecturer in the School of Architecture, Planning, and Landscape at the University of Newcastle upon Tyne, and a member of the Centre for Tectonic Cultures, researching and writing on modern architectural history, and the creation and perception of architectural place. She has published extensively on correlations between music and architecture in the work of Aalto and Sibelius. She is the author (with Flora Samuel) of *Nature and Space: Aalto and Le Corbusier* (2002), a book which utilizes Donald. W. Winnicott's psychoanalytical theories, and is the editor of *Constructing Place* (2003), a book of essays which address the mind and matter of place-making.

Simon Sadler is Assistant Professor of Architectural and Urban History at the University of California, Davis. His publications explore radical tendencies in late twentieth-century architecture. He is the author of *The Situationist City* (1998) and the co-editor of *Non-Plan* (2000). He is currently working on a new book, *Amazing Archigram*.

Brenda and Robert Vale both work at Auckland University, New Zealand. Their publications include *The Autonomous House* (1975) and *Green Architecture* (1991). They have also written numerous academic publications and contributed to many international conferences on sustainable buildings and energy. Their most recent book is *The New Autonomous House* (2000). This provides a concentrated discussion of the issues involved in designing the UK's first autonomous house and explains why the design decisions were made. They are currently working on another book, *The Sustainable House in New Zealand*.

Stephen Walker teaches architecture at the University of Sheffield. His research examines the boundaries between architecture and other art practices. He has published a number of articles on Gordon Matta-Clark, about whom he is currently preparing a monograph. He is also in the process of editing a collection of works and essays on architecture and the contemporary body. This draws together contributions from a wide variety of disciplines, and is entitled *Body-Space*.

David Wood is Lecturer in the School of Architecture, Planning, and Landscape, and a member of the Global Urban Research Unit (GURU), at the University of Newcastle upon Tyne. He is also Managing Editor of *Surveillance and Society*, the international journal of surveillance studies. His current research interests include the social effects of digital surveillance technologies; science fiction and surveillance; the militarization of the city and social life; permaculture and innovative sustainable rural and urban planning and design solutions; landscape and ecology in science fiction; and orbital space policy.

Series Editor's Preface

New Interventions in Art History was established to provide a forum for innovative approaches to, and new perspectives on, the study of art history in all its complexities. This volume expands the horizons of the series to consider recent developments in architecture from a range of interdisciplinary perspectives.

The survey begins with a discussion of the impact of mechanization and industrialization on the production and consumption of the built environment in the mid-nineteenth century, and a consideration of the term "historicism" and its implications for the writing of histories of architecture. The following chapters present moments when the languages of the architecture of the past respond to cultural circumstance by their presence or apparent absence. In this way, revivalist, modern, and postmodern architecture is presented as part of a continuing dialogue between aesthetic criteria and social and cultural imperatives.

The history of architecture is a complex interplay between patterns of living, consideration of what is good architectural form, and what technical means can be deployed. It can seem satisfactory to summarize the architectural achievements of an age with a unified canonical corpus of works, but closer examination reveals that plurality and diversity are indeed very evident. The architecture-world is not coherent and unified, and its histories are plural and diverse. The object is not to arrive at an authoritative "standard" or consensus view of architecture, but to show that different views throw into prominence quite different sets of landmarks to navigate between. In this way, the concerns of this collection of essays both run parallel to and intersect with the broad intellectual base of the series which questions the established frameworks with which we discuss the visual.

The essays provide a rigorous interrogation of the architecture by writers from a variety of disciplines, including architects, geographers, and theologians, as well as architectural historians. It is hoped that this book will provoke future research and debate which will expand the discourses of architecture. As such, *Architectures: Modernism and After* is a very welcome and timely addition to the volumes in this series.

Dana Arnold
London, March 2003

Preface

Architecture is the cultural aspect of buildings, and it happens when buildings and people meet. The essays gathered in this volume put in the fore-
ground various processes in which buildings and architecture are involved,
including education, sustainability, and self-sacrifice. In each chapter
architecture is considered from a different point of view, and from one
chapter to another there is an implied shift in the very idea of what architecture is. Sometimes it seems to be importantly engaged with social issues,
but sometimes it seems to escape them, or to be irresponsible. Sometimes
it seems to be the preserve of an elite, but at others it seems important that
it should belong everywhere, even in the humblest home. Between the
essays there is a sense of volatility, quite at odds with the solidity of buildings and the internal coherence of the perspectives in individual pieces.

The essays are mostly about twentieth-century buildings and twenty-
first-century concerns, sometimes with a longer historical sweep, so that,
for example, we can see the Crystal Palace as a twentieth-century building
that happened to be built in the middle of the previous century, though it
makes better historical sense to argue that the bulk of twentieth-century
architecture was a working-out of nineteenth-century ideas. The title of
the Introduction, "Architectures in the Plural," is an allusion to one of
Michel de Certeau's books, *La culture au pluriel*,[1] which rehearsed, back in
the 1970s, ideas that now seem to be very widespread in cultural studies,
but are still relatively little explored by architectural historians. Architecture
is plural because culture is plural. Each culture produces its own response
to a given object, and in doing so generates a swarm of architectures.

Andrew Ballantyne

Note

1 Michel de Certeau, *La culture au pluriel* (Paris, 1974; 2nd edn, ed. Luce Giard, Editions du Seuil, 1994); trans. T. Conley, *Culture in the Plural* (Minneapolis, MN: Minnesota University Press, 1997).

Introduction: Architectures in the Plural

Andrew Ballantyne

Singing the Habit of Energy

The great machines of the nineteenth century were expressive and thrill-ing. The industrial machines in the factories made a din and produced goods in fantastic quantity to a reliable standard. Locomotives stoked with fire hurtled across the countryside, trailing smoke, linking places that before had been remote from one another. Cities spread, and were blackened by the soot that they produced, so the outskirts on the wind-ward side became the better places to live. The industrial sublime included the engines of infrastructure, such as the huge pumps associated with reservoirs, that could move vast quantities of water, driven by pistons that could crush a man indifferently without hesitation in their thunderous rhythm.

Nineteenth-century machines could make the earth tremble and seemed to be driven by their own imperatives that were as unflinching as the forces of nature, and as unarguable. Where architecture was concerned, it seemed as if the decent thing to do was to mask them with a cloak of respectability. "What is the beauty of a building to us today?" asked Nietzsche in 1878, "The same thing as the beautiful face of a mindless woman: something mask-like."[1] The cotton mills around Manchester, which pounded out fine fabrics, were given towers and turrets, and dressed to look super-ficially like the palaces of a new aristocracy. The thunderous engines that drew into St Pancras Station in London were screened from the city by a cavalcade of pinnacles and pointed arches.

The sublime is never quite polite. Victor Hugo found it in the sewers of Paris, on which he expatiated at length in *Les misérables*, before going on to make use of them in his narrative.[2] In the abstract he thought of them as a farmer might, as taking good fertilizer away from the city, and wasting it by dispersing it in the river and the sea. In their concrete evocation they are the setting for traumatic and gruesome events. In Hugo's day they were still a novelty. For every artistic celebration of the sublimity of infrastructure and machinery in the nineteenth century, there is a whole district of buildings to hide it in. We have, for sure, Joseph Turner's *Rain, Steam and Speed* (1844), but it is a remarkable exception, not a typical picture of the age. Thackeray remarked that "The world has never seen anything like this picture."[3]

Where buildings are concerned the same story can be told. The great building of industrial construction of the mid-nineteenth century was the Crystal Palace of 1851, which became one of the wonders of the age, precisely because the world had never seen its like. It amazed the crowds who flocked to see it, but John Ruskin, the most prominent architectural critic of the day, was not prepared to concede that it made any contribution to the development of architecture. Samuel Laing, the chairman of the Crystal Palace Company, in his address to the Queen at the opening, had claimed that the building ushered in "an entirely novel order of architecture,"[4] and Ruskin claimed that, in doing so, Laing was voicing "the popular view of the facts . . . one which has been encouraged by nearly all the professors of art of our time."[5] To judge by the buildings that were put up during the rest of the nineteenth century, this was certainly an exaggeration. The consensus view among the classes who actually commissioned buildings was much more like Ruskin's own. He was not willing to admit that the Crystal Palace was architecture. "We suppose ourselves to have invented a new style of architecture," he said, "when we have only inflated a conservatory!"[6] Moreover, his voice was not among those asking for a new architecture:

> We want no new style of architecture . . . But we want *some* style. It is of marvellously little importance, if we have a code of laws and they be good laws, whether they be new or old, foreign or native, Roman or Saxon, or Norman, or English laws. But it is of considerable importance that we should have a code of laws of one kind or another, and that code accepted

and enforced from one side of the island to another, and not one law made the ground of judgement at York and another in Exeter. And in like manner it does not matter one marble splinter whether we have an old or new architecture truly so called or not; that is, whether an architecture whose laws might be taught at our schools from Cornwall to Northumberland, as we teach English spelling and English grammar, or an architecture which is to be invented fresh every time we build a workhouse or a parish school . . . Originality in expression does not depend on invention of new words . . . A man who has the gift, will take up any style that is going, the style of his day, and will work in that, and be great in that, and make everything that he does in it look as fresh as if every thought of it had just come down from heaven.[7]

This position is receptive to a degree of novelty in architectural ideas, but stylistically conservative, not because of any failure of the imagination, but as a matter of principle. As a position it can be used to account for how most nineteenth-century architecture looks, when we look back on it with hindsight. Given that the Crystal Palace was such a huge popular success, it is surprising how little impact it had on the artistic productions of its own day. It was not imitated by architects, and had a greater presence in Russian literature than in English. For the Russians it was a symbol of modernization that reminded them of their own backwardness; so, for example, Dostoevsky's reaction to it mixed a certain dazzled admiration with a sense of being reproached by it. It had in his mind an oppressive authority. "I am afraid of this edifice," he said, "because one could not stick out one's tongue at it on the sly."[8] The building is the source of the Modernist vision of a spiritualized glass architecture, developed by Bruno Taut and others,[9] but at the time that it was built it was seen as belonging exclusively to the cultural province of the engineers, and so far as architects were concerned it was beyond their pale.

There is a distance between noticing the technical possibilities of building and their cultural assimilation. It is the cultural assimilation that makes it possible to use the buildings gesturally, and for them to become architecture. It is not necessarily the case that a new technical possibility ever will be culturally assimilated into architecture. A new system of construction might be used experimentally, with satisfactory results, but never be taken up more generally. A building's services, such as its ventilation ducts, can be incorporated invisibly into the building, hidden away behind ceilings, or they can be used gesturally, by making them visible and painting them bright colors. Nineteenth-century theaters, for example, often had sophisticated ventilation systems, using huge gas burners up above ceiling level to heat the air, which therefore rose up out of the building through vents, and lowered the air pressure in the auditorium, so fresh air was drawn in lower down. All this happened out of sight. What the theatergoer saw was a ceiling covered in decorative plasterwork, with a great chandelier hanging down from it. Around the edge of the ceiling's central area there would be a ring of pierced metal, which might seem to be there to embellish the decorative scheme, but which acted as a grille to allow the passage of air. The mechanisms of the building were incorporated into a decorative scheme that derived from rococo ballrooms, and could be lost among the ornament. There are nineteenth-century buildings where mechanisms and structures are more evident, but they were buildings where the usual decorum did not apply. In polished architecture it was seen as necessary to clothe the building in a fabric that showed knowledge of admired buildings of the past, so that the new building reflected some of their accomplishment, and showed that the building securely belonged in polite company.

At some point this changed. The Italian Futurists were successful in drawing attention to the cult of the machine as an object of aesthetic interest. They sang "the love of danger, the habit of energy and fearlessness," and affirmed that "The world's magnificence has been enriched by a new beauty: the beauty of speed. A racing car whose hood is adorned with great pipes, like serpents of explosive breath – a roaring car that seems to ride on grapeshot is more beautiful than the *Victory of Samothrace*."[10] This dates from 1909, when the motor car was still a novelty, and compares the machine with a masterpiece of Hellenistic sculpture, the canonic reputation of which is all the more secure for its being in the Louvre. The art of ancient Greece had been revered for as long as there had been anything that called itself "civilization," and the Futurists' displacement of it from the pinnacle of aesthetic achievement was intentionally radical.

If their message had not struck a chord with others, then we would have forgotten them long ago. If they were noticed at all now, then they would be seen as adolescents letting off steam, in a way that is mischievous rather than important. The enthusiasm for the machine, to which they gave early expression in the art world, was not theirs alone, but was taken up by others in various ways, in architecture most famously by Le Corbusier, who called the house a *machine à habiter* ("machine for living") and designed what he called a "Citrohan" house for mass production – the name evoking the automobile manufacturer "Citroën."[11] By the middle of the twentieth century it seemed feasible to think that we were living in the "machine age," as if machines were now the planet's dominant life-form, and if that were so, then it was proper that art and architecture should give expression to the fact.[12]

If we subscribe to this view and look back at the nineteenth century, then what we see is a story of progress, as the burgeoning machine age took shape, first of all in technological devices that made new things possible, but which had no presence in the world of polite culture, where art, architecture, and literature belonged. It was only later that the truth of the machine was allowed its full glorious expression, without being disguised by the irrelevant trappings of historically derived ornamentation. On this view buildings such as the Crystal Palace are prophetic. They are treated as if their designers could see the future, and being exceptionally gifted, they built it early. In such a mind-set, the Crystal Palace belongs more truly to the realm of architecture than the general run of nineteenth-century buildings, even though this was not recognized at the time. Ruskin, being blind to the building's epoch-making qualities, becomes a critic of marginal interest, whose time has passed.

The way in which architects routinely use the word "historicist" is to mean the use of historical ornament, in buildings that would be better without it;[13] and it is a term that is never used of buildings older than the nineteenth century. It somehow seems to be accepted that eighteenth-century architects would imitate Palladio, or that eleventh-century church builders would aspire to build Roman vaults, but after the Crystal Palace had shown the way forward, then it was somehow irresponsible of architects not to follow where it led. On this view "historicism" is plainly a bad thing, something that architects learned to cast off, and the story of architecture from the middle of the nineteenth century onwards is the story of how it was cast off, first in the case of exceptional buildings, later more generally, as even mainstream buildings could "be themselves" without being seen as barbaric or uncultivated.

Historicism, Irony, and Redescription

The problem with this view of the matter is that it tells us nothing at all about the sensibilities of nineteenth-century architects, or any other nineteenth-century people, which might be a legitimate concern for an historian of nineteenth-century architecture. What it tells us is what in the nineteenth century was of interest to later architectural commentators.

This connects with another use of the same word, "historicism," in the sense that Karl Popper used it in his book *The Poverty of Historicism*, where again "historicism" is a bad thing.[14] Its title is an allusion to Karl Marx's *Poverty of Philosophy*, and its principal aim is to show that, for strictly logical reasons, the future cannot be known. Popper was particularly driven to dismantle the Hegelian sense of destiny that underpinned some of Marx's writings, and the book is dedicated to the "memory of the countless men and woman of all creeds or nations or races who fell victim to the fascist and communist belief in Inexorable Laws of Historical Destiny."[15]

In this sense of the word, much of the architectural historiography of the later twentieth century was historicist, even when it condemned the use of historical ornament in modern buildings. David Watkin made a study of Popper's kind of historicism in writings about architecture, especially in texts by Nikolaus Pevsner and Sigfried Giedion, two of the most authoritative and influential critics read by twentieth-century architects.[16] On Popper's reading, it is an abuse of history to suppose that we can use it to predict the future. In ancient Greek legend, Oedipus killed his father. He did not know that the man he fought was his father, and the reason for that was that he had been cast away as an infant because it had been predicted that he would kill his father. Without the prediction, the event would not have happened: Oedipus would have recognized his father, and would not have killed him. Popper coined the term "Oedipus effect" for "the influence of a prediction upon the predicted event (or, more generally, for the influence of an item of information upon the situation to which the information refers), whether this influence tends to bring about the predicted event, or whether it tends to prevent it."[17] Historicism in this sense is something that any rigorous historian would take pains to avoid falling into. It is nevertheless used when an historical account is set out with a view to establishing the validity of a particular "next step forward." In such cases, even when the historical method is flawed, one might in practice be prepared to indulge the author if the case presented were supportive of a cause that one endorsed. It might after all persuade an audience to do the right thing. If the historical account supported an unacceptable course of action then the methodology's incoherence would be very evident. Popper's argument theoretically makes all such uses of history unpersuasive for those who have read him, independently of whether the ends to which they are used are good or bad.

There is a third sense of the term "historicist" in circulation, which means something else again, and this time the term can cheerfully be adopted by those to whom it is applied, as descriptive of their approach. It is set out very clearly and embraced by those whose work it describes. It is set out clearly and concisely by James Conant, in an essay about Richard Rorty, whose position he is here describing:

> Historical processes are not governed by laws. They are fundamentally *contingent*, influenced by human agency and unforeseeable chance events. Historical understanding is always *situated* and necessarily coloured by our present values and interests. Historical accounts are stories we tell to pro- vide a coherent narrative about who we are and how, through interacting with each other and the world, we got here. Such stories are inherently *retrospective* – each community in each age will tell the story differently – and they are *constructed*. The only sense in which a historical narrative can "get things right" is by telling a story which proves to be both acceptable and enabling to the members of a community; and the only sense in which one such narrative can be "better" than another is – not by offering a more faithful description of the objective sequence of events, but rather – by *redescribing* the events in a novel and helpful way.[18]

Conant's italics here signal words that are used in a particular sense and have special importance in Rorty's vocabulary. It is plain that the histor- icism embraced by Rorty steers clear of the historicism condemned by Popper. There is no "destiny," but some things happen, while others do not. Some of the things that did not happen, might have happened, with- out violating any law. A rigorous history will do its best to take account of any relevant evidence, but the evidence that is relevant will depend on the story to be told. And the stories that we tell each other and ourselves will depend on who we think we are and what we are trying to do.

The collection of essays gathered in this volume was shaped by a con- cern to explore a range of possible ways of conceiving architecture, and to show a variety of possibilities for the kind of story one can tell. Each essay tells us something about an aspect of architecture, and is in accordance with some kind of evidence: the facts that each essay makes use of should all be verifiable and correct. Each, however, generates its own world of facts, which may be incommensurable with others. There is little mention of architectural style here. The essays tend to deal with processes rather than discussing buildings as finished objects. Some essays discuss aspects of the production of architecture, while others discuss aspects of its consumption – which is to say, the ways in which it is used. In them we are often a long way from common sense, the received wisdom of the age.

Here again it is helpful to draw on Rorty's vocabulary and position myself as an "ironist," which means the same thing as an "anti-essentialist" in the vocabulary of critical theory.[19] The essentialist conflates common sense with self-evident truth, and mistakes ingrained habits of mind for reasoning. Architecture is complex and can be approached in many different ways, and no single way can make an exclusive and permanent claim on our understanding. Some ways, however, have been used repeatedly, and have yielded up as much of interest as they are likely to do, while others, such as those presented here, can open up fresh possibilities and new directions in enquiry.

The process of *redescription*, mentioned above, is at the heart of the enterprise. We redescribe a building (or whatever) when we situate it in a story that is not the habitual story of routine common sense. A single building can be redescribed in many different ways, and when that happens it will have various different cultural connotations, and can therefore be said to produce different architectures. The Crystal Palace, for example, was both a shimmering vision of future possibility, and a nightmarish reproach. It was experienced as a radically different kind of thing by Ruskin, Dostoevsky, and Samuel Laing (of the Crystal Palace Company), who seems to have had the general public on his side. "The Crystal Palace" as a cultural construct, which is to say as architecture, was quite distinct in each of their redescriptions, even though they were all looking at one and the same building.[20] A building's cultural value is volatile, and will depend on the story into which it is asked to fit.

In a given culture (or "community," to use Rorty's word for it) there will be various shared points of reference, which everyone involved in that culture is more or less expected to know. These are the landmarks that give us our bearings in the culture, and while some of them may be personal and idiosyncratic, others are known to everyone who seems to belong to that culture, and they therefore come to have the status of a canon. For example, the traditional canon of Western architecture would certainly include such buildings as the Parthenon in Athens and the Pantheon in Rome, and we would be surprised if a Western architectural historian had not heard of them.

If culture these days seems to be more pluralist than in the past, it is at least partly because we now feel that a wider range of people have a right to make their voices heard.[21] At times there seems to be a very great gulf between educated and popular culture, but it is often the case that an individual who has a highly developed "high culture" view in one field, turns out to have a "popular" view in another, and there are "low-brow" and "high-brow" ways of engaging with any given cultural artifact. For example, a recent film aimed at a popular audience, *Minority Report* (2002, directed by Steven Spielberg and starring Tom Cruise), was discussed at some length in *The Times Literary Supplement* under the heading "The Commodification of Paranoia."[22] (The narrative is, incidentally, about a self-fulfilling prophecy, and is a clear example of the "Oedipus effect" in action.) There is a "high culture" of architecture, and, while it is not altogether unified, there is a surprisingly high degree of consensus among architects as to which buildings are important and which ones beside the point. It is a consensus that breaks down somewhat as we look at buildings of the recent past, but even there we can find a general acceptance of examples of "good design" of buildings, which can be quite different from what the generality of public opinion would have selected. In just the same way as there can be a distance between "serious" and "popular" music, there can be a distance between the buildings that are promoted by the architectural profession as representing "good design" and those that are intuitively enjoyed by others. "Architect" is a protected title, and can only be used by someone who has completed an extended course of socialization in the architecture-world, developing a range of knowledge and skills, and usually being formed with a certain range of tastes and proclivities in design.

A Modernist Canon

There is scope for a Modernist academy, which would take iconic examples of twentieth-century buildings into its canon, and include such important "precursors" as the Crystal Palace. It would be possible for such a school to work in much the same way as the old École des Beaux-Arts used to, with the students learning to incorporate gestures from Le Corbusier into their work, instead of learning their repertoire from Roman ruins. There is plenty of evidence that this is just how architects give meaning and status to their work. If I look out of my window here at the university (and it is a *fenêtre longue*, as promoted by Le Corbusier) I can look across to a building raised on *pilotis*, with bands of window running across it, and a balcony inset near the top which brings some columns into view and makes the top part of the building echo the general arrangement of the Villa Savoye (but in bands of brickwork rather than white stucco).

Robert Venturi and Denise Scott Brown have drawn attention to the way in which various prominent buildings have echoed the massing of Le Corbusier's monastery of La Tourette.[23] And La Tourette is echoed again in the headquarters building that Richard Meier designed for the French television company Canal +. One side overlooks the Seine and is highly glazed, but the other has narrow strip windows at eye-height, apparently held up by cuboid blocks. These buildings make use of form in such a way as to show that they are immersed in the culture of the architecture-world, in just the same way as late eighteenth-century buildings showed knowledge of recent publications of the antiquities of Athens. On another reading, though, Modernism is concerned not with the transmission of a culture of approved building form, but with constant re-invention and experiment. The idea of an avant-gardist academy is more problematic, and is examined in Simon Sadler's essay (chapter 1). How does one transmit a culture of unorthodoxy?

In the nineteenth century there was a fierce debate about architectural style, with outlandish claims made for the merits of classical or Gothic architecture. By the early years of the century there was already, within the general view of classicism, the idea that the ethos of ancient Greece had a high cultural value, and drew together the artifacts and way of life in that society in an ideal way that should be emulated if at all possible.[24] The artistic products of ancient Greece, and even everyday objects, were caught up in the ideal way of life and could therefore be valued, alongside the morals, philosophy, and literature. The crucial point here is that the artistic products were seen to be intimately linked with the way of life, so that there was a conflation of ethics and aesthetics. In theory it might be possible to follow an ideal "Greek" line of thought, and come up with a highly original artifact that responded in an entirely appropriate and harmonious way to the changed culture and circumstances of the present day. (On the other hand, what architects did much more readily was to incorporate recognizably "Greek" elements in their designs: Doric columns, meanders, acanthus leaves.)

This kind of argument was taken up by A. W. N. Pugin, who displaced the Greek paganism with Christian morality and argued in favor of "Christian or pointed architecture," by which he meant what we think of as Gothic.[25] With the construction of the Palace of Westminster from 1836 he seemed perhaps to have won the argument, but in 1857 George Gilbert Scott's Gothic designs for the new Foreign Office building in Whitehall were rejected by the Prime Minister, Lord Palmerston, who wanted a classical design. The controversy that followed became known as the "battle of the styles." Scott kept the commission but changed the design for the Foreign Office to an Italianate style.

It was against the background of such stylistic disputations that Ruskin wrote, apparently believing that the outcome of the battle would not be crucial to the quality of the architecture. In France, Eugène Viollet-le-Duc proposed that a new nineteenth-century style of architecture would develop from the serious consideration of new building materials, especially iron, and the Art Nouveau movement of the 1890s was an attempt to overcome traditional stylistic quarrels by proposing a fresh start and an architecture derived from first principles. The great success of the Modernist architecture of the 1920s stemmed at least in part from the fact that it could be presented as the resolution of these, by then traditional, problems. The quarrel about which historical ornament was best was dispatched by saying that all historical ornament was to be avoided. The exorbitant cost of Art Nouveau decoration was avoided by favoring machine-produced artifacts and mass-produced housing. The spirit of the age revealed itself through the machine, and anything that did not engage with the imperative to make this manifest in·the world was beside the point and could be ignored.

Sigfried Giedion's hugely influential work, *Space, Time and Architecture: The Growth of a New Tradition*, located the new architecture in a cultural framework that showed why it had to be taken seriously.[26] The story he told showed how the new architecture was prefigured in such buildings as the Crystal Palace and the Eiffel Tower, and, going further back, how the fluid sense of space to be found in open-plan interiors was prefigured in Baroque churches. Giedion's story therefore shows how, by looking at the architecture of the past, we can see how it points the way to the future. The book was revised and more buildings were included once they had been built, fulfilling the prophecy. As architectural polemic, persuading architects to design in a particular way, the book was staggeringly successful. As history it is methodologically dubious, and "historicist" in Popper's sense.[27] As an account of nineteenth-century architecture it is extraordinary because it involves ignoring almost all nineteenth-century architecture, acknowledging only the very few buildings that helped him to make his points, while neglecting to draw attention to the fact that they were exceptional rather than typical, and would not have been accepted as belonging in the architecture-world of the nineteenth century, when they would have been seen as the work of engineers. On this view of architectural history, the eighteenth-century's rational decorum was set aside by the architects of the nineteenth century, who went careering off on an erratic course, and things were brought to rights and a sobriety restored in the 1920s.

One thing that was not undermined in the course of this change was the way in which the buildings that found their way into the history books, defining epochs and styles, tended to be a procession of cathedrals and palaces: buildings for the bourgeois elite who could afford to follow fashions in architecture, which has always been an expensive thing to do. Individual architects, such as Michelangelo and Christopher Wren, worked for princes, popes, and financiers, and were seen as heroes and geniuses. Some of the projects presented in *Space, Time and Architecture* were more modestly aimed at housing less wealthy people, but the majority were for modern princes – the captains of industry and commerce, in their public and private capacities. Modernism was stylistically but not politically radical. Indeed, Le Corbusier in *Vers une architecture* makes it explicit, with his slogan "architecture or revolution," which promises that the stylistic change will make unnecessary the radical political change that might otherwise be on the way.[28]

Giedion's book had tremendous influence in giving shape to a Modernist canon that was generally accepted in the architectural profession and in the schools of architecture, even if it went unnoticed elsewhere. There was a politics of inclusion and exclusion from this orthodoxy (which Colin St John Wilson has examined)[29] that shifted a little as the book went through its various editions, and it expanded to include some of the more serious omissions, such as Alvar Aalto, who was allowed in as an "irrationalist." There is no doubting the quality of Aalto's buildings, or the fact that he deserves to be treated as the equal of Le Corbusier and Mies van der Rohe, but, as Sarah Menin's essay (chapter 2) shows, the presentation of architecture as the work of heroic individualist geniuses is far from being the whole story. She examines the role of others, specifically of women, in the production of Aalto's work. It involved love, hero-worship and self-sacrifice on their part, but gave him the emotional support that he needed in order to produce the work that he did.

Gerard Loughlin's essay (chapter 3) is a parallel analysis of one of the great hero-monsters of fiction: the architect Howard Roark, from the novel *The Fountainhead* by Ayn Rand.[30] Rand gives us a compelling portrayal of a particular complex of ideas embodied in the figure of the architect whose only drive in life is to see his vision realized in the world. Nothing else really matters to him. He was inspired by the real architect Frank Lloyd Wright, whose egomania was notorious, but Rand's fictional character's progress is uncomplicated by Wright's foibles and setbacks. Rand was born in Russia, detested the collectivism of the Soviet era, and, after emigrating to the US, made it her mission to promote the cult of the strong individual.

The narrative describes the triumph of the architect's will, and has disturbing overtones because it was written before the defeat of fascism in Europe; it was published in 1943 when fascism was still mobilizing populations by means of the exhortations of charismatic, iron-willed leaders. It remains compelling because it sees its ideas through to their conclusion without compromise, or any sentimental concessions to weak-minded human feeling. Its psychology is breathtakingly politically incorrect and out of tune with the liberal consensus that now predominates. The fictional portrait makes Aalto's actual behavior look relatively reasonable, or at least comprehensible given his human weaknesses. Whether one judges the sacrifices made by those close to Aalto to have been worthwhile will depend on one's scale of values, as the loads in the scales cannot be measured in the same units. How much human suffering can legitimately be weighed against artistic accomplishment? And does it help, or make matters worse, if those who suffer are one's closest companions rather than unseen minions? If the ethos of production is to see a happy team at work, does one then lose the vision, commitment, and drive to see the very best work realized?

A Radical Orthodoxy

The story that Brenda and Robert Vale outline in their essay (chapter 4) proposes a radically different agenda for the assessment of the qualities of buildings, by judging them against the criterion of sustainability. The "green" agenda is now an orthodoxy for thoughtful, educated people in the West, and the recycling of bottles and refrigerator coolants is fairly routine. For architecture, the implications are so radical that they almost amount to undoing the discipline. Nietzsche called for "the revaluation of all values,"[31] and the project of sustainability calls for something equally radical if it is to be thoroughgoing.

The architectural works that have dazzled and amazed across the centuries have all been extravagant in their ways, from the pyramids and Stonehenge onwards. The societies that produced the buildings we admire spent vast quantities of their resources on them, whether it be money, labor, or materials. If in the third millennium BC, our forebears had taken the decision that it would, given the circumstances, have been potentially ruinous folly to undertake an enterprise such as the building of Stonehenge, then they would, very reasonably, have decided not to go ahead with the project, and its absence would not have been felt. Nor would these forebears have been remembered. People decided that in fact the undertaking was worth it. We do not know now who these people were, still less what their motives were for building, but given the state of development of technology and civil society at that time, it certainly amounted to a major undertaking, and must have consumed all that the society could spare. It was in all probability the most extravagant thing that could have been done at the time.

The same can be said of the procession of cathedrals and palaces that are the backbone of the story that is told in conventional architectural history. If we look at this story from the point of view of sustainability, then what we see is a story of one reckless extravagance after another, and it will look like a catalog of awful warnings, not of fine examples to emulate. The technical criterion for establishing merit (does the building make effective use of the earth's resources, or does it dissipate them extravagantly?) could lead to a new canon being established, throwing into prominence the works in which the general project makes a leap forward. In fact, the tendency is to call into question the very idea of artistic merit in buildings because it almost inevitably leads to the expenditure of more resources on a building without in itself bringing any improvement in the technical criterion being used as the basis of valuation. The Sistine Chapel would not be artistically improved by being better insulated. Michelangelo's embellishments made no significant difference to its technical performance, but did use up some materials and energy. The point to be made here is that, as the issues connected with sustainability become increasingly important in international politics, as they have done steadily over the past thirty years, then the kind of story that the Vales set down here is one that it is increasingly necessary for us to hear. At some point a change in consciousness could mean that the heroes of the traditional canon, whether classical, Gothic, or Modernist, will all come to be seen as contributing to a reckless headlong rush into the abyss, and to have helped to sustain the momentum of a mechanism that is hurtling us all toward destruction. At that point the scale of values suddenly inverts, and yesterday's heroes become today's specious monsters.

Sacrifice

What, then, makes sense of this extravagance? It has been so deeply traditional in buildings that it seems unlikely that we shall be able to shake it
off in a generation or two. The great theorist of extravagance was Thorstein
Veblen, who published his masterwork *The Theory of the Leisure Class* in
1899. He coined the term "conspicuous consumption," and proposed that
the value system that he could observe in operation in those of the highest
social rank around him could be understood with reference to the idea.
The more wastefully one consumed, the higher the honor and status that
would accrue in consequence. Buildings had their part to play, especially
religious buildings:

> Obviously, the canon of conspicuous waste is accountable for a great por-
> tion of what may be called devout consumption; as, *e.g.*, the consumption of
> sacred edifices, vestments, and other goods of the same class. Even in those
> modern cults to whose divinities is imputed a predilection for temples
> not built with hands, the sacred buildings and the other properties of
> the cult are constructed with some view to a reputable degree of wasteful
> expenditure. And it needs but little either of observation or introspection –
> and either will serve the turn – to assure us that the expensive splendour of
> the house of worship has an appreciable uplifting and mellowing effect
> upon the worshipper's frame of mind. It will serve to enforce the same fact
> if we reflect upon the sense of abject shamefulness with which any evidence
> of indigence or squalor about the sacred place affects all beholders. The
> accessories of any devout observance should be pecuniarily above reproach.
> This requirement is imperative, whatever latitude may be allowed with regard
> to these accessories in point of aesthetic or other serviceability.
>
>   It may also be in place to notice that in all communities, especially in
> neighbourhoods where the standard of pecuniary decency for dwellings is
> not high, the local sanctuary is more ornate, more conspicuously wasteful in
> its architecture and decoration, than the dwelling-houses of the congrega-
> tion. This is true of nearly all denominations and cults, whether Christian
> or Pagan, but it is true in a peculiar degree of the older and maturer cults.
> At the same time the sanctuary commonly contributes little if anything to
> the physical comfort of the members. Indeed, the sacred structure not only
> serves the physical well-being of the members to but a slight extent, as
> compared with their humbler dwelling-houses; but it is felt by all men that
> a right and enlightened sense of the true, the beautiful and the good demands
> that in all expenditure on the sanctuary anything that might serve the comfort

of the worshipper should be conspicuously absent . . . There are few persons of delicate tastes in the matter of devout consumption to whom this austerely wasteful discomfort does not appeal as intrinsically right and good.[32]

This is very close to the view that Ruskin expressed in 1849 at the beginning of his *Seven Lamps of Architecture*. The first of his "lamps," or guiding principles of architecture, was "sacrifice" (the others being truth, power, beauty, life, memory, and obedience). It is part of Ruskin's definition of what architecture is, as distinct from building, that it includes an element of sacrifice, or extravagance:

Let us, therefore, at once confine the name [of architecture] to that art which, taking up and admitting, as conditions of its working, the necessities and common uses of the building, impresses on its form certain characters venerable or beautiful, but otherwise unnecessary. Thus, I suppose, no one would call the laws architectural which determine the height of a breast-work or the position of a bastion. But if to the stone facing of that bastion be added an unnecessary feature, as, a cable moulding, that is Architecture. It would be similarly unreasonable to call battlements or machicolations, architectural features, so long as they consist only of an advanced gallery supported on projecting masses, with open intervals beneath for offence. But if these projecting masses be carved beneath into rounded courses, which are useless, and if the headings of the intervals be arched and trefoiled, which is useless, *that* is Architecture. It may not be always easy to draw the line so sharply, because there are few buildings which have not some pretence or colour of being architectural; neither can there be any architecture which is not based on building, nor any good architecture which is not based on good building; but it is perfectly easy, and very necessary, to keep the ideas distinct, and to understand fully that Architecture concerns itself only with those characters of an edifice which are above and beyond its common use. I say common; because a building raised to the honour of God, or in memory of men, has surely a use to which its architectural adornment fits it; but not a use which limits, by any inevitable necessities, its plan or details.[33]

Extravagance is the piety of architecture, and its defining feature. It was exactly the expenditure of excess that raised the building above the level of mere utility, and allowed it a place in the realm of art. In Veblen's world it is this sacrifice that makes the building "pecuniarily decent" for polite society. It is traditionally the most extravagant buildings that bring their builders glory. Very tall buildings are never the most efficient in terms of land use, but it is possible for them to be commercially viable because people are prepared to pay higher-than-usual sums of money to work in them because of the prestige that they bring. They bring prestige also to the cities in which they are sited, and this is undoubtedly a significant factor in their being built. The tallest buildings in the world from the Woolworth Building to the Sears Tower were in the US, and something significant changed when they were overtopped by the Petronas Towers in Kuala Lumpur, funded by Malaysia's then rapidly developing economy. The significance had nothing to do with the buildings' effectiveness in providing accommodation, but in the extravagant display. The Bible describes an early example of this yearning for glory in the project to build the tower of Babel, on a plain in the land of Shinar: "Come," they said, "let us build ourselves a city and a tower with its top in the heavens, and make a name for ourselves . . ."[34]

There is no question that the extravagant building was for the sake of reputation, not for the sake of the accommodation it would provide. The way to win respect was to devote one's excess to non-utilitarian ends. This notion was explored in a wide-ranging way by Georges Bataille (1897–1962) in a work on political economy, *The Accursed Share*.[35] It opens with a section headed "The Dependence of the Economy on the Circulation of Energy on the Earth," which is remarkable for a work of its date, before the rise in oil prices that brought energy up the political agenda in the early 1970s.[36] Architecture, especially extravagant non-utilitarian architecture, has an important role in this economy because it takes energy out of useful circulation and either burns it up or embodies it in buildings from which it cannot be released. A particularly pure and direct sacrifice was staged as an art event, when one million pounds worth of bank notes were set on fire.[37] The procedure involved is usually less direct, but non-utilitarian deeds in general amount to a sacrifice of the energy involved, and the point connects strongly with the issues in Brenda and Robert Vale's essay (chapter 4). The tower of Babel and the Petronas Towers are sacrifices every bit as exuberant as that of the Aztec priest, ripping the still-beating heart from his victim and holding it out to the sun.[38] Indeed, the Aztec's ziggurat, on which the sacrifice took place, involved the consumption of much more energy than could be had from a single man through his working life, and it was therefore a greater sacrifice to build the temple than to dispatch the man, who was chosen for his beauty and treated like a lord for the year before his death. The whole point of sacrifice is to sacrifice the best, not the most negligible.

Stephen Walker draws on Bataille's ideas about sacrifice in his essay on Gordon Matta-Clark (chapter 5), an artist who worked with houses, taking them out of the realm of utility, and making them unusable by slicing them apart in visually and viscerally arresting ways. In fact, though, the usual way in which buildings enter into the general economy of sacrifice is by consuming lives and resources in their construction rather than in their destruction. Insurance companies can put a figure on the number of lives statistically likely to be lost in a construction project, and there is a monument in Simcoe Park in Toronto (by John Scott and Derek Lo, 2001) that aims to heighten awareness of the dangers of the building site and the sacrifices made of people who work there. A low wall carries small plaques, each one naming a construction worker killed on a building site, one from each of the past hundred years. A life-size bronze figure dressed as a construction worker seems to be at work adding another name to an empty plaque. We know from statistics that the death will happen, but we (as a society) do not suspend building operations. Therefore, although individually we might be horrified to think it, nevertheless, collectively we might be said to will the sacrifice.[39]

Off Limits

The powerful mechanisms that seemed so characteristic of nineteenth-century machinery are still evident on the building site, and they are still in their way driving things along. The enthusiasm for machinery, which was avant-garde when the Futurists expressed it, has now been absorbed, finding its fullest architectural expression in the "hi-tech" movement of the 1970s and early 1980s.[40] Buildings continue to be technical mechanisms, of course, but the fact that they are such no longer seems to make the best architects as excited as it did. We now tell ourselves that we are in the digital age, or the information age, and heavy machinery no longer seems to embody its spirit. Where the most impressive nineteenth-century machines had a monumental presence, today's most impressive devices have no determined form and are often invisible to human eyes.

The atom became culturally and symbolically enormously important from August 6, 1945, when the first atomic bomb was dropped, destroying the city of Hiroshima. The conversion of matter into energy had moved from being arcane theoretical physics, to being a military secret, to being central on the world stage. The astonishing power source was harnessed for peaceable civilian ends in nuclear power stations, which have not proved to be the unequivocal blessing that it once seemed they might be. The excitement about events at the molecular scale does not easily translate into convincing architecture. The Atomium in Brussels, an exhibition structure in the form of a vastly enlarged molecule, is an understandable response, but lame because it remains a large engineering structure in the same nineteenth-century tradition that gave us the Eiffel Tower and the Crystal Palace. It does nothing extraordinary at the molecular level, but makes a crude representation of a tiny thing at 165 billion times life-size. It is fun, but its significance is as an index of the state of culture at the time, not as an application of any of the technical breakthroughs on the path that led us from the bomb to genetic modification. Nanotechnology does not work at 165 billion times life-size.

Buildings have not been able to join the tendency to miniaturize because people have remained resolutely more or less the same size that they have always been. As the subsidiary technology has become more manageable, it has become less directly expressive. Large rooms in old houses used to need large fires to heat them, and some parts of the room would be more comfortable to be in than others. Nowadays, we can arrange for the heating to be invisible and constant across even a very large room. If there is an elaborate fireplace then its role is largely or completely symbolic.

The building complex that is the subject of David Wood's study in chapter 6 is calculated to be inexpressive. It is shrouded in secrecy and surrounded by razor wire. Some of the buildings are earth sheltered, which makes them visually blend in with the natural scenery. Visually the more arresting elements of the ensemble are geodesic domes, which shelter and screen sensitive apparatus that tracks satellites. They help to mask the activities of the base, and, if we are to understand them architecturally, then we should see them as a gesture of concealment. For the viewer who comes across them, there are various possible redescriptions, as Wood explains. He also sets out the "official" story of the base, which takes us away from Rorty's neopragmatist philosophy into the world of practical politics, where redescription is usually called "spin."

The essay serves strongly to make the point that the different redescriptions are not value-neutral and interchangeable. Some might be benign, but others might be seen as unhelpful, challenging, or dangerous. The power politics that then come into play can be supportive of one description, undermining of another.[41] The intellectual mechanism here is the same as that involved in making a poetic image – remember that it was

Shelley who propounded the idea that poets are the unacknowledged legislators of the world.[42] What is at stake here is not aesthetic pleasure, but a much fiercer contestation of meaning, which makes something like poetry into a matter of life and death, just as the Romantics told us it was. Our "spin doctors" have dispensed with any avowed concern with the aesthetic appeal of their descriptions, but they are the heirs of Shelley's original legislators.

Gaston Bachelard (1884–1962) made a celebrated series of studies of the poetic imagination. His enterprise had as its starting-point a concern that "poetic" apprehensions of things might influence the ways in which scientists think. For example, if one imagines the gentle application of heat with reference to images of digestion, then one might be found specifying a stomach-shaped vessel as suitable for gentle heating, and this raised the question of how "objective" scientific thinking can be said to be.[43] His first book in this line of thought was *The Psychoanalysis of Fire* (1938).[44] The one with most direct application to architecture is *The Poetics of Space* (1958) which shows us how we imagine and have come to value certain sorts of spaces.[45] The cellar and the attic are not interchangeable rooms, but engage our imaginations in different ways.

New Domesticities

A traditional dwelling in the French countryside, such as the one that Bachelard took as his model, would have had far more in it than the "presentable" rooms that one expects in a modern urban apartment. They might take up as little as a quarter of the volume of the building. Alongside there would typically be a barn and other outbuildings. The roof space that ran across the whole building could be huge, with a visible structure of heavy beams and the underside of the roof-tiles, with chinks of daylight showing here and there. The principal living rooms would be sheltered from the heat of the sun by this roof, and by a thick layer of earth insulation between the rooms and the attic. Beneath the rooms was a cool, damp, vaulted cellar. The Bachelardian dwelling, then, has its polite sociable rooms at its heart, but is surrounded by more evocative spaces: primitive instinctual *caves* below, and warm dry intellectual stores above.[46]

The German philosopher Martin Heidegger (1889–1976) had a contemporaneous engagement with poetics, and moved between an urban house and a rural hut.[47] His late writings, such as "Building, Dwelling, Thinking" and "Poetically Man Dwells . . . ," considered the act of dwelling more as a mental process than as a matter of finding shelter,[48] and reflected on his experience of living in primitive conditions in the hut, near Todtnauberg in the Black Forest.[49] For Heidegger, the important thing was to have a rapport with one's surroundings, to learn to "dwell"; not only to be habituated to living somewhere, but to be at home there – a condition of mind that he felt was being undermined in modern urban living. Both Bachelard and Heidegger can sound like romantic daydreamers, and discussed poetry and poetic effects, but their concerns were carefully reasoned analyses of their own human experience of dwelling.

It is something that we all have to learn to do, in one way or another, and while we learn a good deal from the circumstances in which we grow up, we can still adapt to changed circumstances when we arrange our living patterns to suit our needs in our adult lives. The patterns of domestic life change, and Elizabeth Cromley's essay (chapter 7) charts some elements of this change in a range of twentieth-century domestic buildings. The examples that she draws on here show how buildings have adapted to these changes and express them. Often, though, the buildings themselves continue in use over the course of several generations, perhaps without their fabric changing very much.

There are many nineteenth-century houses still in use, which are used now in ways that are utterly different from the ways in which they were designed to be used. There are no longer servants in most of them. The relationships between parents and children are very different. People entertain informally in the kitchen, which is now used as an important part of the living space, whereas earlier in the twentieth century the kitchen would be treated as an adjunct to the living space, kept quite separate from it. Even if there were no servants, and the woman of the house prepared all the food, the spatial arrangement meant that food would be brought out from what was clearly designated as a "service zone" into the dining room. Decorum then dictated that one behaved, in effect, as if one had servants, whereas now most of us do not expect to find them, and if they were not in evidence then we would hardly ever assume that they were having the night off.

Those of us who have not had a house designed to our own particular needs, or had them accurately anticipated, occupy spaces that we might adapt, but equally we might adapt to them. There is a relationship of reciprocity between a house and its inhabitants, and it is the house and people together that make it into that complex organism "the household," which will have an identity and character of its own that grows out of the interpersonal relationships and the person–building relationships. The household can have its own psychology, which might be productive of great happiness or corrosive paranoia, and it can be modified either by changing the people, or by changing the building, so that the people come into contact in different ways (by building walls or opening up doorways). We do not all live in new buildings, designed to our own particular needs.

Moreover we do not all want to live in new buildings. Old buildings have their own cultural value, and in the historic centers of European cities they outnumber the new buildings. There are times when architects seem to wonder whether this is a happy state of affairs, as it means that the sites for spectacular new buildings are usually out of the center, in less prominent locations. But there is no doubt that the general population values the presence of old buildings in prominent locations, even if they are not particularly fine buildings. They can come to symbolize continuity and stability if they have "always" been there – which is to say, if they have been there for as long as we can remember, which might actually be a surprisingly short time. Clapped out old buildings can be refurbished, and when that happens they can turn into "heritage" and have an increased cultural value.

Andrew Law's essay (chapter 8) examines how the idea of "Englishness" informed the growth of the architectural-conservation movement in England in the mid-twentieth century. Old buildings connected with a sense of nationhood and contributed to the sense of the individual being bonded to the place. Since then the heritage industry has become a hugely significant cultural and economic force. The National Trust, a charity which conserves historic buildings, is now the UK's largest landowner. Nostalgia is nurtured and cultivated in the popular leisure activity of visiting stately homes, which could have developed into an activity that promoted radicalism, if one imagined oneself overburdened below stairs while the life of leisure went on above.

In fact, though, almost everyone who visits a grand country house identifies with the landed aristocracy, and we come away thinking that life was wonderfully refined in the old days. The likelihood is that, if we do not have connections at court now, then we would not then have had education, disposable income, a vote, or long life. The elegant surroundings work their charm and leave the visitors daydreaming happily of an England that seems to have been lost only recently, and perhaps can be recaptured.

Certainly it can be called back to mind by something bought at the gift shop on the way out. The particular nostalgia does not play in everybody's mind, but is culturally fairly specific, as Law argues. It is manifested in designs for some new buildings, but is much more widely prevalent in the enthusiasm for the preservation of old buildings, and the cultural pilgrimages and devotions that are made there, by some sections of society. The architecture is consumed in a way that was not anticipated by its builders, but which is immediate and instinctual for the range of visitors who have been through a socialization that prepares them for these experiences, which therefore prompt perfectly genuine feelings. It would be possible to say a good deal about the groups who feel excluded by this process, or whom it leaves indifferent, because the culture that is being conserved is not one that they feel to be their own.

Architectural history need not be the history of styles adopted by people putting up fashionable new buildings. There is more than one history to be written discussing people's engagement with and interpretation of buildings no longer new. As always in Western culture, this is to be found first of all in relation to classical antiquity, for example in the relationship between travelers and monuments visited on the Grand Tour;[50] or back in antiquity itself, with the evocations of foreign parts at Hadrian's villa at Tivoli. Buildings that adopt the forms of admired buildings of the past increase the cultural capital that they embody, borrowing prestige from the high-status models. This means that one can trace a pattern of influence from one building to another.

The various mechanisms of identification, introjection, and consumption are less regularly discussed, but they could be. Freud used Rome as an image of the unconscious.[51] Joseph Rykwert's great work, *The Dancing Column*, is a sustained analysis of the habit we have of projecting our human form into inanimate buildings,[52] a habit mentioned more briefly by Nietzsche, who noticed that "We wish to see *ourselves* translated into stone and plants, we want to take walks *in ourselves* when we stroll around these buildings and gardens."[53] Once we alert ourselves to this process, then any building can acquire a cultural dimension, and can be co-opted into the realm of architecture.

Architecture links the tangible and the intellectual worlds, in ways that can be primitive and visceral, or involve the most recondite learning. Discussion of it may involve an analysis of the physical form of buildings and their construction, or may gravitate toward a discussion of the mental operations with which we deal with our surroundings. Architectural history at its most satisfying informs us about both, so that we can relate the built forms to the mental operations, and compare our own responses with those of the people under discussion, whether they were the original occupants of the buildings in question, or latecomers who responded differently. There are parallel histories of buildings as objects and of architecture as ideas, and each makes possible the other, but they are not fixed together and can continually be rearranged. This reconfiguration can be made as a creative act of an individual's will, but often it is a slower and more collective process, which moves without anyone noticing it, until one looks around and finds that the intrusive additions to the neighborhood have mellowed into their place, and now seem like trustworthy landmarks.

Architectural Histories

Architecture is produced when buildings and minds meet, and the stories we tell about architecture are as much about minds as they are about buildings – our own minds come into the picture, as well as other people's. When Pyrs Gruffudd points out that the sky was once a part of an "RAF pastoral,"[54] he is not claiming that the sky is architecture, but there is a similar process at work when we see honesty and virtue in traditional vernacular architecture, or suppose that a Modernist building expresses the spirit of our age.[55] In all these cases an "object" (if we can call the sky an object) comes into contact with a mental apparatus, and is configured in such a way as to be culturally significant. When the object is a building, then we are securely in the realm of architecture. When the object is a cloud, then we call it poetry. There are all sorts of marginal cases, such as the appreciation of forest landscape, or expansive views of farmland, which can be considered as "landscape architecture," and has been since the eighteenth century.[56] In order to experience architecture we must be in the presence of a real building, with our head stocked with appropriate ideas. Then we will properly connect, and the architectural experience will seem to be immediate and visceral. If we make the connection by way of reading about the buildings, or seeing pictures of them, then the experience is not actually of architecture, though we might sometimes be able to imagine quite well what the architectural experience would be. In that way writing about architecture, and even filmic and televisual representations of architecture (which always take away an important dimension of experience),[57] can never be architecture, but in promoting an understanding of architecture can amount to "advertisements for architecture," in Bernard Tschumi's phrase.[58]

Histories of architecture have often in the past tended to be stories about the shapes of buildings, which change over the centuries. Where one can assume that the designer of the building, its users, and the reader all share the same cultural formation, then one can use a single frame of reference to discuss the work, and it will seem to be an uncomplicated matter of self-evident truth that some buildings are better than others, and that the best buildings are simply beautiful. One feels the need for a more complex and sophisticated explanation only when one tries to account for a diversity of cultures and experiences. Then it becomes necessary to account for the fact that, although I respond to a building as a refreshing novelty, I find that another person whom I want to treat with respect can only feel that it is an affront to civilized values. An alternative is to discount the dissident view (the view that is not my own), and to rule it out of consideration. If, collectively, those of us with power on our side agree to exclude all views that are not our own, then we develop an impression of our culture as having a high level of coherence, and with the passage of time its values are naturalized and come to seem innate and self-evident.

If, however, we pay attention to the way in which different groups in our society can develop distinct cultures, then it is possible to feel that it is necessary to give an account of things that gives serious consideration to the responses of the working classes, ethnic minorities, women, and other groups who might traditionally have found themselves excluded from "high culture" on account of having gone through a different cultural formation from that of the normative hegemony. Although there are certainly stories to tell about architecture that give prominence to these issues, there is often a degree of cultural hybridity involved. If an individual might have expected to be excluded from occupying a recognized position of authority because she was a women, she might nevertheless have been able to overcome that exclusion by belonging to an elite group such as the aristocracy, and therefore be able to influence events in ways that men from more humble backgrounds could not. There are commonalities in women's experience and culture, but there are also vast differences, and depending on the particular issue being considered, it might be the similarities or the differences that actually mattered to the story being told. Similarly, there have been attempts in recent years to give an account of "queer space," which would tend to encourage an essentializing idea that all homosexuals have something in common that tends to separate their experience from that of the mainstream.[59] There is a danger here of undervaluing the contribution that homosexuals have made in shaping high culture, from Michelangelo, William Kent, and Winckelmann, to Charles Moore and Philip Johnson: there are more differences between their cultural backgrounds than there are similarities.

I would want to suggest that the stories we have liked to tell about architecture have tended to give priority to moments of inventiveness, which seem to have changed the direction in which architecture developed. These are the moments that seem like crucial points in the plot, and they can be achieved by various means. Usually, though, they were moments when commerce and efficiency were not the highest priorities. This might be because the inventive individual had leisure, on account of having a privileged social position, or might have been inclined to devote unpaid hours to the necessary work on account of being seized by an inexplicable passion for it, maybe living in poverty in order to find the time (although architects themselves have always needed to make contact with individuals with money to burn, in order to realize experimental projects). In the traditional accounts of "high culture," the type of man least likely to figure is the man of modest means who needs to work in order to have an income to support a family and who is ambitious for that family's standing in society. He will be interested in finding a commercial return on his labors, and will not allow himself the leisure to cultivate highbrow tastes, even if good education and affluence seem to put them within reach. The term "philistine" was coined in the nineteenth century to describe his culture, and by this means his views could easily be marginalized, even if they were to be found everywhere. With the general advance of populism, these cultural values seem to be being treated increasingly with respect, and have every prospect of becoming normative – in which case they become the values by which other sets of values are to be judged. In that case it is not only the old aristocratic values that are marginalized, but also all those that act against the ways of the world of commerce, such as the sacrificial logic of religion and high culture, along with "academic" values and any understanding of the ironizing inversions of camp. It would seem to make the world a mediocre place, where nothing would be any better than it need be, and excellence would be irrelevant as a goal.

Thorstein Veblen, however, described how, even in a commercial society, there is room for highly developed culture, if it carries the mark of exemption from engagement in industrial production.[60] "High culture" takes time to acquire, and has no direct commercial value, and is esteemed in a commercial culture because that is the case – because it is expensive. Curiously, this or some such mechanism has meant that the buildings and other cultural artifacts that have the least cultural value are exactly the ones that most of us choose most of the time because they best serve our needs. It is the middlebrow, mediocre, and philistine that are ignored most comprehensively in the stories we tell each other about art and architecture, and yet it is exactly these things that surround most of us as we go about our daily lives. They have high utility, but low levels of embodied cultural capital.[61] The buildings that have the highest cultural value seem to fly in the face of "common sense," which for us usually means commercial sense. It is here that the idea of sacrifice, as explained by Ruskin, reappears as a way of differentiating between the buildings that are constructed for the sake of commerce, and the buildings that are constructed because somebody or some institution has made money and wants to consume it in a way that brings reputation. This makes for a magnificent display of fine buildings in one's story, but it works against the values not only of commerce, but also those of sustainability and those of social inclusion, for example, that would be represented in a narrative that told the story of the development of "community architecture," and the political empowerment of people of modest means to shape and control their own surroundings.

The architecture-world is not unified with a single set of values and cultural expectations, but has a multiplicity of them that are indifferent to the validity of the others. Of all of them, perhaps the value system of commerce comes closest to being a general all-encompassing hegemony, but even it undermines itself by allowing some prestige to attach to the costly accomplishments of high culture. Commercial culture involves all of us in some part of our lives (and some people perhaps in the whole of their lives). Other cultures tend to be more narrow in their range of influence, and we move between some of them quite freely, depending on the role that we are playing at a given moment. The way in which we assess the merits of a building will on some occasions depend on its performance as a visual spectacle, but if we are looking for somewhere to go and meet with friends, or to make an announcement to the press, then we will bring different values to bear and will make different choices. The best building for one might not be the best building for the others, and depending on what we are doing at a given time, we will have one set of ideas uppermost in our minds, while the others are somewhere in the background.

The meaning we attach to buildings can be highly volatile. It will depend not only on what cultural grouping we belong to, but also (because in fact we each belong to more than one cultural group) it will depend on our current range of concerns and preoccupations. Buildings include some of the most solid and permanent artifacts ever made by humans, but the architectures that these buildings produce when they come into contact with people's minds – cultivated in multifarious ways – are more difficult to identify and establish. They do not inhere in the buildings, and are never permanently fixed, because even where there is cultural continuity, there can be continual change. A Doric column by a twenty-first-century architect is a profoundly different cultural event from a Doric column of the same size, shape, and materials, produced in the fifth century BC. A white cubic house raised off the ground on concrete columns is a different cultural event if it dates from the 1920s or the 1990s. The permanence of buildings, and the persistent repetition of particular built forms across time, are no guarantee against the changing ways in which they are understood, from one time to another, and in different cultural groups at the same time. Many vectors pass through a single point, taking us on a multitude of possible trajectories on their lines of flight. There are always multiple perspectives and a multiplicity of architectures.

Notes

1   Friedrich Nietzsche, *Menschliches Allzumenschliches* (1878), trans. R. J. Hollingdale, *Human All Too Human* (Cambridge: Cambridge University Press, 1986), p. 218.
2   Victor Hugo, *Les misérables* (1862), trans. N. Denny, *Les Misérables* (Harmondsworth: Penguin, 1982), pp. 1061–75.
3   William Makepeace Thackeray, "May Gambols; or, Titmarsh on the Picture Galleries," in *Ballads and Miscellanies* (London: Smith Elder, 1899), pp. 419–45, p. 440.
4   John Ruskin, "The Opening of the Crystal Palace," in *The Works of John Ruskin*, ed. E. T. Cook and A. Wedderburn, 39 vols (London: George Allen, 1903–12), vol. 12, pp. 417–32, p. 419.
5   Ibid.
6   Ibid.
7   John Ruskin, *The Seven Lamps of Architecture*, ch. 7, s. 4, in *Works*, vol. 8, pp. 252–3.

8   Marshall Berman, *All that is Solid Melts into Air* (New York: Simon and Schuster, 1982), p. 236; Fyodor Dostoevsky (1864), trans. J. Coulson, *Notes from Underground* (Harmondsworth: Penguin, 1964), ch. 1, pt 10, p. 42.

9   Iain Boyd Whyte, *The Crystal Chain Letters* (Cambridge, MA: MIT Press, 1985).

10   F. T. Marinetti, "The Founding and Manifesto of Futurism" (1909), trans. R. W. Flint, in *Marinetti: Selected Writings* (New York: Farrar, Strauss and Giroux, 1971), p. 41; also (the same translation) in *Futurist Manifestos*, ed. Umbro Apollonio (London: Thames and Hudson, 1973), p. 21.

11   Le Corbusier, *Vers une architecture* (Paris: Crès, 1923), trans. F. Etchells, *Towards a New Architecture* (London: Architectural Press, 1987), pp. 225–65, esp. p. 240.

12   Reyner Banham, *Theory and Design in the First Machine Age* (London: Architectural Press, 1960).

13   This is the fourth meaning of the word given in the Addenda to the *Shorter Oxford Dictionary*, vol. 2, p. 2635.

14   Karl Popper, *The Poverty of Historicism* (London: Routledge and Kegan Paul, 1957).

15   Ibid., p. iii.

16   David Watkin, *Morality and Architecture* (Oxford: Oxford University Press, 1977); 2nd edn: *Morality and Architecture Revisited* (London: John Murray, 2001).

17   Popper, *Historicism*, p. 13.

18   James Conant, "Freedom, Cruelty and Truth: Rorty versus Orwell," in *Rorty and his Critics*, ed. Robert B. Brandom (Oxford: Blackwell, 2000), pp. 268–342, p. 276. Rorty clearly situates himself as "historicist" in Richard Rorty, *Philosophy and the Mirror of Nature* (Oxford: Blackwell, 1980).

19   Richard Rorty, *Contingency, Irony, and Solidarity* (Cambridge: Cambridge University Press, 1989); and see Conant, "Freedom, Cruelty, and Truth," p. 277.

20   For the purposes of this argument, they might as well have been looking at the same building. On another description, they were not, because when Dostoevsky visited London the Crystal Palace had been moved to Sydenham, and had been enlarged.

21   By "we" here I mean our society as a whole, and do not mean to suggest that you as an individual actually hold this view.

22   John Sutherland, "Can You See the Precog Turning? Spielberg, Philip K. Dick and the Commodification of Paranoia," in *The Times Literary Supplement*, July 12 (2002), pp. 18–19.

23   Robert Venturi, Denise Scott Brown, and Stephen Izenour illustrate a sequence of Modernist buildings that have drawn on the model of Le Corbusier's

monastery of La Tourette, which is very securely part of the Modernist canon. Richard Meier's more recent headquarters building on the banks of the Seine in Paris (rear elevation) could now be added to the list. Robert Venturi, Denise Scott Brown, and Steven Izenour, *Learning from Las Vegas* (Cambridge, MA: MIT Press, 1977), pp. 146–7.

24   Andrew Ballantyne, "Space, Grace and Stylistic Conformity," in *Framing Formalism: Riegl's Work*, ed. Richard Woodfield (New York: Gordon and Breach, 2001), pp. 83–106.

25   Augustus Welby Northmore Pugin, *Contrasts: or, A Parallel Between the Noble Edifices of the Middle Ages and Corresponding Buildings of the Present Day* (London, 1836); and *The True Principles of Christian or Pointed Architecture* (London, 1841).

26   Sigfried Giedion, *Space, Time and Architecture: The Growth of a New Tradition* (Cambridge, MA: Harvard University Press, 1941; 5th edn 1967).

27   It is one of the principal works discussed in Watkin, *Morality and Architecture*.

28   Le Corbusier, *Vers une architecture*, trans. Etchells, pp. 267–89.

29   Colin St John Wilson, *The Other Tradition of Modern Architecture: The Uncompleted Project* (London: Academy Editions, 1995).

30   Ayn Rand, *The Fountainhead* (New York: Bobbs Merrill, 1943).

31   Friedrich Nietzsche, *Götzen-Dämmerung* (1889), trans. R. J. Hollingdale, *Twilight of the Idols* (Harmondsworth: Penguin, 1968), p. 21.

32   Thorstein Veblen, *The Theory of the Leisure Class* (1899) (New York: Dover, 1994), pp. 73–4.

33   Ruskin, *Seven Lamps*, ch. 1, s. 1, pp. 27–8.

34   Genesis, 11: 4.

35   Georges Bataille, *La Part maudite* (Paris: Les Éditions de Minuit, 1967); also *L'Histoire de l'érotisme* and *La Souveraineté* in Georges Bataille, *Oeuvres complètes*, vol. 8 (Paris: Gallimard, 1976), trans. R. Hurley, *The Accursed Share: Volumes 1, 2 and 3*, 2 vols (New York: Zone, 1988 and 1991). Note: the English translation is published in two volumes; the title of volume 2 is *The Accursed Share: Volumes 2 and 3*.

36   Bataille, *Accursed Share*, vol. 1, p. 19.

37   Chris Brook (ed.), *K Foundation Burn a Million Quid* (London: Ellipsis, 1997).

38   Bataille, *Accursed Share*, vol. 1, pp. 49–51.

39   This is a version of the argument set out by Michel Serres in "Le Fusil," in *Statues: Le second livre des fondations* (Paris: Bourin, 1987), pp. 13–34.

40   Martin Pawley, *Theory and Design in the Second Machine Age* (Oxford: Blackwell, 1990).

41   This point is particularly associated with Michel Foucault; see, for example, Michel Foucault, *Power/Knowledge*, ed. Colin Gordon (New York: Harvester Wheatsheaf, 1980).

42 Percy Bysshe Shelley, "A Defence of Poetry" (composed 1821, first published 1840), concluding sentence, in *Shelley: Selected Poetry and Prose*, ed. Alasdair D. F. Macrae (London: Routledge, 1991), pp. 204–33, p. 233. See also Richard Poirier, "Why do Pragmatists Want to be like Poets?" and Louis Menand, "Pragmatists and Poets: A Response to Richard Poirier," both in *The Revival of Pragmatism: New Essays on Social Thought, Law, and Culture*, ed. Morris Dickstein (Durham, NC: Duke University Press, 1998), pp. 347–69.

43 Gaston Bachelard, *Le nouvel ésprit scientifique* (Paris: Presses Universitaires de France, 1934), trans. A. Goldhammer, *The New Scientific Spirit* (Boston: Beacon Press, 1984); Mary Tiles, *Bachelard: Science and Objectivity* (Cambridge: Cambridge University Press, 1984).

44 Gaston Bachelard, *Le psychanalyse du feu* (Paris: Gallimard, 1938), trans. A. C. M. Ross, *The Psychoanalysis of Fire* (London: Quartet, 1987).

45 Gaston Bachelard, *La poetique de l'espace* (Paris: Presses Universitaires de France, 1958), trans. M. Jolas, *The Poetics of Space* (Boston: Beacon Press, 1969).

46 Bachelard, "The House. From Cellar to Garret. The Significance of the Hut," chapter 1 of *Poetics of Space*, pp. 3–37.

47 See Adam Sharr, "Heidegger's Hut," unpublished PhD thesis, University of Cardiff, 2002.

48 These two pieces, translated by A. Hofstadter, are in Martin Heidegger, *Poetry, Language, Thought* (New York: Harper and Row, 1971).

49 Andrew Ballantyne, "The Nest and the Pillar of Fire," and Neil Leach, "The Dark Side of the *Domus*," both in *What is Architecture?*, ed. Andrew Ballantyne (London: Routledge, 2002), pp. 15–26, 88–101.

50 Frank Salmon, *Building on Ruins* (London: Ashgate, 2000); Dana Arnold, "The Illusion of Grandeur? Antiquity, Grand Tourism and the Country House," in *The Georgian Country House: Architecture, Landscape and Society*, ed. Dana Arnold (Stroud, Gloucestershire: Sutton, 1998), pp. 100–16.

51 Sigmund Freud, "Civilization and its Discontents," in *Civilization, Society and Religion*, ed. A. Dickson, Penguin Freud Library, vol. 12 (Harmondsworth: Penguin, 1991), pp. 251–340; cited by Arnold, "Illusion of Grandeur," p. 112.

52 Joseph Rykwert, *The Dancing Column* (Cambridge, MA: MIT Press, 1996).

53 Friedrich Nietzsche, *Die fröliche Wissenschaft* (1882), bk 4, s. 280, trans. W. Kaufmann, *The Gay Science* (New York: Vintage, 1974), p. 227.

54 Pyrs Gruffudd, "Reach for the Sky: The Air and English Cultural Nationalism," Department of Geography Working Paper no. 7, University of Nottingham, 1990; see chapter 6.

55 Andrew Ballantyne, "A Face in the Cloud: Anthropomorphism in Architecture," in *The Routledge Companion to Architectural Thought*, ed. Ben Farmer and Hentie Louw (London: Routledge, 1993), pp. 294–9; and "Space, Grace

and Stylistic Conformity," in *Framing Formalism: Riegl's Work*, ed. Richard Woodfield (New York: Gordon and Breach, 2001), pp. 83–106.

56 Andrew Ballantyne, *Architecture, Landscape and Liberty* (Cambridge: Cambridge University Press, 1997).

57 Andrew Ballantyne, "Architectonics of 'the Box': Television's Spatiality," in *Television: Aesthetic Reflections*, ed. Ruth Lorand (New York: Peter Lang, 2002), pp. 127–38.

58 Bernard Tschumi, "Advertisements for Architecture," in *Architecture in/of Motion* (Rotterdam: NAi Publishers, 1997), pp. 104–7.

59 Aaron Betsky, *Queer Space* (New York: William Morrow, 1997).

60 Thorstein Veblen, "The Higher Learning as an Expression of the Pecuniary Culture," in *Leisure Class*, ch. 14, pp. 223–44.

61 As explained in chapter 8.

1

An Avant-garde Academy

Simon Sadler

Teaching Radicalism in European and North American Architecture

Modernism is a contradictory idea because the word "modern" implies something that is bang up to date and still in formation, but the suffix "ism" implies the opposite, a doctrine, a method that is now comfortably codified. The conundrum is more than a semantic quirk. It is sometimes perceptible in Modernist designs,[1] and it became institutionalized, notably in the schools of architecture in Western Europe and the USA.

It is possible to trace a story of how Modernism became an orthodoxy and how it became internally challenged again by those determined to perpetuate the Modernist revolution. In this chapter, the story is broken into three historical periods. The first covers the years between the two world wars, when Modernism's status shifted from avant-garde provocation to taught methodology; the second is the period from the end of World War II to the resurgence of radicalism in the 1960s, an era in which Modernism was accepted as the architectural mainstream taught in architectural schools and practiced in architectural offices. And, as such, it became an establishment target for a *new* avant-garde or "neo-avant-garde." The final section, surveying the period since the 1960s, considers whether the neo-avant-garde has started the cycle again, its own "revolution" settling into another methodology for the ever-new.

Modernist, postmodernist, and various other avant-garde procedures have frequently been played out *within* the architectural schools (and more institutionally the "academy"), although the special attention paid to the role of the academy in this chapter is slightly unusual. Modernism and the avant-garde are conventionally explained against a background of social, economic, technological, and artistic changes, and these must be duly acknowledged. Yet the academy provided a position of relative autonomy to social, economic, and technological factors, creating a space in which architects could creatively reflect upon their practice, undistracted by the immediate pressures of clients and work on site. The academy requires all its disciplines to do the same – to produce better science, more incisive understanding of the humanities, and so on. Perhaps, then, there has been a natural symbiosis between "Modern-ism" and the academy. Both claim to subject their procedures to continual revision.

The Rise of a "Modernist Academy"

Modernism actually became "academic" very early in its life. While its roots stretched back as far as the eighteenth-century Enlightenment, it is conventional to date the emergence of a self-conscious "avant-garde" to the late nineteenth and early twentieth centuries. Cubism, Futurism, Expressionism, Constructivism, and De Stijl were fired by the belief that the creative techniques of the past had to be overturned. Often encouraged by Marxism and anarchism to expect that their radical art was the harbinger of a new way of life, the avant-garde believed that they were preparing for another world, dynamic and made by all, not just by the bourgeoisie with its hands on the reins of production.

By the 1920s, such diverse modernizing tendencies were coagulating into an assertive architectural "Modern Movement" in art and architecture. And with that title, "Modern Movement,"[2] we already have something smacking of a "call to order." The Modern Movement took the revolutionary, firebrand mission of the avant-garde and packaged it as reasoned, methodical, and authoritative. Its program can be summarized as one of breaking down barriers between aesthetics, technology, and society so that appropriate design of the highest visual and practical quality would be produced for the *mass* of the population. Its vision was of the *universal* – universal design solutions, universal standards of living, and universal aesthetic principles (prioritizing volume and transparency over mass and ornament, the regularity of the grid over symmetry, and an aura of technical refinement).

In the wake of World War I, the Modern Movement hoped to turn swords into plowshares, redressing the brutalization of the modern world through a sort of socialism by design. In effect, the Modern Movement believed it could transform mass consciousness by improving productive and environmental conditions. The stress now was not on independent and diverse activity, but on a *consensus* and, quietly, working with capitalism in the hope of reforming it. It was a regulating tendency that had been pioneered by the Deutscher Werkbund, founded in Munich in 1907 to promote the integration of art and industry, and providing a definitive group ensemble of the new architecture at its live show of housing, the Weissenhof Siedlung in Stuttgart, in 1927. Many of the architects working at the Weissenhof were to be linked with the two institutions which came to epitomize the Modern Movement in architecture: the Bauhaus (1919–33)[3] and the Congrès Internationaux d'Architecture Moderne (International Congresses of Modern Architecture, or CIAM, 1928–59).

To enact their velvet revolution, the Bauhaus and CIAM had to supplant the influence of the French École des Beaux-Arts, an architectural education system which had been the paradigm of the nineteenth century. On the one hand, the Modern Movement was indebted to the way in which the Beaux-Arts had helped professionalize architecture and promote its supremacy as the umbrella of all the arts. Moreover, the principles of Beaux-Arts education were a lot like those of the Modern Movement, since they stressed the importance of function, context, and structural rationality. Having said that, the Modern Movement interpreted these principles rather differently. It insisted upon the austerity of the "machine aesthetic" as the twentieth-century corrective to nineteenth-century classicism, ornament, and historical precedent. Anticipating a classless society, it preferred a universal, technological solution to all building types over the hierarchical categorization of buildings that the Beaux-Arts found appropriate to a hierarchical, class-bound society. The stiff formality of Beaux-Arts training earned it the derogatory epithet "academic" for Modernists, who preferred a more dynamic, intuitive, scientific, creative training of the sort pioneered at the Bauhaus. The rivalry between the insurgent Bauhaus system and the remnants of the Beaux-Arts system would linger until the 1960s, some critics of the Bauhaus/CIAM legacy arguing that Modernism was subject to the same "academic" orthodoxies that had beset its Beaux-Arts predecessor. By the 1970s and 1980s, the influence of the Beaux-Arts was widely resurfacing in postmodern architecture.

The Modern Movement was embodied, aesthetically and pedagogically, when the Bauhaus moved to its new building and syllabus at Dessau in 1926. Within its irregular plan, glass curtain walls and steel and reinforced concrete frame beat an interdisciplinary heart so that all the departments – furniture, theater, architecture, textiles, and so on – collaborated. Its *Vorkurs* educational technique encapsulated the contradiction between methodology and innovation that made Modernism, instructing the student to "intuitively" handle the established "science" of form. This ability would then be allied to manual, industrial, and building competencies. It was a message transmitted internationally by CIAM, which numbered amongst its first guiding lights Bauhaus architect and director Walter Gropius, his successor Mies van der Rohe, French renegade Le Corbusier and the historian Sigfried Giedion, who had first met Gropius and other members of the Bauhaus in 1923.

Not only did CIAM and the Bauhaus bring together practitioners to agree on some aims and methods, they also began to organize the *discourse* of Modernism through academic and quasi-academic texts. Like those other movements of the era (such as communism and the emergent fascism, though of course without the violence) the Bauhaus and CIAM were devoted to the wholesale reorganization of the world and its culture, operating as if the world was to be changed through a vanguard party with a clear line that lapsed, when needs be, into dogma and propaganda. Figures such as Le Corbusier and Giedion were masters of polemic. Giedion, for example, argued that the Modern Movement's unification into a single field of all techniques, materials, buildings, and space was the summation of a creative process stretching back to the Renaissance. Giedion went further, suggesting that Modernism was one of the great themes of history itself, since the designers of the Modern Movement were like receptacles for something bigger – "men in whom the spirit of an age crystallizes."[4] The Bauhaus likewise presented itself as though it were an inevitable outcome of history and the progress toward rationality.[5]

The "united front" of the Modern Movement was itself something of an historical construct, maintained by freezing out practitioners who favored "subjective" intuition over "objective" analysis.[6] From about 1923 Gropius stealthily aligned the Bauhaus school with the Modern Movement, as with the publication of *The New Architecture and the Bauhaus* (1935), which marginalized any trace of the more outlandish avant-garde inputs into the Bauhaus such as Futurism (1909) and Expressionism (*c.*1918). Nikolaus Pevsner's powerfully titled 1936 book *Pioneers of the Modern Movement* (republished in 1949 by the Museum of Modern Art in New York, an influential apologist for Modernism) conveniently avoided explaining the riotous early avant-gardes by suspending narrative from around 1910.[7] Only when Pevsner's pupil, the historian Reyner Banham, published *Theory and Design in the First Machine Age* in 1960 were these livelier elements of early Modernist history decisively edited back into the account, calling into question the claim that Modernism was historically predestined through the *Zeitgeist*, the "spirit of the age." In truth, Banham argued, it was the *thrills* of modernity, the embrace of the expressive aesthetics of modern life, whether of machinery or popular culture, that motivated Modern architects quite as much as rationality. It was an allegation that the neo-avant-garde would find compelling in their own work, as we shall see later in the chapter.

CIAM's agenda had been fleshed out during its first few meetings and it provided the keynote for mainstream Modernist architecture and planning until the 1960s. In 1929 CIAM held its conference in Frankfurt in recognition of the mass housing achievements there. A year later, 1930, in Brussels, we can find CIAM boldly extending its remit still further, to the problems of land usage and town planning in their entirety. CIAM even devised a system by which the various national branches of the organization could overcome language barriers, and thereby spatial separations, exchanging information through sign systems and grid displays. And yet CIAM became strangely remote from reality. CIAM's fourth meeting in 1933 took place on a cruise ship, blissfully distant from the critical political situation in Europe. The ship was headed for Athens, and the conference findings became known as the Athens Charter. Under the influence of Le Corbusier, this was the most important document to come out of CIAM. The main clauses demanded the rigid functional zoning of cities and high-rise, high-density apartment blocks surrounded by green space.

CIAM's Athens Charter was the unfortunate source code of many of the worst features of town planning after World War II. Indeed, a "new generation" of Modernists after the war would complain that the Modern Movement had become so enamored with its belief in universal design solutions that its understanding of *actual* technology and the *variety* of modernity had ground to a halt. Modernism appeared more concerned with *representing* rational order than with producing real "machines for living in" or dynamic urban spaces. These objections would sow the seeds of CIAM's own undoing after World War II, when younger architects felt that CIAM itself represented an attempt to make Modernism into a new "academic discipline." Moreover, it seemed that the increasing number of Modernist architectural schools had truly made Modernism into an academic discipline, replacing Beaux-Arts-derived syllabuses with Bauhaus-derived ones; and that their graduates in municipal offices had homogenized city centers from Eastern Europe to the USA. Thereby the avant-garde, open-ended creativity that had launched Modernism had also been defeated by Modernism.

Soon after the so-called International Style emerged in the mid-twentieth century as the "new tradition"[8] of architecture, it was challenged by an internal architectural vanguard determined that the only tradition of the Modern should be that of the ever-new.

"Academic" and "Anti-academic" Modernism after World War II

If before World War II the "Modernist Academy" was somewhat notional, after the war it was a reality, stylistically, institutionally, and through construction. The architects of the Modern Movement found themselves commissioned to build both corporate America and state socialist Europe, endowing Modernism with tremendous authority and responsibility for accommodating the very institutions of society – schools, universities, hospitals, government headquarters, and banks as well as housing.[9]

North American Modernist tastes were initially formed by the home-grown frontier spirit of Frank Lloyd Wright rather than the dictates of European rationalism. Yet, with the appointment of Gropius to the faculty at Harvard in 1937 and Mies van der Rohe to the Illinois Institute of Technology (IIT) the following year (with Laszlo Moholy-Nagy endeavoring to found a New Bauhaus in Chicago at the same time), "academic" Bauhaus Modernism arrived in the USA to thrive with a technical competence that had been unimaginable to the European vanguard of the 1920s.[10] What once had been the fantasy of the glass skyscraper was to be engineered with brilliant effectiveness in the 1950s by the big Modernist practice of Skidmore, Owings, and Merrill (SOM, founded 1936). The story of main-stream Modernism's historical destiny was perfected at the same time, with the 1941 publication of *Space, Time and Architecture*, based upon a series of lectures given by Giedion at Harvard University at the behest of Gropius. Discussion at the time about a "New Monumentality" mirrored Modernism's growing sense of civic responsibility, even reinstating an architectural hierarchy for public architecture that was reminiscent of Beaux-Arts attitudes. It was a far cry from Futurist and Expressionist rebellion.

Across Europe after World War II, the politically radical ancestry of Modernism was forgiven for the sake of national Reconstruction.[11] This was demonstrated, for example, at the Festival of Britain in 1951, which CIAM visited. The nascent British welfare state championed Modern architecture as an economical mode of building that visually represented a forward-looking nation, perfecting the science of building in order to house people, school their children, and care for their health to standards never before attained. For the ambitious British architect in the late 1950s and early 1960s, there were ever-fewer alternatives to "academic" Modernism. The architect would be trained at a university or equivalent institute of higher education (rather than through pupillage) and in 1958 the Royal Institute of British Architects (RIBA) confirmed the ascendancy of what has been dubbed the "Official System" in the Schools.[12] This energetically asserted the role of the architect as being not so much a creative designer as a policy-making "expert," project-managing new buildings and towns.

Yet, for all the technocracy of international mainstream Modernist culture in the 1950s and 1960s, there obviously *was* an unofficial *style* to which the architect was expected to adhere. It was a little bland, perhaps because of the way in which team-working (as championed in private practice by Gropius's firm, The Architects' Collaborative (TAC), and in public practice by the big municipal offices) tended to bury individual expression. The severity of the Functionalist Modern architecture of the 1920s was being tempered by the example of Scandinavia, on the one hand (where since the 1930s architects such as the Finn, Alvar Aalto, had been "softening" and "humanizing" the machine aesthetic into something more organic and tender), and, on the other hand, by the "people's detailing" hailing from the Soviet bloc.

Reaction against this prosaic version of modernity came in the 1950s from young architects in touch with the tough new post-war culture of Beat literature, Angry Young Men and Abstract Expressionism. For them, Modernism sounded yet again as a clarion-call to creative innovation. They were increasingly suspicious that this ideal had been suppressed by the "Modern Movement" and that its pioneers were becoming greying establishment figures. To whom should they look? To Mart Stam, once the inventor of ruthlessly functional and forward-looking buildings, but now the architect of the neoclassical Shell Center (1942) in The Hague?

To Gropius, whose Harvard conservatism seemed to be surfacing in his American Embassy, Athens (1956–61)? Or to Mies van der Rohe, whose neo-Platonic repertoire of form was unlikely to yield any more surprises but *was* likely to prompt imitators looking for a design "formula"?

Only Le Corbusier remained truly inspirational to young architectural "rebels." He had no qualms about revising his principles until they were unrecognizable. He now offered what would become known as a "New Brutalism" of raw, shuttered concrete, exposed brickwork, and primitive, handcrafted-looking building techniques. Massiveness replaced the old Modern Movement impression of lightness. In buildings such as the monastery of La Tourette near Lyons (1956–9) sculptural elements protruded in "poetic" formations that, in their utter rebuke of the machine aesthetic of which Le Corbusier had once been the arch prophet, appeared to brood upon the "human condition" and a world recently torn apart by technological atrocity. Modernism's claims to being functional and rational had always been a bit far-fetched anyway. After the initial shock, architects such as Britain's rising star James Stirling read Le Corbusier's new direction as an invitation to artistic license and heterogeneity, much as Baroque architects had absorbed the Mannerist lesson of Michelangelo.

Some young architects began to confront the Modernist "establishment" itself. The turning point was CIAM's ninth meeting, which took place in 1954 near a building that no Modern architect in the world could ignore: Le Corbusier's Unité d'Habitation near Marseilles (1946–52). It was obvious that, with the Unité, Le Corbusier had himself abandoned the "radiant towers" of the Athens Charter in favor of an inward-looking, self-contained block. It was obvious too that this was no longer a machine aesthetic, but an "expressive," sculptural structure. CIAM 9 wound up with younger members having a party on its roof, and it was to such younger members that the organization of the next meeting, CIAM 10, was entrusted, in the hope that the Modern Movement would be forced to regenerate. So completely did it do so that, though CIAM met for an eleventh time in 1959, it in effect came to an end with the termination at CIAM 10 of a singular "Modern Movement" agenda. Under the youthful leadership of figures such as Alison and Peter Smithson from England and Aldo van Eyck from Holland, their discussion group Team 10 and practices like France's ATBAT, the supposed founding principles of Modernism were revisited in a "Brutalist" manner and new attention was paid to *local* rather than *universal* constraints. Put another way, it was possible to be in some way "avant-garde" again.

Team 10 associates wanted to deliver CIAM from what they regarded as its general "academic" impasse. No more impersonal rote-learnt architecture: they wanted an architecture sensitive to everyday human situations. No more schemes that treated a city in Brazil the same way as a city in Sweden: Team 10 wanted an overt appreciation of local factors, climate, and customs. Design solutions would be achieved by *feeling* rather than rationalizing. Enough mechanical tempo and machine-age metaphors: Team 10 wanted an architecture that created a sense of habitat. And habitat was the theme given to CIAM 10, which met in Dubrovnik in 1956. Alison and Peter Smithson had taken to CIAM 9 a "study Grille," a visual presentation of their ideas for the benefit of other delegates. It fitted the grid format that had been suggested by Le Corbusier and the French contingent of CIAM back in 1949, but its contents were of a different spirit, celebrating not the "ideal universal" but the nitty gritty reality of everyday life in the street. The Smithsons called their method "urban reidentification," which concentrated not on zoning and circulation in the manner of the Athens Charter, but on community. And although the Smithsons adored Le Corbusier and his Brutalist manner, they were uncertain whether even the Unité d'Habitation was really the way to go, seeing it as isolating rather than connecting communities.

Attention would instead be paid to anthropology and the details of everyday life – "the doorstep between man and men" as Aldo van Eyck put it. In his designs he was attempting to recover something of the close-knit intimacy he felt had been part of old Dutch village life or the Dogon villages in Africa. Van Eyck studied poetry, philosophy, Structuralist anthropology, and children's play in the effort to understand ever more deeply, and ever less rationally and crudely, what it is that people really seek in their habitat – security, community, playfulness, the unexpected, emotional involvement. His Amsterdam Children's Orphanage of 1961 intermeshed spaces and functions so that functional circulation (a prime consideration of both Beaux-Arts and Modern Movement designs) was of strictly secondary importance; what mattered was the psychological quality of the space.

The Team 10 avant-garde had, then, split with mainstream Modernism by emphasizing the micro over the macro, the real over the ideal, the spontaneous over the planned. In other words, "New Brutalism" harbored ambitions to be more than a change in Modernist aesthetics; it suggested an inversion in the *ethos* of Modern architecture. Whereas the Modern Movement had aimed to bring architecture and society to a level of universal rational perfection, the New Brutalists would address the world *as it is.* For instance, Alison and Peter Smithson wrote in 1957 that "Brutalism tries to face up to a mass-production society, and drag a rough poetry out of the confused and powerful forces which are at work."[13]

It is this aspiration to be poets of a modernity pieced together from the detritus of art, science, and society that we find inherited by the vanguard of architects during succeeding decades – be it the Archigram group in the 1960s or Rem Koolhaas in the 1990s. A certain graphic panache accompanied it, suitably collage-like – from the Smithsons' CIAM Grille (1954) and *Parallel of Life and Art* show (1953) to the little magazine *Archigram* (1961–70) and Koolhaas's book *S,M,L,XL* (1995). Graphics were used as a cheap, high-impact formula that prepared the public for the cost and commitment of actual building by first seducing and dazzling with visions of heightened modernity. The new wave of architectural graphics echoed those of mass media (which were enjoying exponential expansion during the same period) in order to broadcast the message of vanguard modernity beyond narrow professional architectural audiences. Graphics portrayed the experience of modernity as fractured, simultaneous, and transitory, a reversal of the "call to order" in the 1920s which had turned avant-gardism into a Modern Movement. Modernity was returned to the "raw" condition in which it had been met by the turn-of-the-century avant-gardes.

Unhampered by the cultivation of "good taste," and of all its associated hierarchies, inspiration could now be sourced from areas officially out of bounds to architects, particularly popular culture. The Smithsons and James Stirling were amongst the participants in the highly successful art exhibition "This is Tomorrow" held in London in 1956, which introduced the possibility of a Pop aesthetic, an "aesthetics of plenty." Pop acknowledged the role played by consumer taste, science fiction, cinema, and advertising in the shaping of mass culture. It admitted that the Modernist pioneers of the 1910s and 1920s could have had no inkling of the technologies that were shaping the world of the 1940s, 1950s, and 1960s, like the atomic bomb, electronic computers, television, and manned space flight. While the European Modernist avant-garde had admired the USA in the 1920s, the homage paid to the American Way by the European Pop avant-garde in the 1950s and 1960s was markedly different. Critical attention shifted from the grand industrial abstraction of concrete silos and Chicago steel frames to the chromium-plated details of automobiles and refrigerators. To some extent, the Pop mentality would be imported back into the USA itself, so that practitioners like Venturi and Scott Brown in the 1960s could celebrate the European legacy and American Pop simultaneously.

Moreover, the post-war avant-garde was starting to relax the old European-Modernist ideological stricture that said that while American technology was impressive, the consumer capitalism that sponsored it was beyond the pale. The mass consumer lifestyle of the USA was now *in itself* the subject of some reverence, for the way in which it had seemingly achieved the worker utopia that decades of European socialism and communism had yet to deliver. Concurrently, increasing awareness of Stalinism deprived the Soviet Union of a great deal of its countervailing moral authority. This marked a shift from Marxist/socialist "commitment" to economic liberalism amongst progressive architects that we will return to in the next section.

The full impact of Pop was felt in the 1960s when the Archigram group surfaced in London, just as the revisionist impulses of Brutalism and Team 10 were on the wane. Archigram tried to show that "automobile-styled" houses were not an experimental proposition for twenty-five years hence, as the Smithsons had been at pains to explain with regard to their sensational House of the Future (1956),[14] but for the here-and-now. Archigram thereby foregrounded the Pop impetus behind Brutalism which had been overshadowed by the rough concrete austerity of actual Brutalist buildings. Archigram renewed the avant-garde as wild and posturing in a Futurist way that Team 10, which more eagerly sought credibility, did not. In fact, Archigram cultivated a laissez-faire approach to the organization of ideas and allegiances that distanced them from those Modernist maxims to which Team 10 and the Brutalists still subscribed. Team 10 had stormed the palace of Modernism by taking control of CIAM, dissolving it, reopening debates about housing estates and the like, whereas Archigram largely *ignored* the Modernist "establishment" and the debates with which it had been preoccupied. Pop was the casual, expendable style of a leisured consumer society, and Team 10's nostalgia for traditional, close-knit social structures and mass housing seemed less and less relevant to Archigram and fellow-travelers such as the Japanese Metabolists (founded 1958).

Avant-garde and Neo-avant-garde

This chapter has tried to draw distinctions between the avant-garde (those pushing for radical sociocultural transformation) and the Modern Movement (which was the product of avant-gardes become increasingly respectable, academic, and paradigmatic). A further nuance is apparent. Since the late 1960s, the status and purpose of the avant-garde has come under closer scrutiny, prompting commentators to distinguish between "avant-garde" and "neo-avant-garde." In fact, critics started to agree that the "true" avant-garde, the one that thrived from the 1910s to the 1930s, driven ideologically by the will to overthrow bourgeois society, had become practically extinct.[15] The art and architecture presenting itself since World War II as "avant-garde" was actually an artistic institution, a "neo-avant-garde" which traded radical *forms* as an artistic rather than social challenge. Far from overthrowing the institutions of capitalism, neo-avant-garde production had become a valued commodity sponsored by the bourgeoisie as evidence of its educated taste and commitment to innovation.

This final section of the chapter accepts that the neo-avant-garde label is as useful in architecture as it is in other art forms, and then argues that an architectural neo-avant-garde expanded from the 1960s in order to reassert the importance of dissent from worldwide Modernist "orthodoxy" – returning Modern architecture to something closer to its dynamic, heterogeneous roots. A neo-avant-garde circuit stretched from Japan to Western Europe and the USA, facilitated by the decreasing costs of international travel and the expansion of architectural publishing. While accepting that the neo-avant-garde was operating in a different context from the pioneer avant-gardes, however, this section of the chapter questions whether the dream of changing society and the economy entirely disappeared from architecture. Marxism, for example, periodically resurfaced amongst architects. Just as significantly, architects have looked at ways of tapping into capitalism so as to alter society at a micro level, and while this represents a reining-in of ambition to something close to liberalism, it nonetheless indicates the persistence of the belief that architecture is a social instrument as well as a utility and an art form.

Nowhere has the neo-avant-garde intrigue been more powerful than in the schools of architecture. For instance, when passing through London virtually every foreign architect of note, especially those of radical inclination, visited the Architectural Association (AA), the prestigious and proudly independent teaching institution with which Archigram was as intimately involved as had been the Brutalists before them.[16] A neo-avant-garde network would be sustained from the 1970s onwards by ambassadorial figures such as AA alumni Zaha Hadid, Rem Koolhaas, and Bernard Tschumi[17] as they shuttled between high-profile European and American schools of architecture (including Harvard, IIT, and Columbia).

The emergence after 1961 of the *Archigram* magazine and its affiliates provided initial confirmation of the desire for a new (or neo-) avant-garde. The Archigram group demanded a circuit of thinking and teaching that looked skeptically at the "architecture-as-service" mode that had been espoused, variously, by the Bauhaus's successor, the Hochschule für Gestaltung in Ulm (1955–68), through the syllabuses of the governing professional bodies of architecture (like the RIBA in Britain and the AIA in the USA), through the massive expansion of public offices, and through the slick "finishing schools" of commercial offices like Skidmore, Owings, and Merrill in the USA. *Archigram* hoped to link up and radicalize architectural students in the UK and abroad, and was distributed by architectural students as if in emulation of the illegal *samizdat* literature circulating behind the Iron Curtain. *Archigram* spawned further student-oriented architectural little magazines and vigilante groups in the mid-1960s, prompting the historian Reyner Banham, himself a supporter of Archigram, to talk of "the Movement,"[18] as though it were a shadow of the 1960s' counterculture at large, the student an agent of long-lasting change in architecture as well as society.

It was appropriate then that the factious rejection of Archigram's increasingly institutionalized neo-avant-gardism in the late 1960s and early 1970s would be led by still more radicalized students. The faultline emerged between those who believed in a Pop consumer revolution, and those demanding a more politically grounded response. Radicalized students turned to alternative sources of inspiration, notably French Marxist revisionism and the Paris-based Situationist group (1957–72), which at the time epitomized the cultural resistance to capitalism. The Situationists, though not architects in the conventional or professional sense,[19] were deeply interested in the potential of architecture and the city to instigate radical social change, as was apparent in the design of a "New Babylon" (*c.*1958–74) by the self-styled Situationist "architect" Constant. Whereas Archigram believed in liberation *through* consumerism, the Situationists demanded liberation *from* consumerism, and the overthrow of the rational instrumentality of design – thus questioning who designs and plans, and by what mandate.[20]

In this way the Situationists were like the Marxist- and anarchist-inspired avant-gardes of the 1910s and 1920s, and a new wave of avant-gardes emerged from French and Italian architecture schools in the late 1960s, wavering under the dual influence of liberals like Archigram, on the one hand, and ultra-leftists like the Situationists on the other. Radical

Italian groups showed particular flair for designing objects that confused accepted capitalist-rationalist meanings and functions. Superstudio,
for example, parodied the ambition of the Modern Movement with its
No-Stop City project (1970), an uninterrupted built environment for
production and waste disposal. Italian radical architecture groups began
to take part in direct political action, as when the UFO Group deployed
its pun and riddle-daubed inflatables to block Florentine traffic and make
way for protesters. This incident was in 1968, the year that widespread
student and youth insurgency was kick-started from Paris; design students
contributed to the disorder by occupying the European showcase for
industrial design, the Milan Triennale.

Pure, direct creativity freed from industrial society was the lodestone
of the 1968 cultural revolution. As Italian radical architecture group
Archizoom's Andrea Branzi has put it:

> it had been discovered that doing architecture did not just mean making
> houses, or constructing tasteful things in general, but signified expressing
> oneself, communicating, arguing and freely creating one's own cultural
> habitat, according to the instinctive right that every individual has to create
> his own environment, but from which the division of labour in society has
> totally alienated him.[21]

The most rapidly radicalized young architects were to be found close to the
source of revolution in France. The Utopie group formed in protest at the
syllabus of Paris's Beaux-Arts school in 1967, and by March 1968 had
realized a provocative exhibition at the Musée d'Art Moderne of the sort
of inflatable structures that Utopie believed could provide the basis for a
revolutionary architecture – cheap, lightweight, an architectural medium
for directly lived space. Utopie's increasingly abrasive pamphleteering,
inspired by the Situationists and philosopher Henri Lefebvre, recognized
that the chink in Archigram's armor was that of coherent theory and
explicit social rationale.[22] Reaction against capitalism was similarly marked
amongst the eighty staff and 120 students who defied the French Ministry
of Cultural Affairs' reorganization of the Beaux-Arts school after the May
Events of 1968. Refusing to be co-opted into one of the five new teaching
units ("Unités pédagogiques" or "UPs"), the most intransigent students
and staff gathered as UP6, denouncing "the class segregation perpetuated
and augmented by present bourgeois urbanism."[23] Its strike in the winter
of 1969–70 took teaching "to the streets" and into the decision-making

institutions of building production, including the offices of the Ministry of Services and Housing.[24] UP6 students experimented with the education of the architect, accepting work as site laborers[25] in a social reordering of architectural production.

Some of this radical spirit was even exported from Paris into the syllabus of the more moderate Architectural Association in London.[26] Embarrassed by the liberalism bequeathed to the AA by his former employers, Archigram, Bernard Tschumi (who like Koolhaas had witnessed the Paris Events of May 1968)[27] endorsed squatting[28] and cultivated contacts with the Irish Republican Army (a project eventually dropped after bomb threats against the AA).[29] Apparent in all these revisions to the syllabus was a virulent disdain for the traditional role of the academy as an institution separated from the rest of urban space and society. Modern architecture, the new radicals argued, had caricatured its users as proletarians with just a few basic biomechanical needs, wage-slaves to the circulation of labor and commodities.

And yet most of the architectural radicals of *c*.1968 quickly returned to architecture as it was traditionally practiced; the call to build tended to be more enduring than the call for absolute resistance to bourgeois society. "I was . . . aware of the limitations of our position as intellectuals and architects who were unlikely to find ourselves loading guns and hiding explosives in underground networks," Tschumi confesses about the evolution of his own architectural radicalism.[30] After 1968, the neo-avant-garde fared well, as seen in the startling creation in Paris itself of the Centre Pompidou (Renzo Piano and Richard Rogers, 1971–7). Inspired by a heady combination of Archigram images and the direct democracy of '68, Lefebvrian and even Situationist thinking was being steadily incorporated into official French urban policy in the early 1970s.[31] Even within UP6, the ambition of some of its members to graduate had to be policed with increasing violence, so that, as the course came close to awarding diplomas in 1971, radicals followed the example of the rioting students of Yale in 1968 and burnt down the school office.[32] Utopie split at about the same time, three of its members lured back to practice.[33]

Individual participants had their own reasons for abandoning the architectural revolution, but there seemed little alternative in any case as the wider revolutionary movement of 1968 dispersed. The revolutionary mood of '68 survived no longer than its forebear in the 1920s; it may be the case that the dalliances with radicalism have been *exceptional* phases for Modern architecture, and that liberalism has provided it with more fertile soil. Just a decade later the way was clear for a return to neo-conservative social values and neo-liberal economic principles, espoused by such leaders as Margaret Thatcher and Ronald Reagan, with the further global expansion of capitalism seemingly unstoppable after the collapse of the Berlin Wall in 1989. Above all, the architectural profession had to adapt to the shrinkage in publicly funded building projects, like housing, that had indemnified a post-war generation of architects and had put them in close proximity to the mechanisms of the state.

The switch from unbridled optimism about radical architecture to a suspicion of it was one of the signal qualities of so-called postmodernism. The American postmodernists Robert Venturi and Denise Scott Brown, recognizing the delusion that architecture can or should change the world through ruthless modernization, were already disavowing the pretensions of the avant-garde in their teaching seminars at Yale in 1968 (which would lead to publication of their seminal *Learning from Las Vegas* in 1972). For them, a relevant architecture now meant not the perpetual change of super-technological consumerism, nor a dissembled architecture of revolution, but a "homecoming," a "retrenchment," a new interest in meaning and legibility, a new *vernacular*, a true expression of "everyday people."[34]

Venturi and Scott Brown reinstated the historical devices of architecture and the authorial role of the architect. A renewed air of professionalism was noticeable about the architectural vanguard as it gravitated toward the USA. No more "little magazines," lucky dips of zany ideas chaotically produced and distributed in the manner of *Archigram*; Robert Venturi's *Complexity and Contradiction in Architecture* was sleekly produced and distributed by MOMA in 1966. *Oppositions*, launched in 1974 and edited by Peter Eisenman from the Institute of Architecture and Urban Studies in New York, was as formidably produced as it was titled.[35] The cost of this professionalism and critical rigor was, it could be argued, the carnival spirit in which the neo-avant-garde had thus far reveled. This coincided with a nay-saying amongst architecture's most incisive critics, the most outspoken of whom in the early 1970s was the Italian Marxist historian Manfredo Tafuri, who argued that architecture was only ever a superstructural phenomenon of bourgeois society, and could thus be nothing more than a bourgeois implement of repression in all its guises, avantgarde or mainstream, Modern or postmodern. Much of the neo-avantgarde in the 1970s seemed to agree with Tafuri's sentiment, and began jettisoning claims to its architecture being able to change the world. Peter

Eisenman and his colleagues in the so-called New York Five (Michael Graves, Charles Gwathmey, John Hejduk, and Richard Meier) declared themselves free to concentrate on what they knew architecture to still be capable of – form – reworking the 1920s' Modernist achievements of Le Corbusier and Guiseppe Terragni under the mandate of "autonomy" from overt social and political motivations.

Paradoxically, an avant-garde critique of form at this time *reinvigorated* Modernist form. Eisenman was particularly interested in deconstruction, a philosophy spearheaded by French philosopher Jacques Derrida to pick apart the construction of meaning. Two built projects of the early 1980s exemplified "deconstructivist" architectural (anti-) form – Eisenman's Wexner Center, Columbus, Ohio, in 1983–9, and Tschumi's Parc de la Villette, Paris, in 1984–9, the latter like a "trace" of the presumed purposes of a public park, the former a "deconstruction" of such norms as the grid. Yet deconstructivism sat comfortably in the canon of Modern architecture because it foregrounded – in an inventive, graphic, almost parodic manner – such long-standing preoccupations of Modern architecture as the difference between inside and outside, and drew inspiration from the Constructivist and Cubist styles of the 1920s. In a show of 1987, deconstructivism acquired recognition by the same institution and under the same curatorship (Museum of Modern Art, New York, Philip Johnson) as the International Style had enjoyed back in 1932. The challenges posed in designs such as Daniel Libeskind's Jewish Museum (2001) and Frank Gehry's Bilbao Guggenheim Museum (1997) were easily smoothed out as magazine images and tourist destinations.

Neo-avant-garde ideology retained an enigmatic, non-committal, and even ironic aura, as if the architect with the least commitment was the best prepared to survive and respond socially and aesthetically to a world undergoing the rapid transformations wrought by free-market capitalism, scientific change, and accelerated communications. Critic Ellen Dunham-Jones aptly described figures like Koolhaas and Tschumi as "surfing" late capitalism rather than opposing it: "Koolhaas's research of Manhattan, Atlanta, and Asia, has since been in pursuit of the perfect wave."[36] The neo-avant-garde stance became very problematic, though caution should be exercised before dismissing it as ethically rootless: it sought less to endorse capitalism as to recognize it as a potentially *renewing* force in the world. Perhaps, it was mooted (for instance by the postmodern philosopher Jean Baudrillard, formerly of Utopie), the ascendancy of the masses was likely to come about not by the utopian dreams of the avant-garde and the left but by consumption. The neo-avant-garde was receptive to a poststructuralist intellectual climate that questioned the ethics and efficacy of retaining old "certainties" like the prospect of class war, while dissenting feminist, ethnic, and sexual perspectives, previously subsumed by the rhetorics of class, also began to be heard. "Despite all earlier warnings to the contrary," wrote architect Nigel Coates about the cultural background of his design in the late 1970s and early 1980s, "social fragmentation added a new vitality to things."[37] Such willingness to look at the contemporary world without prejudice reminds us of an observation made in the previous section of this chapter – that a pivotal change in the post-war avant-garde was to recognize the world *as it is* rather than project upon it the abstraction of *what it is not-yet*. It is easy to create the impression that the post-war neo-avant-garde was less politically effective than the pre-war avant-garde. But could it, or should it, have better resisted the developments in economics, technology, and culture that made a singular agenda for architecture – of the sort maintained by the Modern Movement – less and less credible?

Le Corbusier's slogan, "architecture or revolution," was an early indicator that what Modern architecture really wished to provide was a built *order* or *image* appropriate to a *changing world*. Perhaps the avant-garde architects that faired best were those who provided the most convincing representations of often frightening or invisible forces of modernization, "making them safe" (just as the opposite strategy of historicism sought to deny them). In an age when technology threatened global destruction through the A-bomb, for example, Archigram reassured its audience that technology might yet be the savior of civilization (as had been believed by some of the first avant-gardes). Two decades later, in a world menaced by the decline of industrial production and governance through barely perceptible networks of capital and information, architects like Tschumi, Koolhaas, and Gehry created a powerful, somewhat macho post-industrial aesthetic that rejoiced in immateriality, disjunction, and flow.

While neo-avant-garde activity of deconstructivist and postmodern ilk tended to disavow the social earnestness of the late 1960s – and indeed of the Modern Movement – the spectral hope of liberation persisted. No longer, it was true, liberation from the capitalist economy as hoped for by the radicals of '68, but still some sense of liberation from the norms of architecture and the ways in which it is used. Deconstructing familial space and comfort in his series of Houses built in the early 1970s, Peter

Eisenman challenged the norms of domesticity. The desire to reshape social space was apparent in work carried out at the AA by the teaching units of Bernard Tschumi and Nigel Coates,[38] the fading inspirations of 1968 supplemented in the late 1970s by the anarchic culture of Punk and the rediscovery of the bestial disorder and transgression celebrated in the 1930s' writings of renegade Surrealist Georges Bataille. Rem Koolhaas's classic 1978 book, *Delirious New York,* turned conventional planning on its head by endorsing the pleasures of congestion. In the 1980s Koolhaas and Tschumi typically inserted into their designs gaps and ramps which tempted visitors into "transgressive" and "crossprogrammed" movements and activities. By the 1990s, the pursuit of functional and typological ambiguity had emerged as the nearest thing to a program for the neo-avant-garde – an exact inversion of Modern Movement urbanism, and offered with just the same sense of public-spiritedness.[39]

Out of the conferences and publications of the architectural schools, meanwhile, emerged a sort of neo-avant-garde syllabus urging students to consider not so much how architecture is produced, but how architecture produces – how it produces meanings, behaviors, social distinctions, and subjective experiences. In this, "theory" (adapted from philosophy, literary criticism, Frankfurt School Marxism, phenomenology, and psycho-analysis) was often found to be more useful than that traditional staple of architectural humanities, history.[40] The academy continued to offer laboratory conditions for successive neo-avant-gardes. Zaha Hadid admitted in 1992 that "as actual professional practice becomes ever more circumscribed by codes, standards and stereotypes, architectural education – the arena of the experimentalist fringe – becomes ever more unrestrained in its self-indulgent 'radicalism.'"[41] The prominence given to "radical" ideas in architectural training, it was often argued by critics, was completely disproportionate to the "two percent" return of "radical" architecture actually getting built.[42]

Indeed, the neo-avant-garde may have been in part a product of the academy, just as the Modern Movement before it. There was, it could be argued, an element in '68 and its aftermath which was an academic project, spilling over from the University of Nanterre into the Sorbonne and a host of other teaching institutions across Europe and the USA, inspired by a succession of sometime academic gurus: Barthes, Leary, Marcuse, Chomsky, Laing, Lefebvre, Foucault. Faculty members at Columbia in 1968 enjoyed the student rebellion, it has been alleged, vicariously reliving the communist agitation of the 1950s.[43] "'Destroy the University' was a popular slogan both during and after the May events," Martin Pawley and Bernard Tschumi reported in 1971. "But," they concluded in defence of the academy, "to close the school utterly and completely was to destroy any real possibility of systematic analysis and critique."[44] Against a rising tide of conservatism, the 1970s–1980s was an era when the neo-avant-garde, such as it was, needed the institutional support of the academy more than ever. It is probably no coincidence, meanwhile, that so many key "avant-garde" buildings of the post-war decades have been sponsored by universities (for instance, Candilis/Josic/Woods' Free University, Berlin, [1964–79], James Stirling at Cambridge and Leicester [1963, 1968], Peter Eisenman's Wexner [1989], Frank Gehry at Loyola [1986], Tschumi at Columbia and Florida [2001, 2002]).

One could even venture that the academy itself has been a utopian model, an arena for free thought, by increments more socially inclusive through the expanding provision of higher education, endowed with massive resources of knowledge, a space that is relatively autonomous from the spectacular-commodity city at large.[45] In the 1960s it was wondered whether university culture anticipated the dwindling away of work into a life of leisure and learning, its refectories replacing the intellectual space of the cheap city cafés being driven out by escalating rents. The fact that the academy is, at the same time, an exclusive and conservative institution, marshaling thought, a prison of its own paradigms, may only add to its allure. Locked into a contradiction of its own making – the claim to authority, on the one hand, and intellectual regeneration on the other – the academy has created a disjunctive space of its own, its laws providing, to paraphrase Tschumi (who became a Dean at Columbia), an erotic effect of bondage to be violently transgressed, usually only intellectually, but sometimes physically.[46] It is a characteristic that echoes the conundrum of "Modern-ism."

We need to be aware, too, of a special political dilemma that besets all architecture, and that is that building provides infrastructure to the world *that is*, rather than the world that is to come (in this way, a building is unlike, say, a piece of avant-garde music or poetry that may have a prophetic quality to it). The best place where architecture can talk of the things-to-come is the Schools, where so many of the architects mentioned in this chapter have waited for their opportunity to build, while implanting their ideas onto a student body, the "next generation" of architects through whom it is possible to live vicariously.

Notes

1 See *Non-plan: Essays on Freedom, Participation and Change in Modern Architecture and Urbanism*, ed. Jonathan Hughes and Simon Sadler (Oxford: Architectural Press, 2000).

2 Common usage of the term Modern Movement can be traced back amongst English practitioners at least as far as 1936: see Nikolaus Pevsner, *Pioneers of the Modern Movement* (London: Faber and Faber, 1936). However, the idea of a "movement" clearly developed earlier, between Le Corbusier's coining of "l'Esprit nouveau" ("the new spirit," the title of Le Corbusier's journal of 1920–5) and the Weissenhof Siedlung (1927) and CIAM (1928). The term Modern Movement as such, with its messianic associations, probably originates in the British literature after 1928 (for instance in the *Architectural Review*), and its stylistic principles acquired the label "International Style" in 1931–2, provided by the Americans Alfred Barr, Henry-Russell Hitchcock and Philip Johnson. The nearest equivalent to "Movement" in German is the word *Weg*, which occurs in art and architecture throughout the 1920s, though the word *mouvement* does not occur in French until much later. (Prof. Tim Benton has provided me with much of this clarification.)

3 Note, however, that while all the directors of the Bauhaus were eminent Modernist architects (Gropius, Meyer, Mies van der Rohe), a separate department of architecture was not established until 1927.

4 Sigfried Giedion, *Space, Time and Architecture: The Growth of a New Tradition*, 4th edn (Cambridge, MA: Harvard University Press, 1963), p. 27.

5 The Bauhaus chose not to teach history for the first three years of its existence (1919–21) for fear that it would pollute its project.

6 See, for instance, Eric Mumford, *The CIAM Discourse on Urbanism, 1928–1960* (Cambridge, MA: MIT Press, 2000) and Colin St John Wilson, *The Other Tradition of Modern Architecture: The Uncompleted Project* (London: Academy Editions, 1995). Examples of "excluded" figures include Johannes Itten from the Bauhaus and Hugo Häring from CIAM.

7 The title of Pevsner's book was toned down to *Pioneers of Modern Design* when it was reissued again in 1960, acquiring its subtitle: *From William Morris to Walter Gropius*.

8 See the subtitle of Giedion's book, *Space, Time and Architecture: The Growth of a New Tradition*.

9 Documentation for this period of history is to be found in *Architecture Culture 1943–1968: A Documentary Anthology*, ed. Joan Ockman and Edward Eigen (New York: Columbia Books of Architecture/Rizzoli, 1993).

10 For detailed discussions of the avant-garde in the US, see *Autonomy and Ideology: Positioning and Avant-garde in America*, ed. R. E. Somol (New York: Monacelli Press, 1997).

11   For detailed discussion, see John R. Gold, *The Experience of Modernism: Modern Architects and the Future City, 1928–1953* (London: Spon, 1997).

12   See Mark Crinson and Jules Lubbock, *Architecture, Art or Profession? Three Hundred Years of Architectural Education in Britain* (Manchester: Manchester University Press, 1994).

13   Alison and Peter Smithson, "The New Brutalism," *Architectural Design* (April 1957): 113, quoted in Reyner Banham, *The New Brutalism* (London: Architectural Press, 1966), p. 66.

14   See Peter Smithson, interview with Graham Whitham, November 22, 1982, in *The Independent Group: Postwar Britain and the Aesthetics of Plenty*, ed. David Robbins (Cambridge, MA: MIT Press, 1990), p. 37.

15   See Peter Bürger, *Theorie der Avantgarde* (1974), trans. M. Shaw, *Theory of the Avant-garde* (Minneapolis, MN: University of Minnesota Press, 1984).

16   Peter Smithson, James Gowan, John Killick, and John Voelcker amongst others.

17   Both Koolhaas and Tschumi were at the AA by 1970 (Tschumi as a young teacher). See Ellen Dunham-Jones, "The Generation of '68 – Today: Bernard Tschumi, Rem Koolhaas and the Institutionalization of Critique," *Proceedings of the 86th ACSA Annual Meeting and Technology Conference* (1998), pp. 527–33, p. 528.

18   Reyner Banham, "Zoom Wave Hits Architecture," *New Society*, March 3, 1966, reprinted in Reyner Banham, *Design by Choice*, ed. Penny Sparke (London: Academy Editions, 1981), pp. 64–5, p. 64.

19   Two architect members were in fact expelled in 1960.

20   See Simon Sadler, *The Situationist City* (Cambridge, MA: MIT Press, 1998).

21   Andrea Branzi, *The Hot House: Italian New Wave Design* (London: Thames and Hudson, 1984), p. 60.

22   Jean Aubert, in conversation with Tim Benton, Paris 1998.

23   Manifesto of the group Environnement Mai '68 (1969), in Martin Pawley and Bernard Tschumi [Tchumi], "The Beaux-Arts since '68," *Architectural Design* (September 1971): 553–66, p. 553.

24   Ibid., pp. 554–5.

25   Ibid., p. 566.

26   An AA delegation visited the École des Beaux-Arts in January 1971.

27   In 1968 Koolhaas and Tschumi were both twenty-four years old, living in Paris, Koolhaas as a journalist and Tschumi with the Candilis/Josic/Woods practice that was sympathetic to student protests at the École. See Dunham-Jones, "The Generation of '68 – Today," p. 527.

28   See Bernard Tschumi, "The Environmental Trigger," in *A Continuing Experiment: Learning and Teaching at the Architectural Association*, ed. James Gowan (London: Architectural Press, 1975), pp. 89–99, p. 96.

29   See Bernard Tschumi, *Architecture and Disjunction* (Cambridge, MA: MIT Press, 1994), p. 7.

30 Ibid., p. 10.

31 See Eleonore Kofman and Elizabeth Lebas, "Introduction," in Henri Lefebvre, *Writings on Cities*, ed. and trans. Eleonore Kofman and Elizabeth Lebas (Oxford: Blackwell, 1996).

32 See George Baird, "1968 and its Aftermath: The Loss of Moral Confidence in Architectural Practice and Education," in *Reflections on Architectural Practices in the Nineties*, ed. William S. Sanders (New York: Princeton Architectural Press, 1996), p. 64.

33 See *The Inflatable Moment: Pneumatics and Protest in '68*, ed. Marc Dessauce (New York: Princeton Architectural Press, 1999), p. 8.

34 For an account of the wider urge for "homecoming" within the intelligentsia, see "The 1970s: Bringing it All Back Home," in Marshall Berman, *All that is Solid Melts into Air: The Experience of Modernity* (London: Verso, 1983).

35 For more on *Oppositions*, see *Oppositions Reader*, ed. K. Michael Hays (New York: Princeton Architectural Press, 1998), and Joan Ockman, "Resurrecting the Avant-garde: The History and Program of Oppositions," in *Architecture-production: Revisions no. 2*, ed. Beatriz Colomina and Joan Ockman (New York: Princeton Architectural Press, 1988), pp. 180–99.

36 Dunham-Jones, "The Generation of '68 – Today," p. 531.

37 Nigel Coates, "Narrative Break-up," in *The Discourse of Events* (London: Architectural Association, 1983), pp. 12–17, p. 15.

38 See ibid.

39 See, for instance, the "snapshot" of ideas and projects provided in *The End of Architecture? Documents and Manifestos*, ed. Peter Noever (Munich: Prestel, 1993).

40 The production of theory was particularly intense around the schools on the East Coast of the USA, a fact reflected in compendiums of recent architectural theory: *Architecture Theory since 1968*, ed. K. Michael Hays (Cambridge, MA: MIT Press, 1998) and *Theorizing a New Agenda for Architecture: An Anthology of Architectural Theory, 1965–1995*, ed. Kate Nesbitt (New York: Princeton Architectural Press, 1996).

41 Zaha Hadid, "Another Beginning," statement to the Vienna Architecture Conference, June 1992, in *The End of Architecture?*, ed. Noever, pp. 25–8, p. 25.

42 An estimate from the Vienna Architecture Conference, June 1992. See "Roundtable," in *The End of Architecture?*, ed. Noever, pp. 99–127, passim.

43 Dan Leab, paper to the Open University '60s seminar, April 1997. Leab was a Dean at Columbia at the time.

44 Pawley and Tschumi, "The Beaux-Arts since '68," pp. 564–5.

45 As Tschumi acknowledges in *Architecture and Disjunction*, p. 252, of the development of deconstructivism, "Much of this work benefited from the environment of the universities and the art scene – its galleries and publications

– where the crossover among different fields allowed architects to blur the distinctions between different genres."

46   See Tschumi, *Architecture and Disjunction*, p. 88: "the game of architecture is an intricate play with rules that one may accept or reject. Indifferently called système des Beaux-Arts or modern movement precepts, this pervasive network of binding laws entangles architectural design . . . When manipulated, however, they have the erotic significance of bondage."

2

Aalto and the Tutelary Goddesses

Sarah Menin

Human Costs of "Humane Modernism"

Alvar Aalto was one of the most admired twentieth-century architects, praised as a pioneer of humane Modernism. However, the production of his architectural sensitivity toward the "little man" (as he called the users of his buildings) was costly. This cost was paid by those close to Aalto, who gave him his stability when the mantle of his manic-depressive personality crippled him and made him unable to act in his self-appointed position as "top dog," holding him almost in psychosis at times. When running creatively, he seemed often to find his footing by trampling on the hearts of those around him. Yet when ridden with tortured depression and often childish neediness,[1] he drained the life blood of those same dedicated individuals. This chapter will examine the shadow side of Aalto's humane Modernism, the architecture sculpted out of his own pain, and the lives of those around him.

True Architecture and the True Self

In 1958 Alvar Aalto wrote that "True architecture exists only where man stands in the centre. His tragedy, and his comedy, both."[2] In accord with his compatriot, architect and theorist Juhani Pallasmaa has suggested that "architecture is not primarily about theory, technique or function, but about the world and life," going on to suggest that "[w]e are able to conceive only what our unique life condition at large makes possible and architecture provides one of the most important horizons of experience and understanding."[3] By invoking the "life condition," Pallasmaa invites an examination of Aalto's "life-world" (*lebenswelt*) to use Husserl's notion.[4] Indeed, by focusing on Aalto's personal realm the discussion is directed toward what is most fecund in his work, but also the nature of the sacrifices that facilitated it.

Göran Schildt, in his biography of his friend Aalto, describes the rift in Aalto's personality between a hard, precocious shell and a nervous, repressed ego. The humanism, which resulted in sensitivity to the psychosocial aspects of human experience being purposefully accommodated in Aalto's architecture, and his deep agenda to design for the "little man" who is too easily hidden or forgotten in the generation of fine architecture, can be shown to be rooted both in the repressed side of himself and, ironically, in the care and sensitivity shown by those he often treated less than well in adult life.

Aalto's was therefore a very costly humanism in human terms. Ironically, investment in this humanism had been made unwittingly in his childhood. The tragedy therein began to draw to itself the lives of others, who, by supporting Aalto at times of psychological vulnerability, equally invested themselves in the production of "humane" Modernism. However costly, they were sometimes very moving, holding environments in which the vulnerable Aalto was supported, made strong again, and able to perform creatively for the "little man" outside and beyond himself.

As Anton Ehrenzweig suggests in his study of *The Hidden Order of Art*, "Art's conscious superstructure may be largely composed by intellectual effort, but its vast substructure is shaped by (unconscious) spontaneity, as indeed is any creative work."[5] Thus mental processes of which the person is not aware exert a powerful influence on behavior. Drives, fantasies, and difficult memories are repressed and made unconscious because of their unacceptable nature. While accepting, with other scholars, that psychology cannot completely explain art,[6] this chapter will explore the link between Aalto's "life-world," his creative drive to humanize what he saw as harsh Modernism, and his capacity to draw life from those around him to sustain his own creativity (both personally and artistically). A connection between his personal pain, the pain that he inflicted (advertently or inadvertently), and the product of his creativity (i.e., humanized architecture) will be established. It is also important to recognize that Aalto's life story is not unique, and that the experiences which may have caused or stimulated subsequent creativity are all too common.

Architecture and the Cessation of Intimacy

Aalto experienced a deep trauma in childhood which left him with a strong, highly defended personality which was, nonetheless, extremely vulnerable to breakdown. The roots of this vulnerability are important both to the specific discussion of his relationships, and to the direction and deep nature of his architecture.

Alvar was born in 1898 at Alavus, seventeen miles from Kuortane near Alajärvi in Southern Ostrobothnia. His family moved to Jyväskylä, Central Finland, in 1903. Alvar's father, J. H. Aalto (as, according to the tradition of the times, he was called), was from peasant farming stock in Häme, yet was lucky enough to attend the first Finnish Lyceum (grammar school) in Hämeenlinna, also attended by Sibelius. After much hard work, he went on to train as a land surveyor, becoming district surveyor in Jyväskylä. Alvar's mother, Selma Mathilda Hackstedt, came from an educated Swedish-speaking family, and was keenly interested in issues of women's emancipation. She bore five children, of which Alvar was the second. The first died in infancy; the last, Selma (known as Piu), remained weak throughout childhood.

Alvar enjoyed close physical intimacy with his mother beyond his infancy. He slept in her bed while his father was away on surveying expeditions. Though not uncommon, nor unhealthy, this is less usual for the oldest child. What is most significant is the fact that this intimacy was severed by her sudden death from meningitis, in 1906, when Alvar was eight, causing what was to become a deep-seated trauma, manifesting itself as a terror of death which haunted him throughout his life. His maternal grandfather, who had moved to be close to the family and with whom Alvar had an important relationship, then died in 1909. This paints a picture of the imminence of death, the tone of which was to become still darker. Indeed, his younger brother, Einar, killed himself in response to the call up at the outbreak of the Winter War, in 1939, when Russia invaded Finland's eastern border. In response to the same historic event Aalto ran away. This contradicts Schildt's comment that the Aalto children's "security was not shaken by their mother's demise."[7] On the contrary, therein lies the fault line which led to immeasurable pain and suffering, yet out of which indirectly, it will be argued, grew his great compassion for the "little man."

Alvar's aunt, Flora, who lived with the family already, soon stepped into her sister's shoes, and married his father. The picture Aalto painted is of continuous security and contentment, with the happy memory of the two mothers becoming fused. What Aalto does not recall is that from which he could never find release: the gaping wound of his mother's sudden demise.

Alvar's father believed in safe and stimulating provision for children. He was also extremely conscientious about his work, often undertaking long surveying trips, on which he took Alvar after Selma's death. However, J. H. Aalto was also undemonstrative, reserved, and cool in character, making "an appearance now and then and ordered the boys about but otherwise he was away, at work, or drinking toddies with the other gents," according to Hanni Alanen.[8] It seems that he was completely unable to compensate for the loss of his wife's warmth. The lack of Alvar's birth mother's physical and emotional warmth may have been ameliorated by Flora (known as Mammu), but it seems that she was unable to provide a sufficiently healing environment through which the trauma of his mother's death could be healed, and therefore through which Alvar would learn to adjust to reality and to experience healthy boundaries; in short, to know himself as being separate from others.[9] Instead, as a child, Alvar apparently learnt to dislocate feelings and expression, from which a persistent sense of inner weakness and inadequacy soon took root, around which the manic defenses he exhibited later in life grew.

Anxiety and the "Gap"

The Finnish semiotician Eero Tarasti succinctly suggests that "The existence of anxiety is a *sign* for something."[10] The prolific psychiatrist and writer Donald W. Winnicott sought to move the psychoanalytical movement of Freud and Klein from concentration on conflicts within the individual to understanding the experience and environment of the individual.[11] Winnicott might therefore respond to Tarasti by saying that anxiety is a *sign* of a break or a "*gap*," which he defined as a failure of the infant's environment.[12] In a "good enough environment" (i.e., that which basically facilitates rather than prevents primary, pre-sexual creativity) there should be no "gap." This is helpful here, assisting analysis of Aalto's life.

The first environment, Winnicott believed, is the experience of being held, starting before birth and progressing through the nursing period, facilitating psychosomatic integration, and "natural" growth processes.[13] To grow, clearly both child and adult must be inherently creative, rejecting, changing, and ultimately integrating the fragments of order which are experienced into individual inner worlds. Concurring with Pallasmaa above, Winnicott championed the effect of cultural and environmental factors in the human growth (i.e., creative) process, writing: "When one speaks of a man one speaks of him along with the summation of his cultural experience. The whole forms a unit."[14] For Winnicott, the paradox of the infant–mother relationship lay in the fact that the environment (mother) *makes* the *becoming* self of the infant feasible.[15] There seems to have been some interruption or schism in this process of Alvar's development. Other psychoanalysts were exploring factors of environment, recognizing that "in the beginning one's mother is, literally, the whole world."[16] Selma may, for some reason, still have been "the whole world" for the eight-year-old Alvar, and therefore her demise shattered his life. Perhaps it was this that he sought to recreate in his relationships, and what is more in his architecture. It will be argued that early childhood deprivations may also create drives which unconsciously motivate other behavioral patterns, which may include the "inner urge" to create, and the agenda of this creativity.

Primary Creativity

It can be demonstrated that there is often a link between severance within the psyche and the development of a pattern of behavior where creativity is central. Here the argument draws closer to Aalto's case. Winnicott believed that the very earliest stages of development were intrinsically creative. Creation, so conceived, is not a mystery, but a phenomenon experienced when the self acts freely. Thus, at odds with Freudian analysis, Winnicott promoted "the idea of primary psychic creativity," suggesting that if "good-enough" maternal care was forthcoming, integration, personalization, and realization would follow.[17] So, although Aalto is perceived as an extrovert creative individual in artistic terms, in personal, psychological terms, it may be argued that he was not free, having not "grown" sufficiently in emotional terms in childhood. It is as if he sought to recreate his own freedom through his work.

Integration, which has taken the infant from primary un-integration (being without ego), then takes him to integration in which the experiences coming from outside and inside are united. In an un-integrated state the infant needs the security to be safe "in bits," so to speak.[18] If the safety needed to do this is not forthcoming, disintegration occurs, in which the infant creates inner chaos which may replicate the failure or the unreliability of the environment.[19] Such breaks or early cessation of integration can cause dissociation, in which un-integrated parts of the self lose touch with the developmental process, and are then adrift as "unknowable deficits."[20] It was the connecting of these drifting parts that Winnicott saw as the purpose of psychoanalysis, and which Ehrenzweig recognized as the core of the *Hidden Order of Art*. This is fascinating at the level of analogy with architectural form, since Aalto's work famously draws together seemingly disparate elements into a precarious whole.

Believing that the mother facilitates the infant's growth, Winnicott argued that the disruption of the environment (the "gap") interferes with the growth of the individual, and with the "Potential Space" the individual might occupy; i.e., the space carved out of a "place" without impingement or a "hypothetical area that exists (but cannot exist) between the baby and the object (mother or part of mother) during the phase of the repudiation of the object as not me, that is at the end of being merged in with the object."[21] This notion, which grew from Winnicott's belief that play and creativity were linked in the transitional world, between subjectivity and objectivity, strongly countered Freudian assumptions of sublimation, wherein creativity is a substitute for instinctual expression.[22] Such a primary process of identifying self and non-self is a central context for creative (human) development because with sufficient trust in the environment (initially *mother*), there can be creative (potential) space which the individual might inhabit (both internally and externally); i.e., exploration of the interplay between inner and outer reality. It becomes apparent that there was a lack of development in this area of Aalto's personality, and that, indeed, this developed into a "gap." At this point the individual feels that, as Winnicott puts it, "The only real thing is the gap,"[23] which, therefore, they seek to fill through fantasy and indeed creative endeavor; i.e., drawing the fragmented parts into a union, however difficult a whole this transpired to be.

Altering the "Gap"

Winnicott believed in the need for basic "good-enough Mothering" (by the primary person in infancy) to sustain "going on being." If the "gap" was central to life in childhood, then addressing the "gap" in one way or another (defending it, denying it, or seeking to ameliorate its effect) also becomes the central preoccupation later. Winnicott saw, for example, any anti-social acts as attempts by the child to return to a point at which the environment failed him; a return to examine or dwell in the "gaps" in himself.[24] Children also react to insecurity by repeatedly testing the goodness of their environment, their parents or substitutes.[25] Such behavior, for instance, includes the split between the withdrawn ego and the very weak inner ego (i.e., a schizoid split or what Balint called a "basic fault.")[26]

Adult children (those who have not established sufficient object relations, nor have reached emotional maturation) do the same. Indeed, despite the threat of withdrawal of approval and affection by his wives, Aalto openly wove a pattern of flirtations and frequent affairs (to which Schildt repeatedly refers).[27] For instance, on a journey to a conference in Norway, Aalto openly flirted with a young colleague in the car, despite the presence of his wife Aino, and another. When he refused to stop the blatant petting, his wife insisted the car was stopped, and the young woman was kicked out.

Contiguous to Winnicott's famous phrase "we are poor indeed if we are only sane,"[28] Jean Sibelius wrote to a friend, "He is richest who can suffer most."[29] Aalto, too, suffered, but not with any great humility it seems, rather drawing others into his pain, and (like Sibelius) on occasions acting out childish, insensitive, and sometimes cruel behavior. Aalto established a survival strategy in the form of relational structures which would shore him up when his ego collapsed, but which he would consciously or unconsciously abuse when his ego was "strong." Without these sacrificial lives he could not cope, evinced by his trips abroad, in which he seems either to have to be drunk or a philanderer, if he was not to become deeply, even desperately, lonely, crying out for help. For instance, from one trip in 1932 he wrote to Aino, "It was as if I begged you to help me."[30] Aalto's inability to experience being content alone was profound. Without the support of either those relationally committed to him, or temporary "lifeboats," either human or liquid, he seems to have collapsed either psychologically or physically. At such times the "gap" was too big to be ameliorated. For instance, in a letter to Aino from the CIAM meeting in 1933 Aalto relayed his conquering of an American millionaire's young daughter in Marseilles, actually describing her accurately as a "lifeboat," and boasting into old age of how he cured the woman of her "strict Protestant upbringing."[31]

Environment, Experience, and Ideas

Plato believed that knowledge was true opinion bound by the "chains" of recollection,[32] seeking to associate ideas, rather than experience, of being and seeing in the world. Yet, significantly, the notion of chains signifies the connectedness that Suzanne. K. Langer implies in the phrase "the threads of unrecorded reality."[33] Yet these descriptions of chains also infer restriction, two elements of the bank of memories. That Aalto's past could have been the source of both his adult trauma and, to some degree, his soaring creativity is important. Indeed, a person's mental catalog of experiences is like an early bank of perceptual history: abstracted forms of things and experiences are retained as concepts.[34] New perceptions fall into abstract forms, and are filtered through the concepts (their shape, form, and significance) of previous experiences. Therefore, Plato's preference for ideas over experience is not unfounded. Since perception changes as a child develops, incidents which are experienced and recorded as wholes (*gestalts*) before latency (from four or five years to puberty) are felt differently later, at which time abstract analytical faculties develop.[35] Nevertheless, early "concepts" retain their fecundity, and new perceptions become associated with known forms from earlier experience.[36] Indeed, it has been demonstrated elsewhere that it is not illegitimate to conceive of Aalto's experience of the forest as "refuge" in childhood having been translated creatively into form later in life.[37] In *The Ecology of Imagination in Childhood*, Edith Cobb has explored such a link between experience of nature and the development of personality and creativity (both personal and artistic).[38]

Yet, in an ironic comment in 1967, Aalto cited Nietzsche's notion that "only obscurantists look back."[39] His son Hamilkar also recalls that "He never looked back too much. To grieve for something was foreign to him."[40] Indeed, Aalto often seems to seek to obscure details of his past, with what Schildt describes as florid, often fantastical tales, wishing to "reinterpret reality in his own way, transforming the past into myths or at least amusing tales."[41] However, attempts to master painful memories (i.e. "working through") helps a person assimilate the experience and restore emotional balance.[42] In denial, such as that which seems to characterize Aalto's descriptions of his childhood, this cannot happen and the memory is buried alive. In many ways it is as if in his work Aalto was looking to address and reform what he could face in his life.[43]

Failure to adequately address the "gap" head on can result in mental instability, since anxiety results from trauma and rejection, being "lied about."[44] Consequently, the unconscious houses "the potentialities for awareness or action which the individual cannot or will not actualise."[45] The widely accepted concept of anterograde amnesia (loss of memory for specific events and experiences which occurred around trauma), or perceptual blanking, often applies in situations of trauma such as the death of a parent. Such loss may have confused and disturbed the child Alvar, leaving him to grapple to banish the terror and anxiety into which he was thrust by the bereavement.[46] The "gap" widens when the remaining parent cannot offer adequate intimacy, relatedness, or time to the child, for which all infants naturally clamor,[47] as is known to be the case with Alvar's father. It is left to the child to rebuild his or her psychic world. The substitution of Flora for Selma must have been an agent for amelioration, but may also have indirectly helped to seal the memories of Selma's sudden demise.

Testing Structures and Building Worlds

In a letter in 1941, Aalto wrote "I think people psychologically need security."[48] Cobb explains this fundamental need in terms of "world-building," suggesting that "[e]very child tries to structure a world" from which some security is found.[49] In situations where the child cannot comprehend or escape from the environment of excessive early deprivation, Winnicott observed the psychic death of the infant, wherein the healthy development of the child is sometimes inhibited, often resulting in psychosis.[50] Alternatively, the child may grasp hold of a system of order from beyond his or her unpredictable environment, internalize it, and use it to seek to bring some order to the interior chaos; seeking to "structure a world" through creative evolution.[51]

Aalto seems to have requisitioned the natural order around himself from an early age. Such a structure acts as a refuge, and can be an important ingredient in the future direction of a creative journey, demonstrating engagement in world-building to attempt to structure life in analogy with an external system, a notion akin to Eriksen's "natural genius of the child."[52] Indeed, some research suggests that "creative individuals" are much more likely to have suffered trauma, specifically the loss of a parent in childhood than matched controls.[53] It is sufficient here to record that Aalto spent much of his childhood exploring nature, giving free rein to his enquiring imagination in the depths of the woods, and excelling in the intricacies of nature studies at school.

In his childhood the patterns of his father's persona also left the youngster with a strong rationalist streak. This may have encouraged the dichotomy between the desire for rational, unsentimental masculinity and the need for maternal tenderness and the emotional comfort of femininity for which he had an insatiable yearning, relating back, it seems, to the early relationship with his mother: what one lover described as "an incredible longing for tenderness."[54] Schildt reports that Aalto "never talked to anyone about his problems."[55] Although he rarely shared his inner feelings, Aalto seems to have acted out his need for intimacy in both destructiveness and creativity: first, in his innumerable affairs, in which it seems he clamored for affection which hurt his wives,[56] and, secondly in the intimacy and sensitivity of his approach to provision for the "little man" in his buildings.

Aalto's forms are analogous with just such a juxtaposition of the rational and the emotive in their relation of rectilinear and curved elements, epitomized by the undulating plan of Baker House, MIT (1949), in which the serpentine form is yoked to the straight back of the building. It was this unity that best addressed the whole experience of the "little man." Aalto also believed that "exaggerated worship of theory . . . reflects the human predicament and insecurity. We think that in it we can find salvation from the threat of chaos"[57] – those psychic "bits" from childhood mentioned above.

Acting Out the "Gap"

Aalto may thus have found the salvation from the "chaos" he wrote of, in temporary measure, in relationships, but also in the process of designing, in part, around the "gap," the trauma, and the "tragedy" of the little man, and vicariously of himself. The picture emerges of a driven character, who uses those around him for his own well-being, and who designs for the well-being of others, more distant from himself, with whom he need not personally engage.

The Greek word for wound is *trauma*.[58] The symptoms of sudden trauma experiences can clear up quickly, only to resurface when the person is again exposed to severe stress, or acutely reminded of the trauma. Alternatively, the trauma may remain as traumatic neurosis, incapacitating the person permanently. The emotional impact of bereavement such as Aalto's, which smashes a child's schema, has been found to result in three emotional phases: protest, despair, and detachment.[59] Detachment (the pathogenic phase) is key in this case, and is most dangerous, causing permanent personality damage, often arising from long-term or permanent separation. Such damage can disable the development of the capacity to grieve effectively later in life, and encourage the development of strong depend-ent needs related to the terror of abandonment, and disturbed behavior in adulthood.[60] When symptoms continue for many years the person is said to suffer from chronic traumatic neurosis, in which ability to deal with normal activities, phobic reactions, excessive fatigue, and psychosomatic disorders all result from the increased stress levels induced by the original trauma.[61] This describes Aalto's condition, in which the trauma seems to have become fragmented and extrapolated into the development of his character and the direction of his life and work. Aalto suffered from virtu-ally all the symptoms mentioned above, experiencing times of crippling anxiety and rigid defenses, especially when coming close to the subject of death.[62] In such times contact with reality was virtually lost.

Early emotional "gaps" lead to "insufficiencies of the normal control ap-paratus,"[63] and in turn to all neurotic phenomena. Aalto's behavior manifests the denial of trauma, and concomitantly demonstrates the pathological behavior patterns and dysfunctional relationships to which this often leads,[64] and which, in turn, promotes the continuation of the "lies" from the past (the childhood scripts which serve to maintain the status quo of the damaged person), thereby entombing the anxiety in the "gap." Aalto's insistence that his childhood was happy, and his repeated references to his mother's underclothes, as reported by Maire Gullichsen,[65] demonstrate at least the complex web of his memories. Gullichsen suggests that "Mama's underwear" was the inspiration for Aalto's vases and lamps; he did origin-ally call the iconic Savoy Vase "The Eskimo Woman's Leather Breeches."

Aalto's childhood trauma was to be augmented by the early demise of his first wife. When such further trauma comes upon existing emotional disorder recovery is more difficult. In such instances there is great subcon-scious motivation to get rid of unpleasant emotional states and to ward off full awareness of a threat, and the buried trauma it triggers. Uncon-trollable spells of panic-like dread are a common symptom of acute trauma, as indeed is the search for refuge in excessive alcohol consumption (see below). The traumatized person often retains the view that the world is unsafe, and a sense of victimization often persists.

The Trauma of Insecure Structures

Anthony Storr has noted that "the more fundamentally insecure a person is, the more he is likely to fail to grow beyond his earliest emotional attitudes, or to regress into a state where such attitudes become apparent when things go badly with him."[66] When suffering from bronchitis and pneumonia in 1935 Aalto was engulfed by a "nervous crisis," which Schildt seeks to explain as amounting only to the dropping of the "top dog" persona.[67] This expression was learnt from his father, along with the directive that "You don't give orders to an Aalto;" another, which he often failed to act out, was "Always remember you're a gentleman!" Schildt often describes how Aalto was paralysed and bedridden by depression, especially in the darkest months of the year.

Demonstrating more of the deep trauma associated with the subject of death, Aalto avoided being called to the Russian Front in 1939 by secretly running away to a Stockholm hotel. According to Schildt, who wrote on the advice and memories of Aalto's family,[68] Aalto was discovered in a cowering psychosis, completely unable to admit the trauma.[69] Storr suggests that this was more likely to have been a severe panic attack than psychosis, since the latter suggests hallucinations, delusion, or gross disturbance such as catatonia.[70] Here there was a subconscious dilemma at the core of Aalto's being, between his inability to live with the reality of his feelings and the projection of himself as "top-dog." When he recovered from the acute episode in Stockholm he used his connections to get himself transferred to the propaganda office, in Helsinki, and then out to the USA on propaganda business. Maire Gullichsen wrote moving letters, seeking to persuade him to do the right thing, and return to Finland: "We cannot help feeling a little disappointed about the new postponement of your journey and do not understand the reason . . . Frankly I must say that I believe it would be very important for you to come home",[71] but Aalto refused to return, until he received a cable from the government: "RES.2ND LIEUTENANT AALTO ORDERED TO RETURN TO HIS POST."[72] Referring to his psychological vulnerability, Schildt writes: "Aalto was unusually poorly equipped to function during war time conditions."[73]

Since his brother's suicide at this time evinces a terror similar to Aalto's, it is again surprising that Schildt believes that the security of the Aalto children had not been shaken by their mother's death.[74] Such cessation of intimacy must have shocked and wounded the children deeply. Yet again, Schildt writes that "The love, security and appreciation [that Aalto] received from his earliest years from his two mother figures and a whole benevolent family gave him such a basic sense of security that he never seems to have doubted his own worth and ability."[75] He says this of the man who sometimes spent months on end in bed engulfed in psychosomatic illness.

Here Schildt exposes at least a limited, if not prejudiced view of Aalto's life. He goes on to suggest that Aalto had "no need to expose himself, to beg for understanding, or get tangled up in explanations," stating that he was "an unusually open and uninhibited person" who never felt shame after behaving badly in public (and he certainly did this).[76] Nor, according to Schildt, did he feel he owed even his wife explanation for private indiscretions.

Grandiosity and Depression: Creativity as a Mental Tool

Relentless accumulation of stress is known to lower tolerance until every minor upset is perceived as a major threat. In manic-depressive psychopathology the manic phase makes the person overactive, elated, in denial of obstacles, and suffering from illusions of grandeur, which collapse, and with them external sources of narcissistic supply. In the subsequent lurch to the paralysing state of depression, the failure to succeed and achieve is marked. With the air of the tragic loss of self, depression also protects the individual from these feelings and is thus unable to facilitate healing since deep mourning for the emotional losses, or the environmental "gap," is prohibited.

Aalto's life was a record of extremes. He exhibited symptoms of bipolar disorders of a cyclothymic temperament and even, on occasion, manic-depressive illness.[77] Aalto continually exhibited characteristics of neurosis, and, when triggered by the shock of war, death, or illness, or subsumed in the darkest months of the year, was occasionally overtaken by indomitable depression in which he was emotionally and creatively paralysed, suffering from acute, but non-specific illness, drinking excessively, and regressing to the state of a dependent child in which he needed (and wanted) to be pampered in bed for very long periods of time.[78] In such situations he was completely incapable of working, and lost contact with reality. It is at these times that his son-in-law, the psychiatrist Yrjö Alanen, believes Aalto to have been close to psychosis, completely losing his capacity to function as an adult.[79] Yet, despite all this, at other times Aalto demonstrated prolific creativity, enjoyed a wild social life, and was very popular. He had a strong ego which, though cracked, never completely crumbled, retaining the mental safety valve of withdrawal by abandoning adult responsibilities; as Schildt says, "Untiring work was the natural way of life for Aalto."[80] When he could not create he collapsed.

Winnicott believed that "Through artistic expression we can hope to keep in touch with our primitive selves whence the most intense feelings and even fearfully acute sensations derive," following this with the famous insight cited above: "we are poor indeed if we are only sane."[81] Creativity was a tool for Aalto with which he forged symbolic structures which addressed the "gap," in part recreating what he had lacked in his childhood. Aalto avoided his fear of being alone with an "all-but-manic zeal,"[82] tightly corseted by the emotional protection offered by his wives, Aino then Elissa. One who worked in Aalto's office in the 1930s describes something of the manic phase, in which Aalto managed to push the team of assistants into a frenzy of activity, as wine flowed, exhaustion was stemmed, adding that "The real wine that raised us to heights of euphoria was Aalto's personality."[83] She goes on to speculate, quite accurately, that "Part of the secret of his genius must have been this ability to alternate between extremes."[84] His inner pain was often very close to the surface, causing many episodes of hypochondriacal depression. His ability to work manically protected him from the loss of self-confidence and esteem, being scaffolding onto which he was sometimes able to cling when despair threatened, acting like a shoring, or ordering mechanism, manic in nature, but very productive if the right people were on board to service the "top dog."

Lacking the capacity to deal with normal, sober boundaries between himself and others, he became withdrawn and depressed when he could not command the scene as "top dog." Clients of Aalto's have concurred that he was a co-creator, encouraging their ideas, and not a dictator.[85] Yet, this pattern of openness to the needs of others in design terms was often not always matched in his personal relations. Aalto was extremely controlling in his behavior. His children have both related dissatisfaction with their father's behavior in later life, though when they were children he played happily with them. His daughter Hanni Alanen writes, "He loved playing with us . . . he was so kind."[86] She reports that Aalto did not understand his two children when they were no longer playful infants.[87] Hanni also describes how, when she wanted to become either a nurse or a kindergarten teacher, Aalto was not pleased, feeling it was not academic enough: "So I was not allowed to do it. He stopped talking to me."[88] Her mother, Aino, had understood her daughter's wish, but apparently could do nothing.

Some who ceased to think of themselves as friends could not swallow the line of the grand artistic genius without questioning the human side.

One such individual was Nils-Gustav Hahl, with whom Maire Gullichsen, Aalto, and Aino had founded artek. During the war, when Aalto wanted to save Finland with purely verbal patriotism in the form of a journal called, ironically, *The Human Side*, Hahl wrote to Maire:

> Of course I believe in the importance of his idea [of the journal], although I turned down all his proposals for collaboration. Think he should for once carry something through by himself. To be honest, there was another reason for my refusal: all his plans involve a certain measure of fantasy – "artistic" ditto if you will – and his working habits have kept that Bohemian aspect which can be so charming but is dubious right now. For these reasons I find that he does not have the self-discipline and level-headedness that I absolutely require of my working environment for as long as the war goes on.[89]

This is interesting as contemporary criticism from someone who had been close to Aalto. Aalto's son Hamilkar also comments on this: "Many of my father's fantasies were balanced through mother."[90]

Nevertheless, Aalto's patterns of dependency were clearly not limited to creativity and relationships. The deep psychological roots of excessive spending and drinking made any attempt to halt the indulgences futile until their roots were fully examined. Aalto wrote to one important client: "I would like to have talked . . . at the Art Hall party, but I was so blind drunk . . . Grogs internally and women's breasts externally don't seem to do me good."[91] Such dependence results in a relinquishing of responsibility, for which there is a price to be paid, usually in the form of neurosis. Another assistant recalls that Aalto "was a complete bohemian and drank like a fish," observing that "that didn't stop him working."[92] Certainly, alcohol works to lower conscious inhibitions, and it is thought therefore to facilitate primary-process thought, i.e., the thought processes of the unconscious.[93] If, as is accepted, there is a relationship between creativity and the unconscious, although Aalto sought to anaesthetize himself, he may, ironically, have been facilitating access to his hidden realm through the strength of his commitment to (i.e., dependence on) drink. Demonstrating his various dependencies, when traveling to Beirut on business without his second wife Elissa, in 1964, Aalto drank until he was inebriated, becoming unconscious, and was thus unable to attend a lunch given in his honor, at which he was to meet the President of Lebanon. Aalto flew home with a hangover, without completing any business.

"Little Man" and the True Self

Toward the end of his career Winnicott developed the notion of the True Self, which referred to a feeling of being fully alive, of being real, spontaneous, active, authentic, and bodily alive.[94] This instinctive freedom contrasts with what is reactive, which results from excessive failures of the early environment, which brings frustration and a "threat of annihilation" which leads to the development of a False Self (which continues to collect impingements).[95] In other words, a child develops ways of covering up his real (True) self by projecting another, artificial (False) Self to the world. Thus, the True Self can hide behind the False Self, being protected from being swamped or annihilated by others or by circumstances.[96] However, the False Self both seeks to create an environment in which the True Self might grow (i.e., a vital place for creativity and "world-building"), and copies others to hide the vulnerable True Self. In his way Aalto sought to help the true self of the "little man" flourish.

The vulnerable often become contorted in order to hide behind their defense mechanisms. In Aalto's case, this was coupled with the fact that newly independent Finland sought to project onto him the role of omnipotent cultural hero. Consequently, those who met Aalto experienced only part of the truth about the man. The role of pillar of Finnish culture did not cause, but rather fed into, his pre-existing psychopathology of grandiosity and depression, the two sides of the same False Self. Indeed, Schildt's biography repeatedly shows how Aalto acted, wrote, and spoke of himself in terms of Nietzschean superman.

Receiving praise from all quarters on first encountering America in the late 1930s as a famous European designer of the newly opened World Fair Finnish Pavilion, Aalto perceived America as a wonderful country of opportunities and wealth. Yet in the late 1940s, when his fame waned and Aino was dying, he was full of vitriol for the land of the free. As one psychologist has put it, the patient is always suffering from the self-knowledge he has had to deny himself,[97] experiencing the world as hostile, and sliding, in Aalto's case, into hypocondriachal, drunken, or amorous withdrawal.

Aalto named the small boat he designed for his summer house *Nemo Propheta in Patria* as early as the 1950s. He already seemed to believe that he, a prophet, was not recognized in Finland. On occasions, Schildt's biography seems to lack critical distance from Aalto, seeking to defend him for posterity. For example, Schildt wrote that, in the 1960s, a group of young Finnish communist Constructivist architects (which included the young Juhani Pallasmaa and Kirmo Mikkola) took a dislike to what they saw as Aalto's over dominant personality and his extroverted handling of fame, and accuses them of being openly hostile to Aalto.[98] Pallasmaa denies ever having been a communist or a Constructivist, and puts Schildt's accusations down to the attempts of those who surrounded Aalto to fight off anything that threatened or even questioned the architect's stature as indomitable cultural hero.[99] Ironically, Schildt alludes to Aalto as a King Lear character, which is surely one of tragic humiliation and senile confusion, rather than one simply abandoned by ungrateful youngsters.

Patterns of striving for achievement evince life in which self-esteem hangs precariously, leading to torturing dependence.[100] Dependence, a compulsion for over-reliance on something or someone outside the self in order to feel better, arises from the illusion that self-worth comes from the approval of others because of the brilliance of the person's achievements. Thus love is experienced as a reward for doing and achieving, not for being. Breakdown of the cycle of achievement brings recognition of the dependence, and disillusionment regarding the nature of the love, and the concomitant withdrawal.[101] The tragic loss of love arouses grief and despairing longing, frustration, lowered self-esteem, separation anxiety, and loneliness, bringing the downward spiral into depression. Indeed, individuals who become dependent "are typically lacking in self-confidence, unsure of their abilities and willing to allow decision-making in all matters to be taken over by others,"[102] or indeed to take the reins themselves in a controlling manner.

Aalto's thirst for human contact and his inability to be alone seems to have been burdensome. His strong personality and "social temperament" meant that he was at the center of family or social gatherings.[103] Aino was not an extrovert, and not sociable in the same way: "she was shy, and spoke slowly and cautiously."[104] Indeed, Schildt closes his three-volume biography with the phrase "he never did want to be alone."[105] In "The Capacity to be Alone" Winnicott expressed the belief that the experience of being alone in the company of another (particularly the mother) is vital for development and security.[106] Clinging behavior is indicative of insecurity and the roots of dependency, and can be seen to be intertwined with manic-depressive disorders. Indeed, as Storr indicates, "The capacity to be alone thus becomes linked with self-discovery and self-realisation; with becoming aware of one's deepest needs, feelings and impulses;"[107] something many people deny themselves.

Despite Aalto's "unquenchable thirst for human contact," he did not easily share his own feelings.[108] According to Schildt, he was "extremely reticent about personal matters" because he "never communed with himself. Indeed," Schildt continues, "he was so gregarious that he could not bear to be alone. He needed other people around him to be able to function properly. It seemed as if he only really existed when he had another psyche close by to react to, take a stand on, and arouse reactions in."[109] It was this that compounded the myth of Aalto as a happy and confident soul; a myth which, again, at times, Schildt seems to seek to perpetuate.

Having generally concealed his reticence, and his self-declared "sense of alienation in this world,"[110] Aalto sometimes surprised those who only knew a confident and extrovert "top dog." Schildt believes Aalto had an ability to "work" with other people, "a psychological understanding of how to handle them, authority and an impressive public manner."[111] Similarly, elsewhere in the biography, Aalto's most striking characteristic is described as "his adaptability and sensitivity to the psychological climate of his surroundings,"[112] being comfortable with communists like Hans Schmidt, and fascists like Albert Speer during his visit to the Third Reich in 1943. Such adaptability was probably used as a chameleon defense. He certainly flattered those he met with a convivial public face, putting on "his carefree front and 'top dog' attitude."[113] This presented a fallacy of intimacy beneath which he was "critical of virtually all those around him" behind their backs, while actually being deeply "closed and hypersensitive."[114] Again, this is hardly an unusual openness.

Schildt also recalls Aalto's ruthlessness, admitting he was a person "who manoeuvred with considerable shrewdness."[115] An example of this is his relationship with the gregarious Morton Shand in England, to whom he made promises regarding artek furniture which did not materialize. When they met again (when for this and other reasons Shand had fallen into financial ruin), Aalto was no longer Shand's friend, writing to someone else: "A curious nervous old fool – everything's wrong with Shand – himself most of all." Here he shows no compassion, rather seeming to want to deny any responsibility for having played a part in his friend's downfall.

By the third volume of the biography, Schildt does, nevertheless, admit that Aalto's "scintillating personality overwhelmed [him]," making it difficult for him, as biographer, to see the architect objectively, and concedes that he thought of Aalto as "an all too close father figure."[116] He does suggest that work on the biography did begin to change this. Some of Schildt's reading of his subject's life may be explained by his own autobiography, *Lånade vingar: Ungdomsminnen* (*With Borrowed Wings: Youthful Memories*),[117] in which it becomes clear that the effect of Schildt's own father's suicide, when he too was eight, may have colored his reading of Aalto's situation. This may account for the contradictory explanations of Aalto, in what seems to be an underlying attempt to paint a portrait of a sound and capable man, justified in all he did. It also demonstrates the observation of Aalto's contradictory character.

The Realm of the Tutelary Goddesses

Through discussion of Aalto's character, creativity, and the nature of his humane architecture, the cost to those close to him begins to come into focus. Aalto's wives seem to have acted as guardians, serving as protector patrons, watching over their husband as adviser, lover, wife, and, it must be said, mother. It is as if his wives, the tutelary goddesses, were held in bondage, having to support, lead, reassure, and praise Aalto. To understand the nature of this role, it is helpful to explore the characters of his mother and step-mother, into whose image the role for Aino and Elissa was cast.

Aalto's mothers (Selma and Flora) came from a progressive family of Swedish-speaking Finns, all the daughters of which were radical young "professional" women, determined to make their own way in the male-dominated world, but each of whom found themselves relinquishing their independence for the sake of the Aalto children.

Selma was an attractive woman, alert intellectually, with a lively temperament. Unlike her two sisters, who became teachers, Selma was to be a post-mistress with musical and artistic ambitions. Schildt suggests that "the intimacy between [mother and son] and its loss heightened Aalto's craving for maternal approval until it became a recurrent pattern for his entire artistic career: the child's wish to be praised grew into the man's instinct to stay within the magic circle of this special love by repeating the creative act, time and again."[118] This is similar in the creative drive of many artists.

As suggested, the death of Aalto's mother left an emotional and physical "gap" which he tried, unsuccessfully, to fill for the rest of his life. Aalto spoke with great tenderness about his mother, "soaring into descriptions about her lace-trimmed underwear and her curly hair."[119] As demonstrated, Aalto simply refused to confront death, shutting his eyes to the complete psychotic panic which overtook him, and his "irrational" heart, which challenged his "rational" head; perhaps modeled on his father's way of dealing with his mother's death. In a beautiful pencil drawing of Aino on her deathbed Aalto has inscribed the word "Mami," seeming to refer to his mother, Selma.

Four years Selma's junior, Aunt Flora had given up teaching and was working in J. H. Aalto's cartography office, so that she could be on hand to help with Selma's four children. Schildt suggests that she was not as attractive as Selma, but "had the virtues of the good heart."[120] Before Selma died, in the winter Flora shared a room with the youngsters, and in the summer had a room in the attic. Late in life she described how she had no choice but to marry J. H. Aalto; the children (and doubtless J. H. himself) needed it. Flora did not die until 1957, when Aalto was remarried.

The third sister, Aunt Helma, was single, and a "real feminist." According to Schildt, she had a mannish exterior, gruff, but was full of suppressed affection.[121] Having been expected to keep house for her brothers as they trained in Helsinki Polytechnic, aged 29 she entered university herself, eventually gaining an MA, and becoming a teacher. Then she too moved to Jyväskylä to teach, in order to be close to the family. In 1911 she left teaching and moved to Lovisa, on the Baltic coast, renting rooms to wealthy Russians and welcoming the Aalto children on extended summer visits. In 1919 she left Lovisa to serve the children by buying a small apartment in Helsinki as a home for the Aalto boys during their education.

The three Hackstedt sisters thus established a pattern of caring for Alvar which Aino was to follow. The following description of Aalto's first wife, Aino Marsio, by a Japanese acquaintance, Mrs Kayoko Ichikawa, contrasts with the picture of Aalto's character.[122] "Mrs Aalto has a lucid and penetrating mind and a sure instinct . . . she always speaks very calmly; her whole behaviour is well-balanced. She has very deep insight, and her gentle eyes observe everything quietly." Aino, four years Aalto's senior, had begun to work for Aalto in 1924, having graduated two years before Aalto, and therefore being more experienced than him when they met. Aalto joked that they had to marry because he owed her so much money in wages. Aino was a powerful, compassionate woman, large in stature and capacity to "represent a rediscovered security and a substitute for his lost mother," as Schildt put it.[123] But she had no illusions about marriage: "This madness we must all go through at one time or another and perhaps something good might even come of it."[124] As they departed by plane on honeymoon, Aino's sister cried "He's going to take our girl's life, that

Alvar";[125] this referred to their fear of the new invention, but is ironic in terms of the direction of her life.

The couple's characters were very different, which led to many conflicts. In the relationship Aalto was shored up to maximize his creative output, since that process of creativity was so vital for his mental balance. Aino's career did continue, largely in his shadow (with the exception of her glasswork and a few competition entries which found recognition). Aalto's attempts to claim co-authorship for many designs actually overesteems her design input (not her potential) but probably accurately describes her vital (emotional) support in the process. An old assistant of Aalto's recalled how he registered Aino as collaborator on projects in which she had taken no part, but believed that "Mrs Aalto was a real architect. Besides she was also wife and mother to Alvar."[126]

Alvar and Aino complemented each other in some areas. For instance, Aalto was poor at drafting, Aino was skilled; she also had a sharper sense of reality, which anchored Aalto's "ungovernable inventiveness bordering on unrealistic fantasy"[127] into reality in a gentle but firm way. The same was the case with finance. Aino economized around Aalto's extravagance. He could also behave like a bohemian, so Aino saw to it that he came home in the evenings. Indeed, an assistant recalls Aino Aalto's oft-repeated maternal words "No, that's enough, Alvar" when his drinking was getting out of hand.[128] Interestingly, little account is given of the cost of Aalto's behavior in the biography.

Schildt, who never met Aino, describes her and Alvar as an "odd couple – a brilliant husband and a rather morose wife," adding, however, that close friends soon learnt to respect Aino for her "great independence, her sound judgment and, above all, her human integrity."[129] Gregor Paullson describes them more kindly, writing that "Alvar was like an ardent flame, Aino was like still water."[130] Aino's less than jolly persona may, in part, be due to her role as carer – a life dedicated to assisting and shoring up another, volcanic temperament. Her daughter Hanni recalls that through music "she released all kinds of things kept inside . . . a world through which all her joys and sorrows could be expressed. Men are what they are! Never quite grown up. They don't always know how to offer comfort."[131]

Importantly, the nature of Aalto's architecture was more than a little influenced by Aino. For instance, he was hugely influenced by her social vision and commitment. Viola Markelius recalls that Aino took more interest in social issues than Alvar, and that "her talent was deeper than his."[132] Maire Gullichsen concurs, noting that Aino was "very much involved in social matters – even more so than Alvar – I would venture to say. He was the artist but she had the stronger moral conviction about her responsibilities."[133] His famous mission to humanize Modernism can therefore be seen to have been rooted in both her social vision and her costly personal compassion extended to him constantly over the years.

The relationship between Alvar and Aino seems also to have been stormy. She was witness to his flirtations, and doubtless all too well aware of his affairs with family friends. Schildt alludes to these with thinly disguised hints of the real nature of Aalto's relationships with women. For instance, Viola Markelius describes Aino's physique in unflattering terms, and then admits to partner swapping, and having got the more permanent, better deal: "Alvar was a wonderful lover, my goodness! . . . He always tried it on with everybody."[134] Schildt juxtaposes these memories with a nude sketch from Aalto's sketch book of a slim figure (which is clearly not Aino's), commenting that Viola's account "stands in this biography for the many women Aalto met during his long life, with whom he shared his zest for life and who retained a warm memory of him."[135] Schildt continues with an extraordinary comment. "This kind of contact," i.e., love affairs, "was so natural to him that it was rarely misinterpreted either by the other party concerned or by his nearest and dearest, though Aino's patience failed more than once." This is an understatement. Aino clearly did care about these affairs, as Schildt indicates elsewhere.

Personal letters which Aalto sent to his wives provide a rare glimpse of his inner life. In a letter from 1932, Aalto told Aino: "Always when I thought of you in my loneliness, it was as if I had begged you to help me . . . I missed you terribly and at the same time there was something painful about it;"[136] and in November 1945: "you are the source of security and the steady, quiet warmth that gives our life its stability."[137] Aino might have responded with Sibelius's long-suffering wife: "For my part I needed no other son than my husband."[138] But Aino Aalto had to divide her time between her two children (her son Hamilkar and her daughter Hanni), her gregarious and often needy husband, and her own desire to practice as an architect. Hanni (Alanen) describes how Aalto felt that Aino's "main duty was to look after him, to take care of him, after him came the children, after them, her work."[139]

Aalto the man was virtually incapable of functioning without contact with his wife, or other women. Indeed, he had engineered life so that he had virtually never been alone since his mother's death. In the letter from Marseilles, during his 1933 CIAM trip (during which he refers to his young American "lifeboat"), he wrote in his dyslexic German: "*Mir kommt vor dass wir noch unglaublich viel von einander zu bekommen haben. So verstehe ich die Liebe.* [It appears to me that we still have unbelievably much to receive from each other. That's how I understand love] . . . This trip gives a boost to one's self-confidence, but only when we're together can an unexaggerated balance and right attitude be found."[140] This letter is very telling, associating, as it does, his affairs (i.e., the lifeboat), his creativity (i.e., CIAM), his fame (e.g., "We sat together in Marseilles, Le Corbusier and I, every morning"), his mention of less than full self-confidence (despite what Schildt seeks to portray), and his love for and need of Aino.

Aalto's personal life was not insulated from the fantasy which inspired his work. Indeed, his daughter recalls that he was most comfortable with small children and enjoyed being childish himself. This degree of fantasy was an important ingredient of his life. This fantasy moved him ever onwards, away from a static position, but in something of a driven way. In 1947 he had written to Aino just after visiting Falling Water, of his "plan . . . for us to concentrate on the forest life."[141] Having broken with Rationalism, Aalto could return spiritually and creatively to his Finnish environment, to the nature of his childhood, such as the forests of Jyväskylä, but it was also the nature of the acute trauma of his mother's tragic death. Aino's imminent death threw him into deep trauma. Indeed, working to resist the reality of her demise, in 1948 he wrote (from the States) just before her death about how they would "steer" their lives together toward the highlights of collaboration. Interestingly, despite the tone of deep vulnerability, Schildt suggests that Aalto's letters to his dying wife show "more open confidence."[142]

However, demonstrating a moment of painful reality, the archives also reveal a telegraphic response to a desperately urgent enquiry from Aalto in Helsinki to an American friend, John Goldstone, whose cable from New York gives medical details and prognosis regarding such cancers.[143] Aalto's friend, J. M. Richards offers one account of the time of Aino's death: "[Aalto] was totally disorientated, lost his customary ebullience and drank until his friends despaired of his future."[144] Indeed, Schildt describes Aalto's shock at Aino's death as almost pathological, rendering him completely lost and unbalanced, drinking excessively, and incapable of functioning for some years, until he became involved with a young assistant in his office, Elsa (Elissa) Mäkiniemi, to whom he very soon became engaged. As Richards suggests, "He was only rescued by a second marriage," and that Elissa "launched him once more on his career,"[145] like an emotional bowsprit. The "shield against the unresolved pain"[146] was again in place. He could now return to the drawing board, able again to create the most intimate, inspiring spaces and places for the "little man," having moved from paralysing depression to elation, to being "top dog," the center of attention and control, once more able to do "world-building."

Very much his junior, Elissa worked closely with Aalto in his designs, but, again, her more important role seems to have been as a support to her often vulnerable husband. She continued to bear Aalto's creativity after his death, completing some design projects, and fielding enquiries, renovations, and so on, until her death, also from cancer, in 1995. When asked what sort of a husband Aalto was, Elissa has said "In the usual meaning of the word he was not ideal. But he was a very warm person, a stimulating person," while openly acknowledging that "there were problems."[147]

Aalto's relationships with his wives nevertheless failed to ameliorate his deep insecurity, or prevent his devastating depression. Their relationships were bound in dependency. Schildt's suggestion that Aalto learnt that the greatest human happiness comes from contact with others,[148] defies the fact that such a longing is a painful reminder of the trauma which haunted him, and the pain which forbade him the peace and confidence ever to be content alone. Without these strong women there would be no security, and thus it may be said that these relationships were vital holding environments in which enormous pain was borne, and from which some happiness and great creativity was forthcoming, but not without a cost.

Making Spaces: Shoring up the "Gap"

The Finnish poet, Bo Carpelan has written: "Life, it was a mystery, you had to take care, go in and out with your skin like a bruise you couldn't touch."[149] It seems that, despite appearances, in many areas Aalto experienced life in this way. Indeed, as if seeking understanding, Aalto wrote: "Psychological factors must be taken into consideration."[150] The understanding of Aalto herein suggests that the creation of art may be enmeshed in "the threads of unrecorded reality."[151] This is the realm of the artist's life of which he may not be conscious, but which may include the "gaps" resulting from childhood trauma and deprivation. An American friend of Aalto's, Harmon H. Goldstone, has suggested that "Aalto was a great humanist" and that his "lasting appeal" is that in everything he touched there was "this warmth of human understanding."[152] It is, however, apparent that this manifest, material sensitivity had a huge cost to those around Aalto. The person who deeply desired sensitive built environments was the same person who could repeatedly (even addictively) abuse the basic human trust and love of those closest to him. This person was, like many, bedeviled by unresolved drives within. At some level it is as if Aalto knew this, but did not want to face the depth of the reality of it in himself. The relation between these two selves is crucial, since, by revisiting and rebuilding aspects of his past through his design, he could maintain some mental balance and provide "humane" modern buildings.

Aalto wrote a few fragments of what was a spiritual testimony. In one of these, called "The Human Factor," he explored "human weakness" or "man's tendency to err." He found that this was "particularly clearly present in the Christian religion."[153] To conclude, it is telling to cite, alongside this testimony, a design element from his Vuoksenniska Church. Aalto was determined that above the altar should hang the cross on which Christ was crucified, but that this should be flanked by those of the thieves because this represented life in its entirety,[154] the little man, "his tragedy, and his comedy, both."[155]

Notes

1   Aalto's daughter, Hanni Alanen, describes how Aalto left it to his wife, Aino, to be responsible for the children, describing how "He was like a child himself." Hanni Alanen in L. Lahti, *Alvar Aalto: Ex Intimo* (Helsinki: Rakennustieto, 2001), p. 9.

2   Alvar Aalto, "Instead of an Article," *Arkkitehti-Arkitekten* (1958), reprinted in Göran Schildt, *Alvar Aalto Sketches* (Cambridge, MA: MIT Press, 1985), p. 160.

3   Juhani Pallasmaa, "From Metaphorical to Ecological Functionalism," in *Functionalism – Utopia or the Way Forward: Proceedings of the 5th International Alvar Aalto Symposium*, ed. M. Kärkkäinen (Jyväskylä: Alvar Aalto Symposium Committee, 1992), pp. 14–15.

4   Edmund Husserl's notion explicated in *Die Krisis der europäischen Wissenschaften und die transzendentale Phänomenologie: Eine Einleitung in die phänomenologische Philosophie* (1954), trans. D. Carr, *The Crisis of European Sciences and Transcendental Phenomenology* (Evanston, IL: Northwest University Press, 1970).

5   A. Ehrenzweig, *The Hidden Order of Art* (London: Weidenfeld and Nicolson, 1967), p. 266.

6   For example, D. O'Hare, *Psychology and the Arts* (Sussex: Harvester, 1981), p. 304.

7   Göran Schildt, *Alvar Aalto: The Early Years* (London: Rizzoli, 1984), p. 49.

8   Hanni Alanen in Lahti, *Aalto: Ex Intimo*, p. 9.

9   D. W. Winnicott, "On Influencing and Being Influenced" (1941), reprinted in D. W. Winnicott, *The Child, the Family and the Outside World* (Harmondsworth: Penguin, 1964), p. 204.

10 E. Tarasti, "Signs of Anxiety or the Problem of the Semiotic Subject," *Acta Semiotica Fennica*, 2 (1991): 51–7.

11 D. W. Winnicott, "Cure" (1970), in D. W. Winnicott, *Home is Where We Start From: Essays by a Psychoanalyst* (Harmondsworth: Penguin, 1987), p. 114.

12 D. W. Winnicott "Primitive Emotional Development" (1945), in D. W. Winnicott, *Collected Papers: Through Paediatrics to Psycho-analysis* (London: Tavistock, 1958), p. 145. Environment is understood as the set of circumstances or conditions in which a person lives or lived, or as being that which surrounds and influences them. See A. S. Reber, *Dictionary of Psychology* (Harmondsworth: Penguin, 1985), p. 242.

13 D. W. Winnicott "Children Learning" (1968), in Winnicott, *Home is Where We Start From*, pp. 142–9.

14 D. W. Winnicott, *Playing and Reality* (Harmondsworth: Penguin, 1971), p. 116.

15 M. Khan, "Introduction," in Winnicott, *Collected Papers*, p. xxvii.

16 M. Milner, *On Not Being Able to Paint* (London: Heinemann Educational, 1950), pp. 115–16.

17 D. W. Winnicott, "Psychoanalytical Studies of the Personality," *International Journal of Psycho-Analysis*, 34 (1963): 43.

18 Ibid.

19 D. W. Winnicott, "Ego Integration in Child Development" (1962), in D. W. Winnicott, *Maturational Processes and the Facilitating Environment* (London: The Hogarth Press/The Institute of Psycho-Analysis, 1965), p. 116.

20 Ibid.

21 Winnicott, *Playing and Reality*, pp. 2–10, 108.

22 Sigmund Freud, *An Outline of Psychoanalysis*, Standard Edition, ed. James Strachey, vol. 23 (London: Hogarth Press/Institute of Psycho-Analysis, 1963).

23 D. W. Winnicott, "Transitional Objects and Transitional Phenomena" (1951), in Winnicott, *Playing and Reality*, p. 26.

24 D. W. Winnicott, "Primitive Emotional Development" (1945), in Winnicott, *Collected Papers*, p. 145.

25 D. W. Winnicott, "On Influencing and Being Influenced" (1964), in Winnicott, *The Child, the Family and the Outside World*, p. 204.

26 Michael Balint, *The Basic Fault: Therapeutic Aspects of Regression* (London: Tavistock, 1968).

27   Göran Schildt, *Alvar Aalto: The Decisive Years* (New York: Rizzoli, 1986), pp. 50, 52.
28   Winnicott, *Collected Papers*, p. 150.
29   Jean Sibelius, letter to Bo Carpelan, August 10, 1916; E. Tawaststjerna, *Sibelius, vol. 3: 1914–1957* (London: Faber and Faber, 1997), p. 95.
30   Alvar Aalto, letter to Aino, Alvar Aalto Foundation (hereafter AAF), cited in Göran Schildt, *Alvar Aalto: The Mature Years* (New York: Rizzoli, 1991), p. 130.
31   Schildt, *Aalto: Decisive Years*, p. 98.
32   Knowledge, επιστημη, *episteme*; opinion, δοξα, *doxa*; recollection, αναμνησις, *anamnesis*: Indra K. McEwan, *Socrates Ancestor* (Cambridge MA: MIT Press, 1992), p. 127.
33   S. K. Langer, *Philosophy in a New Key: A Study in the Symbolism of Reason, Rite and Art* (1942; reprinted Cambridge, MA: Harvard University Press, 1993), p. 281.
34   M. D. Vernon, *The Psychology of Perception* (Harmondsworth: Penguin, 1962).
35   Ibid., p. 21.
36   C. Fisher, C. Paul and I. H. Paul, "The Effects of Subliminal Visual Stimulation etc.," *Journal of American Psychoanalytical Assignments*, 7 (1959): 38–54.
37   Sarah Menin, "Aalto and Sibelius: Children of the Forest's Mighty God," in *Sibelius: The Forest's Mighty God*, ed. E. Clark (London: UK Sibelius Society, 1998), pp. 52–8, and "Relating the Past: The Creativity of Sibelius and Aalto," in *Ptah: Alvar Aalto Foundation Journal of Architecture Design and Art*, 1 (2001): 32–44.
38   Edith Cobb, *The Ecology of Imagination in Childhood* (Dallas: Spring Publications, 1993).
39   Alvar Aalto, "Conversation" (1967), in Schildt, *Sketches*, pp. 170–2.
40   Hamilkar Aalto, in Lahti, *Aalto: Ex Intimo*, p. 15.
41   Schildt, *Aalto: Early Years*, p. 10. He also refers to this in *Mature Years*, pp. 32 and 321.
42   Otto Fenichel, *The Psychoanalytical Theory of Neurosis* (London: Routledge and Kegan Paul, 1947).
43   This is explicated in Menin, "Relating the Past."
44   Rollo May, *The Courage to Create* (London: Collins, 1976), p. 58.
45   Ibid., p. 55.
46   Clearly, small "gaps" may exist in any parental care patterns where there is no severe tragedy, or before severe traumas occur.
47   D. W. Winnicott, "The Location of Cultural Experience" (1967), in Winnicott, *Playing and Reality*, p. 116.
48   Letter from Aalto to Hélène de Mandrot, host of the first CIAM gathering at La Sarraz, summer 1941, cited in Schildt, *Aalto: Mature Years*, p. 49.
49   Cobb, *Ecology of Imagination*, p. 17.

50   D. W. Winnicott, "Fear of Breakdown" (1948), reprinted as *International Review of Psycho-Analysis*, 1 (1973).

51   Cobb, *Ecology of Imagination* , p. 17, and Henri Bergson, *Creative Evolution*, trans. A. Mitchell (London: Macmillan, 1911). Cobb's final chapter borrows Bergson's wording – "Creative Evolution: A Process of Compassion."

52   Cobb, *Ecology of Imagination*, pp. 17, 53. E. Eriksen, *Insight and Responsibility* (New York: Norton, 1964), p. 45. This is associated with the need to make their mark in the world, explored in R. E. Ochse, *Before the Gates of Excellence: The Determinants of Creative Genius* (Cambridge: Cambridge University Press, 1990).

53   It has been found that many figures at the forefront of history lost a parent by the age of ten, a figure higher than that expected in modern Western populations: J. M. Eisenstadt, "Parental Loss and Genius," *American Psychologist*, 33 (1978): 211–23; R. S. Albert, "Family Positions and the Attainment of Eminence," *Gifted Child Quarterly*, 24 (1980): 87–95; R. S. Illingworth, *Lessons from Childhood* (London: Livingstone, 1969). Indeed, it is suggested that "creators typically suffered some deprivations and distress in childhood": Ochse, *Before the Gates of Excellence*, p. 81.

54   Viola Markelius, in Schildt, *Aalto: Decisive Years*, p. 50.

55   Schildt, *Aalto: Mature Years*, p. 313.

56   Some evidence of Aalto's personal life is available in the letters held in the archives of the Alvar Aalto Foundation, in the anecdotes of those who knew him, and those who observed his life from both close and more impersonal quarters.

57   Alvar Aalto, "The Humanising of Architecture" (1940), in Göran Schildt, *Alvar Aalto: In his own Words* (New York: Rizzoli, 1998), pp. 102–3.

58   τραυμα in Greek.

59   J. Robertson, *Young Children in Hospital* (London: Tavistock Publications, 1958), and J. Bowlby, "Grief and Mourning in Infancy and Early Childhood," *Psychoanalytical Study of the Child*, 15 (1960): 9–52.

60   I. L. Janis (ed.), *Personality: Dynamics, Development and Assessment* (New York: Harcourt, Brace and World, 1969), pp. 176–7, 189.

61   Ibid., pp. 21–2.

62   Aalto reports experiencing the news of Strindberg's death as a "harrowing event": Schildt, *Aalto: Early Years*, p. 49.

63   Fenichel, *Psychoanalytical Theory of Neurosis*, p. 19.

64   J. M. Thorburn, *Art and the Unconscious* (London: K. Paul, Trench, Trubner and Co., 1925), p. 21.

65   Schildt, *Aalto: Decisive Years*, p. 136. Aalto's Villa Mairea (1939) was commissioned by and named after Maire Gullichsen.

66   Anthony Storr, *The Dynamics of Creation* (Harmondsworth: Penguin, 1991), p. 73.

67   Schildt, *Aalto: Decisive Years*, p. 117.
68   The family, with the exception of Elissa, were in favor of the biography; she did, however, cooperate. Aalto's son-in-law, psychiatrist Yrjö Alanen, is cited when discussing some aspects of Aalto's psyche.
69   Schildt, *Aalto: Mature Years*, p. 14.
70   Anthony Storr, letter to Sarah Menin, June 26, 1996.
71   Maire Gullichsen, letter to Alvar Aalto, cited in Schildt, *Aalto: Mature Years*, p. 19.
72   Telegram cited in ibid., p. 20.
73   Schildt, *Aalto: Decisive Years*, p. 186.
74   Schildt, *Aalto: Early Years*, p. 49.
75   Ibid., p. 69.
76   Ibid.
77   The person experiences great mood swings from elation to depression. Manic-depressive personalities experience a much more severe cycle of emotions, often leading from neurotic to psychotic behavior: F. K. Goodwin and K. R. Jamison, *Manic-depressive Illness* (Oxford: Oxford University Press, 1990).
78   Schildt, *Aalto: Decisive Years*, p. 117.
79   Alanen, in Schildt, *Aalto: Early Years*, p. 71.
80   Schildt, *Aalto: Early Years*, p. 140.
81   Winnicott, *Collected Papers*, p. 150.
82   Schildt, *Aalto: Mature Years*, p. 220.
83   Schildt, *Aalto: Decisive Years*, p. 162.
84   Ibid.
85   Schildt describes the process of designing his house in the film *Alvar Aalto: Nature and Technology* (Phaidon Film). Joonas Kokkonen has concurred in descriptions of how Aalto came up with the piano-like plan of his house in Järvenpää in a conversation with the author (Villa Kokkonen, Järvenpää, July, 1988).
86   Hanni Alanen in Lahti, *Aalto: Ex Intimo*, p. 9.
87   Hanni Alanen has described the importance of her nanny, called Anni "who was some sort of substitute mother to us for 25 years" and "was everything to us." Anni looked after the children when Aino and Alvar traveled. "Of course from the child's point of view they travelled too much": Hanni Alanen in Lahti, *Aalto: Ex Intimo*, p. 7.
88   Hanni Alanen, from *Alvar Aalto Technology and Nature* (Phaidon Film).
89   Letter from Hahl to Maire Gullichsen, cited in Schildt, *Aalto: Mature Years*, p. 21.
90   Hamilkar Aalto, in Lahti, *Aalto: Ex Intimo*, p. 13.
91   Letter from Aalto to the head of the National Pensions Institute, Kaarlo Hillilä, 1952, cited in Schildt, *Aalto: Mature Years*, p. 88.
92   Schildt, *Aalto: Decisive Years*, p. 44.

93   R. W. Weisberg, *Creativity: Beyond the Myth of Genius* (New York: W. H. Freeman, 1993), p. 43.

94   D. W. Winnicott, "Ego Distortion in Terms of True and False Self" (1960), in Winnicott, *Maturational Processes*, p. 148.

95   D. W. Winnicott, "Primary Maternal Preoccupation" (1956), in Winnicott, *Collected Papers*, p. 303.

96   R. D. Laing, *The Divided Self* (Harmondsworth: Penguin, 1969).

97   A. Phillips, *Winnicott* (London: Fontana, 1988), p. 53.

98   Schildt, *Aalto: Mature Years*, pp. 307, 312.

99   Pallasmaa denied the accusations in letters to the author, July 1999.

100   Alice Miller, *The Drama of Being a Child: The Search for the True Self* (London: Virago, 1989), p. 57.

101   O. F. Kernberg, "Further Contributions to the Narcissistic Personalities," *International Journal of Psychoanalysis*, 18 (1974): 51–2.

102   Reber, *Dictionary of Psychology*, p. 188.

103   Hamilkar Aalto, in Lahti, *Aalto: Ex Intimo*, p. 16.

104   Hanni Alanen, in ibid., p. 12.

105   Schildt, *Aalto: Mature Years*, p. 323.

106   D. W. Winnicott, "The Capacity to be Alone" (1958), in Winnicott, *Maturational Processes*, p. 34.

107   Anthony Storr, *The School of Genius* (London: Andre Deutsch, 1988), p. 21. Some researchers highlight the intellectual and emotional independence of creators (e.g., Ochse, *Before the Gates of Excellence*, p. 125).

108   Schildt, *Aalto: Early Years*, p. 15.

109   Ibid., p. 70.

110   Aalto in letter to Aino, December 26, 1945 written from Saarinen's home in the States, AAF; cited in Schildt, *Aalto: Mature Years*, p. 104.

111   Schildt, *Aalto: Early Years*, p. 56.

112   Schildt, *Aalto: Decisive Years*, p. 103.

113   Ibid., p. 117.

114   Schildt, *Aalto: Mature Years*, p. 98.

115   Schildt, *Aalto: Early Years*, pp. 13, 126.

116   Schildt, *Aalto: Mature Years*, p. 11.

117   Göran Schildt, *Lånade vingar: Ungdomsminnen* (Helsinki: Söderström and Co., 1995).

118   Schildt, *Aalto: Early Years*, p. 71.

119   Ibid., p. 48.

120   Ibid., p. 49.

121   Ibid., p. 60.

122   Kayoko Ichikawa was the wife of Japan's first ambassador to Finland, who held office from 1933 to 1937.

123   Schildt, *Aalto: Early Years*, p. 71.

124 Letter from Aino to her sister, 1924, cited in ibid., p. 131.

125 Schildt, *Aalto: Early Years*, p. 134.

126 Harald Wildhagen in 1978; Schildt, *Aalto: Decisive Years*, p. 42.

127 Schildt, *Aalto: Early Years*, p. 142.

128 Bjertnaes, an assistant in the Aalto office, in conversation with Schildt, September 3, 1978; Schildt, *Aalto: Decisive Years*, p. 44.

129 Schildt, *Aalto: Decisive Years*, p. 133. Hamilkar Aalto comments that Schildt did not meet Aino and has constructed her image based on hearsay; Lahti, *Aalto: Ex Intimo*, p. 17.

130 Gregor Paullson, in Schildt, *Aalto: Mature Years*, p. 130.

131 Hanni Alanen, in Lahti, *Aalto: Ex Intimo*, p. 9.

132 Viola Markelius, in Schildt, *Aalto: Decisive Years*, p. 50.

133 Maire Gullichsen, from *Alvar Aalto: Nature and Technology* (Phaidon Film).

134 Viola Markelius, in Schildt, *Aalto: Decisive Years*, p. 50.

135 Schildt, *Aalto: Decisive Years*, p. 52.

136 Alvar Aalto letter to Aino, c.1932, in Schildt, *Aalto: Mature Years*, p. 130.

137 Alvar Aalto letter to Aino, November 1945, AAF; cited in ibid., p. 131.

138 Aino Aalto to Jean Sibelius, in S. Levas, *Jean Sibelius: A Personal Portrait* (Helsinki: WSOY, 1972), p. 15.

139 Hanni Alanen, from *Alvar Aalto Technology and Nature* (Phaidon Film).

140 Schildt, *Aalto: Decisive Years*, p. 99.

141 Letter from Alvar Aalto to Aino, AAF; cited in Schildt, *Aalto: Mature Years*, p. 110.

142 Schildt, *Aalto: Early Years*, p. 70.

143 Undated telegram, AAF.

144 J. M. Richards, *Memoirs of an Unjust Fella* (London: Weidenfeld and Nicolson, 1980), p. 203.

145 Ibid., p. 203.

146 Schildt, *Mature Years*, p. 130.

147 Elissa Aalto, from *Alvar Aalto Nature and Technology* (Phaidon Film).

148 Schildt, *Aalto: Early Years*, p. 69.

149 Bo Carpelan, from "The Courtyard," in *Room Without Walls* (London: Forest Books, 1987), p. 62.

150 Alvar Aalto, "The Dwelling as a Problem," in *Domus* (1930); reprinted in Schildt, *Sketches*, p. 29.

151 Langer, *Philosophy in a New Key*, p. 281.

152 Harmon. H. Goldstone, from *Alvar Aalto Technology and Nature* (Phaidon Film).

153 Alvar Aalto, "The Human Factor," AAF (undated).

154 Alvar Aalto, "Vuoksenniskan Kirkko," *Arkkitehti-Arkitekten*, 12 (1959): 201.

155 Aalto, "Instead of an Article" (1958), in Schildt, *Sketches*, p. 160.

3

Becoming-skyscraper: Ayn Rand's Architect

Gerard Loughlin

In dream, everything becomes substitutable, though chiefly the body and its parts, and above all the sexual organs. Sigmund Freud's parapractic account of dreaming tells us that dream images are "ungenuine things, substitutions for something else that is unknown to the dreamer . . . substitutions for something the knowledge of which is present in the dreamer but which is inaccessible to him."[1]

The symbolism of dreams is an ancient concern, and Freud's achievement was not so much to have reclaimed the art of dream interpretation for the twentieth century, nor to have so incessantly sexualized its interpretations, as to have extended the domain of the dream into waking life. Dreams repeat substitutions already established in unconscious thought, already expressed in jokes and allusions, already the "carry-on," the word-play of language.[2] The symbolism of dreams is not reserved to sleep, but shared, as Freud put it, with "psychoneuroses, legends and popular customs;" in short, with culture.[3] Yet Freud's substitutions are comprehensively, though not entirely, sexual;[4] so that the "innervating" effect of the Freudian analysis has been to eroticize all symbolic systems, returning all domains to the body and its desires. Freudian psychoanalysis is a metaphorics of the (social) body, an anagogy of the (contingent) flesh.[5]

After Freud, it is not possible to suppose that any arena of cultural production escapes the erotic, including the three spaces of this chapter: the religious, the cinematic, and the architectural. "It is true that I know patients who have retained an architectural symbolism for the body and the genitals."[6] Thus pillars and towers can substitute for the erect penis, doorways and openings for the vagina, and the descent of stairways for the sexual act. As the process of symbolic substitution is never static, as if following a fixed code, our changing world constantly gives rise to new symbols, requiring pragmatic interpretations. Thus Freud could find Zeppelin airships (new in 1900) symbolic of sexual excitement, the elongated shape of the floating dirigible being a perfect substitute for the erect penis, since in "erection-dreams" flight and flying machines express the "remarkable characteristic of the male organ which enables it to rise up in defiance of the laws of gravity."[7] Thus Freud, if he had come upon it in the dreams of his patients, would not have failed to recognize the skyscraper as a perfect phallic symbol; and we cannot fail to so recognize it in the cinematic dreaming of the city.

Just in so far as the skyscraper symbolizes the architect in the twentieth century, as well as the society and culture that constructs, sustains, and glories in such a building type, then King Vidor's 1949 film of Ayn Rand's *The Fountainhead* is the quintessential "erection-dream" of the American psyche. Ayn Rand (1905–82) was a confirmed Americanist, declaring that "America is the greatest country on earth. No – it's the *only* country."[8] In her three remarkable novels – *We the Living* (1936), *The Fountainhead* (1943), and *Atlas Shrugged* (1957)[9] – she presented a philosophy for America: Objectivism. It argues for a rational egoism that makes for human happiness and provides the only firm foundation for free-market capitalism.[10]

Born Alice Rosenbaum in St Petersburg in 1905, Rand and her family left the city for the Crimea in 1918, only returning to the renamed Petrograd in 1921, where she entered the university. An able student, well read, and increasingly entranced by the movies, she went on to study at film school[11] (presumably at the Technical Institute of Screen Art, Leningrad),[12] before being granted permission to leave Russia for America in 1926, where she disembarked as Ayn rather than Alice Rosenbaum.[13] A little later, while living with her relatives in Chicago, she again renamed herself, after her Remington-Rand typewriter.[14] It is not only fitting that she should be named after a writing machine, but that the proponent of self-making man should herself be self-named, and that in so warmly embracing the New World and its myths of heroic struggle, she should become a life-long opponent of communism and collectivism, a self-declared "radical for capitalism." She would later, at the behest of the Motion Picture Alliance for the Preservation of American Ideals, write a "Screen Guide for Americans," warning against communist ideology in Hollywood films. In 1947 she appeared as a "friendly witness" before the House Un-American

Activities Committee investigating communism in Hollywood. Rand hoped to denounce William Wyler's *The Best Years of our Lives* (1946), a popular and critical success, which nevertheless portrays a banker "with a heart," who advocates loans without collateral.[15]

As soon as she could after arriving in America, in the summer of 1926, Rand made her way to Los Angeles and Hollywood, in order to become a film writer. One of the first original screenplays on which she worked, for Cecil B. De Mille, was entitled *Skyscraper*, a love story about a girl and two construction workers. The film was released in 1928, the same year that King Vidor's *The Crowd* appeared, a celebration of life in the quintessential American city, New York.[16] Rand, in order to gain background knowledge for *Skyscraper*, arranged to visit a building site on Hollywood Boulevard.[17] Later, when working on *The Fountainhead*, she would work in an architect's office, in order to better understand the world of her architect hero. But from her first glimpse of the New York skyline in Russian movie houses,[18] the skyscraper came ready made as a potent symbol of American achievement, imbued with erotic tension in film and life. Left waiting for the superintendent to show her around the building site, Rand visited a library and there met again Frank O'Connor, who would become her husband in 1929.

The hero of Rand's novel *The Fountainhead* is Howard Roark (played by Gary Cooper in the film), a man of such integrity and so possessed of his architectural vision that no one can dissuade him from building how and what he wishes to build, even if this means that his visions of what iron, glass, and concrete can be, are never built. The integrity of man and building are one and the same in Roark. He will not compromise, though all around him are either men destroyed for their integrity or those who destroy them. Roark is Rand's ideal of the self-made man, who produces and adheres to his own values, without resentment of those who oppose him. Roark is answerable to no one, only to architecture. He tells the Dean of the Architecture School from which he has just been expelled: "I don't intend to build in order to have clients. I intend to have clients in order to build."[19]

Roark is chiefly contrasted with Peter Keating, a friend from college days, who has great personal facility, getting on with everyone he meets, and so rising in the architectural profession through casual manipulation of weaker people. But Keating lacks passion and genius for architecture. At key points in his career, it is Roark who provides him with his winning designs. The climax of the story is the building and destroying of Cortlandt

Homes, a federal-funded housing project for the poor. Keating is the architect, but Roark supplies the designs, on the condition that the project is built as designed. When Keating is unable to dissuade his clients from altering the buildings, Roark sets dynamite and destroys his own buildings for the sake of architectural integrity. In his defense, at the resulting trial, Roark proffers a passionate statement of the Rand–Roark philosophy and is acquitted by the jury. As Andrew Saint notes, "there is no pretense of verisimilitude about this acquittal."[20] Rand has chosen to vindicate her hero before the American people, showing that his philosophy can and should be embraced by all. As a glorious wish-fulfillment, the novel, and more especially the film, for which Rand wrote the screenplay, is precisely Rand's dream. It concludes with Roark being offered the contract to build a monumental building entirely to his own design, which will be a monument to Roark himself, to his supremely maintained egoism: "the tallest structure in the city,"[21] which in the film becomes the tallest structure in the world.

More than the early De Mille film, Rand thoroughly researched the architectural world she portrays in her novel, which is that of 1920s' and 1930s' America.[22] Much of the novel's pleasure derives from its sly rendition of contemporary architects and architectural practices. There is little question that Roark as designer is based on Frank Lloyd Wright, while Roark's architectural mentor, Henry Cameron stands in for Wright's own hero, Louis Sullivan.[23] To Cameron is ascribed Louis Sullivan's Modernist dictum "that the form of a building must follow its function."[24] Much of this and other satiric moments are lost in the film, not least because, while Wright was approached to design the film's architecture, he proved too expensive and demanding, and the job went to Edward Carrere,[25] who produced clean but derivative designs in the Modernist manner – more Walter Gropius and the Bauhaus than Frank Lloyd Wright and the Prairie School.[26] Nevertheless, the sets have a stark, Expressionist edge, with counterpoised planes of light and dark, and vast windows giving views of the cityscape and its towers. These, together with Vidor's camera angles, give the film a cold and subtly Surreal quality.[27]

One of the scenes in the novel that does not appear in the film is an arts ball at which Keating and other architects dress up in cardboard models of their most famous buildings. This is based on the actual Beaux-Arts Ball of 1931 at which various famous architects did just that, most successfully William Van Alen as the Chrysler Building. It is a striking image of man-becoming-building, architect-becoming-skyscraper.

That Roark is an independent, uniquely creative architect, producing buildings never before seen, and that the buildings of his that we see in the film are uninteresting as architecture – easily located within a standard history of architectural design, showing all the generality of the collective, of the architectural herd – is more than just a passing irony.[28] It is the visual undermining of Rand's philosophy. Roark says that he owes nothing to anyone, but we can see that he owes everything to others. Film excites the body along two nervous pathways, the auditory and the optical, both of which produce meanings and affects, which in *The Fountainhead* are strikingly out of joint. Moreover, the disjunction is precisely to do with the body. For Rand's philosophy ultimately denies the body and its dependencies.

In order to see how Rand's philosophy is undone, in book and film, and not merely at the level of the image, we must venture our third arena of the religious, and, in particular, the space of sacrifice. In choosing atheism, Rand supposed herself to have refused religion, and in particular self-sacrifice, which, along with faith and collectivism, she saw as the abiding weaknesses of Western society. Yet both sacrifice and religion make a return in her work.

For Rand's Objectivism, each person is singular and of final worth, each is an end in him or herself, and for no other person. Each one is beholden only to him or herself. Each may give to another, but only so as to receive a return. For the rational egoist seeks only his or her own well-being and happiness, and every expenditure should receive an equal if not greater restitution. The actions of the rational egoist may appear similar, even identical to those of the sacrificer; but while the latter will give away what he or she has to give for the sake of the other, the rational egoist will do so for him or herself because, for example, the expenditure of vast wealth will retain that thing or person that gives the rational egoist immense pleasure. Rand's ethics were based on a reading of Aristotle that pressed hard his insight that ethical actions are those that institute the *eudaimonia* or well-being of the actor, that happiness is the goal of ethics. Rand less clearly focused on Aristotle's teaching that friendship and ultimate union with the Absolute were constitutive of human happiness, and she was disinclined to suppose that the practiced virtue of friendship might involve dispossession and sacrificial giving.

Roark, as the self-made man, is uninterested in what others think about him. It is good when they appreciate him and his work, but of no personal consequence when they do not, though it may be an affront to architecture.

At the beginning of the novel we are told that, when he walked through the town, people turned to look at him as he passed. But he did not see them. "For him, the streets were empty. He could have walked there naked without concern."[29] He does not understand how other people think, or why they are resentful of his indifference toward them.

> He always looked for a central theme in buildings and he looked for a central impulse in men. He knew the source of his actions; he could not discover theirs. He did not care. He had never learned the process of thinking about other people. But he wondered, at times, what made them such as they were.[30]

Such autism is for Rand the basis of a rational ethic and society. At the end of the novel, just before Roark starts to speak at his trial, in a moment of silence, we are told that the hostile crowd in the courtroom suddenly knew that he bore them no ill will. "For the flash of an instant, they grasped the manner of his consciousness. Each asked himself: Do I need anyone's approval? – does it matter? – am I tied? And for that instant, each man was free – free enough to feel benevolence for every other man in the room."[31] Roark is free because he needs no one's approval, he depends on no one, he is not a slave or a parasite. The film omits the one line of Roark's speech that Rand considered the most important, but the studio thought the most inflammatory: the line that summed up Roark's and Rand's credo, and is perhaps the most deathly line in the novel: "I am a man who does not exist for others."[32] The line is deathly because if Roark did not exist for at least some others he would not exist at all. Roark imagines that he is most truly himself as a free man when he is most alone, unnoticing and unnoticed by other men: become an almost disembodied consciousness. In book and film, this fallacy is sustained through the image of the architect as someone who alone builds out of raw materials the visions of his mind. Yet, as every builder and most architects will know, architects do not build. The novel is not completely fanciful at this point, since it does reveal the collective labor of the architect's office and the construction site. But Rand imagines this overcome by making the architect the master will.

> No work is ever done collectively, by a majority decision. Every creative job is achieved under the guidance of a single individual thought. An architect requires a great many men to erect his building. But he does not ask them

to vote on his design. They work together by free agreement and each is free in his proper function. An architect uses steel, glass, concrete, produced by others. But the materials remain just so much steel, glass and concrete until he touches them. What he does with them is his individual product and his individual property. This is the only pattern for proper co-operation among men.[33]

It is the architect's unseen touch that produces the building. The same fancy is repeated in the process of producing a film such as *The Fountainhead*, where the director takes the place of the architect, and where the mechanics of film production are always occluded. This was even more the case in 1949 than it is today, when very few of the many people who constructed films were credited for their work. But the fantastical denial of the architect's dependence on others is at its most intense in his sexual relationships.

For Rand, one enters into a sexual relationship not for the other person, but for oneself, and in so far as one develops a concern for the other, it is because it increases one's own happiness to do so. But as soon as one ceases to receive such a repayment, acting for the good of the other becomes irrational, and should cease. In love, as elsewhere, we are to be traders, and self-sacrifice is a bad trade, giving away more for less. Objectivism supposes – with rhetorical appeals to "objectivity" and "rationality" – that the highest value is always the self and its wants, and that any trading on this without equal or greater return is a loss-making venture.[34] In short, Rand's Objectivism seeks to institute capitalism at the heart of the American soul.

Sex is the celebration of romantic love, and romantic love is the union of pride in oneself with admiration for another.[35] They can be united because what one admires in the other is the reflection of oneself: "A man falls in love with and sexually desires the person who reflects his own deepest values."[36] Sex is then an act of celebratory self-esteem, the most concrete joy of being alive and one's own man. The person who seeks in sexual pleasure a confirmation of his or her own worth can only ever confirm his or her want of it. It is only the person for whom sex is an expression of a self-worth already achieved and known who can truly enjoy pleasure as the "reward of self-esteem."[37]

In *The Fountainhead*, these ideas about the sexual relationship are given shape in Howard Roark's relationship with Dominique Francon (played by Patricia Neal in the film). The character of Dominique repeats the disparity I have already noted between Roark's self-declared genius and what we see of his actual building designs, since she is both necessary for, and necessarily occluded by, the fantasy of the self-made man.

Roark has sex with Dominique, but he does not need her, because he is purely potent in his own right. When she first sees him, he is working as a laborer in a quarry, driving his drill into a granite block. Infatuated from the start, she arranges for him to come to her house to repair a broken hearthstone in her bedroom, and it is there that he later rapes her, after an earlier encounter in which she strikes him with a branch that she was at the time using as a horse whip.[38]

> It [Roark's "taking" of Dominique] was an act that could be performed in tenderness, as a seal of love, or in contempt, as a symbol of humiliation and conquest. It could be the act of a lover or the act of a soldier violating an enemy woman. He did it as an act of scorn. Not as love, but as defilement. And this made her lie still and submit. One gesture of tenderness from him – and she would have remained cold, untouched by the thing done to her body. But the act of a master taking shameful, contemptuous possession of her was the kind of rapture she had wanted. Then she felt him shaking with the agony of a pleasure unbearable even to him, and she knew that she had given that to him, that it came from her, from her body, and she bit his lips and she knew what he had wanted her to know.[39]

This scene, uncut from the film, though played discreetly, establishes the sado-masochistic, master–slave relationship between Roark and Dominique. Roark's violent "taking" of Dominique, though an act of "defilement," is yet also an act of sexual love in Rand's sense, since Dominique reflects back to him his own deepest values. "They had been united in an understanding beyond the violence, beyond the deliberate obscenity of his action; had she meant less to him, he would not have taken her as he did."[40] Taking Dominique is an *architectural* act, confirming his integrity and self-worth. "In some unstated way, last night had been what building was to him; in some quality of reaction within him, in what it gave to his consciousness of existence."[41] Roark builds himself in and through Dominique's returned gaze.

We are to suppose the same for Dominique, that her "rapture" at being raped by Roark is because he represents her own deepest values: "had he meant less to her, she would not have fought so desperately."[42] But she has not been building, she has been built upon; and we may wonder if her "passive" act is more akin to the sacrificial in Rand's sense. In the balance of the exchange, has Dominique gained or lost more than she has given?

The self-made man must deny the body, especially his own body, because he must deny that he was born of another, that he received his flesh and his life from another. Like Rand, who forgot the Old World in the New, forgot the language and family in which she was first given herself, so Roark appears fully grown, but without a past. "The boy's entrance papers showed no record of nearest relatives. When asked about it, Roark had said indifferently: 'I don't think I have any relatives. I may have. I don't know.'"[43]

The self-made man becomes immobile because, in refusing his given-ness, he refuses to give in return, lest he lose himself altogether. He fails to recognize that, in order to be, he must give away what he has been given so that it may return, more fully than before. His is a life of dying, becoming-immobile, becoming-monument. Roark – and behind him Rand – knows nothing of a sacrificial economy in which everything is given away so that all may return more abundantly.[44] Indeed, he becomes paralyzed by fear that to give is only to lose.

In order to exist at all, Roark needs someone like Dominique, for he always needs someone to acknowledge his autonomy, to see his indifference. He needs the gaze that can alone assure him that he exists; in short, he needs us, the readers of the novel and the viewers of the film. While much of the film's point of view is unspecific, it imperceptibly becomes that of Dominique herself, and most definitely in the last scene of the film when she visits the construction site of the Wynand Building, taking the open works elevator to the top of the tallest structure in the city.

> She stood, her hand lifted and closed about a cable, her high heels poised firmly on the planks. The planks shuddered, a current of air pressed her skirt to her body, and she saw the ground dropping softly away from her . . .
>
> Flat roofs descended like pedals pressing the building down, out of the way of her flight . . . She saw roof gardens float down like handkerchiefs spread on the wind. Skyscrapers raced her and were left behind. The planks under her feet shot past the antennae of radio stations . . .
>
> The hoist swung like a pendulum above the city. It sped against the side of the building. It had passed the line where the masonry ended behind her. There was nothing behind her now but steel ligaments and space. She felt the height pressing against her eardrums. The sun filled her eyes. The air beat against her raised chin.

She saw him standing above her, on the top of the platform of the Wynand Building. He waved to her.

The line of the ocean cut the sky. The ocean mounted as the city descended. She passed the pinnacles of bank buildings. She passed the crowns of courthouses. She rose above the spires of churches.

Then there was only the ocean and the sky and the figure of Howard Roark.[45]

The film ends with the same scene, concluding with a shot that is exactly Dominique's point of view. As she flies up the side of the building, so do we; as she gazes upon Roark, so do we also: and he knows it. He waves at Dominique and at us, he meets our gaze without flinching, the wind buffeting his clothes and hair, confirmed in his existence and perfectly identified with his skyscraper, defying gravity. This closing scene is one of theophany, since Roark has ascended his skyscraper in order to meet with his god, who is of course himself, and as Dominique approaches, up the side of the man-made mountain, she sees the glory of the self-positing man.[46]

Yet since the significance of the building is Roark, and he and the building are one – he has no other significance – he needs to be seen by Dominique and, through her eyes, by us. He needs the sacrifice of our gaze, lest he cease to exist altogether.

Notes

1 Sigmund Freud, *The Penguin Freud Library, Vol. 1: Introductory Lectures on Psychoanalysis* (1916), trans. James Strachey, ed. James Strachey and Angela Richards (Harmondsworth: Penguin, 1973), p. 143 (hereinafter *PFL 1*).

2 Sigmund Freud, *The Penguin Library, Vol. 4: The Interpretation of Dreams* (1900), trans. James Strachey, ed. James Strachey, Alan Tyson, and Angela Richards (Harmondsworth: Penguin, 1991), p. 462 (hereinafter *PFL 4*).

3 *PFL 4*, p. 461.

4 "The assertion that all dreams require a sexual interpretation, against which critics rage so incessantly, occurs nowhere in my *Interpretation of Dreams*. It is not found in any of the numerous editions of this book and is in obvious contradiction to other views expressed in it [1919]." *PFL 4*, p. 521.

5 Suzanne R. Kirschner, *The Religious and Romantic Origins of Psychoanalysis: Individuation and Integration in Post-Freudian Theory* (Cambridge: Cambridge University Press, 1996), p. 12.

6 *PFL 4*, p. 462.

7   *PFL 1*, p. 188. Freud's airship achieves its apotheosis in the image of Slim Pickens astride the bomb as it falls away from the plane in Stanley Kubrick's *Dr Strangelove* (1964). However, the association of flight with phallic potency predates Freud, and may be found, for example, in late eighteenth-century pornography. In the anonymously published *Parapilla* (1776), a young man with the help of the archangel Gabriel grows a plant of winged penises, which then provide pleasure for a number of formerly unsatisfied women. See further Clive Hart and Kay Gilliland Stevenson, *Heaven and the Flesh: Imagery of Desire from the Renaissance to the Rococo* (Cambridge: Cambridge University Press, 1995), pp. 173–6.

8   As quoted in Barbara Branden, *The Passion of Ayn Rand* (New York: Doubleday, 1986), p. 67. This is a fascinating but possibly unreliable biography since it is written by a former confidante of Rand, who became estranged when Rand discovered from her that Nathaniel Branden (Barbara's husband), with whom Rand was having an affair, was seeing another woman, Patricia. The biography is entirely unreferenced.

9   Ayn Rand, *We the Living* (New York: Macmillan, 1936); Ayn Rand, *The Fountainhead* (New York: Bobbs-Merrill, 1943); Ayn Rand, *Atlas Shrugged* (New York: Random House, 1957). During World War II, *We the Living* was recognized in Italy as an anticommunist tract, and piratically filmed in two parts as *Addio Kira* and *Noi Vivi* (both 1942) by Goffredo Alessandrini. An edited and legal version of the two films, with subtitles, was released in 1986 as *We the Living*.

10   See Wallace Matson, "Rand on Concepts," in *The Philosophic Thought of Ayn Rand*, ed. Douglas J. Den Uyl and Douglas B. Rasmussen (Urbana, IL: University of Illinois Press, 1984), pp. 21–37.

11   Branden, *Passion of Ayn Rand*, p. 57.

12   See Denise J. Youngblood, *Soviet Cinema in the Silent Era, 1918–1935* (Ann Arbor, MI: UMI Research Press, 1985), p. 63.

13   Branden, *Passion of Ayn Rand*, p. 63. "Ayn" is pronounced to rhyme with "mine."

14   Ibid., p. 71.

15   Ibid., pp. 199–203. Other "friendly witnesses" were Adolphe Menjou, Ronald Reagan, Robert Taylor, and Gary Cooper. Of those on the Committee, Rand was most impressed by Richard Nixon.

16   See Colin McArthur, "Chinese Boxes and Russian Dolls: Tracking the Elusive Cinematic City," in *The Cinematic City*, ed. David B. Clarke (London: Routledge, 1997), pp. 19–45, p. 25.

17   Branden, *Passion of Ayn Rand*, p. 83. *Skyscraper* was directed by Howard Higgins and starred William Boyd, Alan Hale, Sue Carol, and Alberta Vaughan. The film was subsequently shown in Russia, where it was praised as "social cinema." Adrian Piotrovskii, while disparaging the film's "philosophy of

success and fortune, the idea that a man can do anything as long as he wants to," admired its combination of plot and ideology, so that the story "unfolds under the direct influence of the actual raw material of the 30-storey building," while its ideological theme "emerges in the consciousness of the audience only as the final emotional sum." See Adrian Piotrovskii, "Zapadnichestvo v nashem Kino" ["Westernism in our Cinema"], *Zhizn' iskusstva* (30 June 1927): 7, in *The Film Factory: Russian and Soviet Cinema in Documents 1896– 1939*, ed. Richard Taylor and Ian Christie (London: Routledge and Kegan Paul, 1988), pp. 267–70, p. 269. American films were immensely popular in Russia, and Soviet filmmakers were greatly exercised by the problem of successfully delivering ideology through narrative. It was a problem that Rand set out to solve in her novels.

18 Branden, *Passion of Ayn Rand*, p. 57. It was while watching American movies in Russia that Rand became prey to what the Russian film director Lev Kuleshov called *amerikanschina* ("americanitis"), and others *inostranshchina* ("foreignitis" or "foreignism"). See Denise J. Youngblood, *Movies for the Masses: Popular Cinema and Soviet Society in the 1920s* (Cambridge: Cambridge University Press, 1992), ch. 3.

19 Rand, *Fountainhead*, p. 18.

20 Andrew Saint, *The Image of the Architect* (New Haven, CT: Yale University Press, 1983), p. 4.

21 Rand, *Fountainhead*, p. 676.

22 Starting in 1937, Rand worked for six months as an unpaid clerk in the New York office of Ely Jacques Kahn. See Branden, *Passion of Ayn Rand*, pp. 143– 4.

23 "The only resemblance between Howard Roark and Frank Lloyd Wright is in their basic architectural principles and in the fact that Wright was an innovator fighting for modern architecture against tradition. There is no similarity in their respective characters, nor in their philosophical convictions, nor in the events of their lives." Rand quoted in Branden, *Passion of Ayn Rand*, p. 140.

24 Rand, *Fountainhead*, p. 37. See Louis Sullivan, *Kindergarten Chats and Other Writings*, ed. Isabella Athey (New York: Wittenborn, Schulz, 1947), p. 43.

25 Branden, *Passion of Ayn Rand*, p. 209.

26 See H. Allen Brooks, *The Prairie School: Frank Lloyd Wright and his Midwest Contemporaries* (Toronto: University of Toronto Press, 1972).

27 See further Donald Albrecht, *Designing Dreams: Modern Architecture in the Movies* (London: Thames and Hudson, [1986] 1987), pp. 18–74; and *Film Architecture: Set Designs from Metropolis to Blade Runner*, ed. Dietrich Neuman (Munich and New York: Prestel, 1996), pp. 126–33.

28 A related irony is that Rand's rejection of tradition and espousal of the modern is presented through conventional narrative forms, in book and film. See

further John A. Walker, *Art and Artists on Screen* (Manchester: Manchester University Press, 1993), pp. 95–105, pp. 102–3. In a further twist, Claudia Roth Pierpont notes that the novel, "in its high legibility, its hectoring force, and its insistence that there were still giants among men," resembles nothing so much as the "officially sanctioned Soviet bombast of Socialist Realism." See Claudia Roth Pierpont "Twilight of the Goddess," *The New Yorker* (July 24, 1995): 70–81, p. 75. I am grateful to Dr Peter Willis for bringing this article to my attention.

29   Rand, *Fountainhead*, p. 8.
30   Ibid., p. 18.
31   Ibid., p. 663.
32   Ibid., p. 670.
33   Ibid., p. 668.
34   "A sacrifice, it is necessary to remember, means the surrender of a higher value in favour of a lower value or of a nonvalue. If one gives up that which one does not value in order to obtain that which one does value – or if one gives up a lesser value in order to obtain a greater one – this is not sacrifice, but a gain": Nathaniel Branden, "Mental Health versus Mysticism and Self-sacrifice", in Ayn Rand, *The Virtue of Selfishness: A New Concept of Egoism* (New York: New American Library, 1964), pp. 36–42, p. 40.
35   Rand, *Virtue of Selfishness*, p. 65.
36   Ibid., p. 66.
37   Ibid., p. 67.
38   Rand, *Fountainhead*, pp. 203–4.
39   Ibid., p. 205.
40   Ibid., p. 206.
41   Ibid.
42   Ibid.
43   Ibid., p. 17. When her finances permitted, Rand sought permission for her family to visit the United States, but without success. Her parents and sister Natasha died in the German siege of Leningrad in 1941–2. Rand's youngest sister, Nora, survived the war, and with her husband visited the United States in 1973. It was not a happy reunion. Branden, *Passion of Ayn Rand*, p. 375.
44   See John Milbank, "Stories of Sacrifice," *Modern Theology*, 12 (1996): 27–56.
45   Rand, *Fountainhead*, pp. 679–80.
46   Colin McArthur finds in this scene a reference to Italian Futurism, since Roark atop his building evokes the "fascist *squadrone* as represented in inter-war Italian graphics, including some by Futurists." In the images of the movie, he also espies fleeting references to the films of Leni Riefenstahl. See McArthur, "Chinese Boxes and Russian Dolls," p. 26.

4

Steps Toward a Sustainable Architecture

Brenda and Robert Vale

Architecture and Sustainability

The practice of an architecture that is sustainable is not new, but the idea of making a sustainable building or deliberately engaging in the practice of sustainable architecture is a modern construct. The Jew's House in Lincoln, a house erected in the eleventh century, is a building that has sustained its function over centuries, yet when this building was constructed there was no intention of deliberately making a sustainable building. The goal was to obtain the best building that met the needs of the time. It was either fortunate that those needs have continued unchanged over the years, so that the building still serves its purpose, or that the building was made in such a way that it could be adapted to meet changing needs. In terms of resource use, the resources that went into making this ancient house have continued to give service over the years, and hence this building could be viewed as sustainable, since it has provided shelter with little impact on the environment.

In contrast, the deliberate design and construction of a sustainable house will set out to minimize its impact on the environment in terms of the resources that are put into making, maintaining, and operating the building. The difference between the buildings of the past that have survived and the sustainable buildings of the present can be summarized as one of intent. This chapter sets out to explore the impact that this difference in intent has on the architecture and buildings that have been produced.

Tradition

The history of architecture is commonly viewed as an analysis of its artefacts. Seldom is the history of architecture and building viewed as a history of the way in which people have used buildings. This exploration has largely been left to people like sociologists and industrial archeologists.[1] If buildings are to be examined in terms of their sustainability, the way in which buildings are used is critical.

In whatever way sustainability is defined, it inevitably impinges upon the behavior of people. It is not buildings that consume resources in the form of fossil fuels to keep internal environments cool or warm, it is the users of the buildings that consume those resources, through the demands that they make upon the internal environment. These demands may be far more sophisticated than the simple action of a user being cold and turning on the electric fire. Many such demands will be subsumed in regulations that society has set up to keep buildings at acceptable internal temperatures. These in turn may be linked to keeping a workforce healthy, since an unhealthy workforce is both unproductive and can also cause other costs to society through a demand for health care. Where a building is and who uses it will also affect its use of resources. The resources to use and maintain it will have to be procured from somewhere and long distances can often be involved in transporting building materials. Energy has to be obtained to operate the building and people will also consume energy in commuting to the building. Much of this expenditure of energy was avoided in the past. How contemporary society makes and uses its whole built environment may be a key issue in the making of more sustainable buildings.

Traditionally, many of the problems outlined above were avoided in the built environment. Buildings were made of local materials and were used by local people. There is plenty of evidence that past societies went to considerable lengths to avoid moving materials. The great European cathedrals were built of stone quarried and dressed at the quarry site, marked and then transported to the building site for assembly. When the cost of moving stone ten miles by horse and cart was the same as the cost of the material, only moving what was absolutely necessary was critical. Coming down the social scale, lesser buildings were made of those materials closest to hand, whether these materials were ideal (limestone) or not (chalk stone). This is the basis of vernacular architecture.

There is a romantic view that vernacular buildings offer a path to the development of sustainable architecture.[2] Vernacular architecture does make use of local materials but such buildings only survive if they are well maintained. A Devon cottage with cob walls, a mixture of mud and straw, will require regular painting of the walls to keep the water from penetrating through them. It will also require a solid waterproof foundation of stone or brick and a good overhang to the roof to throw the rainwater well clear of the walls. Roofs were normally thatched as this minimized the structural load on the weaker walls, and thatch itself is also a material that has to be reapplied on a regular basis. So the use of local materials for walling set up a system that did require the importation of some materials, if only for the stone for the footings to the walls. Moreover, making the walls was not a quick process. The walls could be left for up to twelve months in order to dry out properly, so the investment in materials had a long time-lag before anything useful in the form of shelter could be gained from them. This situation is far removed from the fast-track procurement of buildings that characterizes the present built environment.

Nor were the buildings thus created ideal environments. A mud building is not capable of maintaining a constant internal temperature without the application of energy in the form of heat in the winter. It may remain cool in summer but this is largely a function of the structural properties of the material. Mud is not strong and becomes weak at the corners, which is why external corners were often formed as curves rather than right angles. Any window openings are, of necessity, limited in size. This prevents too much sun from entering the internal spaces in summer and hence the building does not overheat. In fact, the users had to work out the most appropriate strategy for living in the building to keep as comfortable as possible, so behavior was important for comfort, not the building envelope alone.

There is plenty of evidence to support the idea that the buildings of the past did not produce ideal internal environments that would meet the standards of today. It is obvious from reading the contemporary literature that people consumed a great deal more food than is common today. The Warden, Mr Hardy, in Trollope's novel of the same name is described on a visit to London toward the end of the book. He consumes a chop and a pint of port for breakfast,[3] a calorific intake that would ensure obesity if carried out for any length of time in modern society. For a middle-class woman to be comfortable in a Victorian parlor required the wearing at least five layers of underclothes, petticoats, and skirts, not to mention a corset, all of which meant that the average swooning female could be comfortable in air temperatures around 12–13 °C. These were reasonable responses to the environmental conditions that could be achieved in the buildings of the past. Whether such conditions would be acceptable in today's society is questionable. Lighting levels are another example. A rush light makes use of tallow, a byproduct of agriculture, and so could be seen as sustainable. The light from such a lamp would leave most people over fifty unable to see clearly after it became dark. Higher light levels are required for close work as the body ages.

The traditional approach can, in fact, be seen as producing some form of shelter related to available materials and resources, but it required a way of living that was adapted to making best use of the buildings thus produced. It mattered little, for instance, that English farm laborers had cottages with very small windows, since all their waking hours were spent outside in the fields in most weathers. Indeed, where particular craft industries, such as handloom weaving, were carried on in cottages, special adaptations were made to produce large windows in the upper storys, as can be seen in many Yorkshire villages around Huddersfield. However, for crafts such as lace-making, where the equipment was both small and portable (a pillow and bobbins), the user was generally to be found sitting in the open doorway to the cottage so that light and shelter could be obtained together.

Vernacular interiors, like the Victorian parlor mentioned above, failed to provide a great deal of thermal comfort in the winter. An open fire was the means of heating and cooking, the latter possibly being the more important function of the two.

> Fful sooty was hir bour and eke hire halle,
> In which she ete many a slender mele.

This is Chaucer's comment on the situation of a widow woman in her cottage in *The Nun's Priest's Tale*. This situation did not change in the houses of ordinary people until the spread of model cottage building in the early nineteenth century led to improvements in the housing of at least some of the rural poor.

Even if vernacular building did not provide a particularly comfortable internal environment it still made use of local resources and hence could be thought of as more sustainable. It has also been seen to have been produced in conjunction with the local climate to make building forms that married the use of materials to climate mitigation. Examples of such vernacular building range from the shallow-pitched roofs of Scandinavian houses which allowed the snow to settle on them, therefore providing an additional layer of external insulation to keep more heat inside the building, to the cluster of mud brick walled and roofed dwellings that formed the houses of the Pueblo Indians of the south-western states of America. The latter were clustered with no windows in the walls, only an opening in the roof for access to minimize the sunlight reaching the interior. The thick layer of 300 mm of mud overlaying a timber structure that formed the roof of the houses would heat up in the daytime and the heat would begin to migrate through the structure toward the building's interior. Since this took about eight hours to happen, the heat would reach the interior as the sun went down and the cold of the desert night began to encroach. Heat would be lost to the interior (and also to the cold night sky), so that by the time the sun came up again the roof was able to repeat the same cycle of heat transfer.

Such a system worked well in a climate, such as a desert climate, that is perfectly predictable. In a less extreme, temperate climate, people rather adapted to what the shelter offered. In fact, more comfort may have been afforded by sheltering the animals under the same roof as the people so that their thermal benefit could be felt (a cow gives off approximately 1 kW of heat, a person only a tenth of this). This situation is found in many European vernacular buildings, from the large Bavarian farmhouses where the animals are stabled under the main living floor, to the "but and ben" of the Scottish highlands, where people lived in one room of a two-room dwelling with the stock in the adjacent space, just as Chaucer's widow would have done. This practice does not seem to form part of the present call for a return to the vernacular in the name of sustainability, despite its widespread use in the past.

Nor are vernacular buildings necessarily consistent in the forms that are produced within the same climate. Oliver, in writing on the vernacular architecture of Africa, has shown that in a very similar climate and latitude very different forms of mud building are used by different peoples.[4] In Africa, the Nabdam people live in individual circular huts grouped in circular families, with the whole tribe of these groupings sitting in the middle of the land that provides it with its self-sufficiency. The mud walls are incised with decoration and thatched with straw. On the Black Volta, the people also use mud and thatch but here the walls are rectangular with the roof supported by posts on the side that faces a rectangular compound.[5] The huts are large enough for family occupation and the grouping of the huts around the compounds is all basically orthogonal. A third group in a similar climatic region live within a large rectangular mud-walled enclosure, which presents a fortress-like aspect to the surrounding land.[6] It is not the climate and use of materials that drive the building form in these examples, but rather a cultural tradition handed down from generation to generation, and which established a tribal identity in its building form. Within this identity, life is adapted to provide the best conditions possible, and it is this adaptation that becomes enshrined in the cultural traditions. This process is perhaps best summed up by Richard Jefferies, the nineteenth-century writer on the English countryside. In describing the English village he states: "To these houses life fitted itself and grew to them: they were not mere walls, but became part of existence. A man's house was not only his castle, a man's house was himself."[7] In a time of globalization and standardization is it possible to recapture what the vernacular actually enshrined within itself: a way of life that made the buildings, which in turn reinforced the way of life? What way of living is to be associated with a sustainable built environment?

Attempts to Make a Sustainable Built Environment

To answer the question posed above it is necessary to consider the history of buildings that have been deliberately made to be sustainable in recent times. It might also be useful to consider to what extent these buildings use vernacular principles. In addition, how buildings designed to be sustainable are used may also give a useful comparison with the true vernacular.

In one way the history of sustainable buildings begins with a whole consideration of change in life-style. It was this reaction to the dominance of life by modern technology that introduced the idea of alternative technology. What was classified as alternative technology in turn influenced what buildings which used it looked like and how they operated. The idea of alternative or appropriate technology emerged in the 1960s and 1970s when various aspects of modern technological society began to come under increasing criticism. The criticisms covered the three main areas of environmental pollution, the depletion of non-renewable resources, and what were considered to be unacceptable political and social factors.

The pollution problem was first brought to popular notice by Rachel Carson.[8] She sought to demonstrate the effects of man-made pesticides in the environment. Her arguments concern new chemicals developed for warfare that were finding other uses in peacetime. These insecticides were different from the largely plant-derived products used in the past because even very small doses had carcinogenic or toxic potential.

In terms of buildings, the whole Building Biology Movement (*Baubiologie*) that originated in Germany relates back to the discussions of Carson. The movement seeks to remove all materials and systems within a building that could in any way pollute the indoor environment. A simple thing would be to avoid the use of solvent-based paints, since such solvents are known to cause health problems.[9] Organic or water-based paints can be used in their place. Some of these will not have the covering power or life of traditional paints but this change will be acceptable because of the lack of pollution associated with their use. More questionable would be the avoidance of electricity in certain forms because of the magnetic fields associated with its use. The effect on health of such phenomena is unproven to date but alternative ways of house wiring will be preferred, which may add additional cost to the house. At no point, however, is the suggestion made to go without any electricity at all. There is no indication of avoiding a problem; what is presented is an alternative and more expensive way of replacing what is done conventionally. This whole area seems to be more one of personal preference rather than looking for sustainable ways of building. This is not in the vernacular tradition. However, where real costs can be put on illnesses caused by indoor pollution then society may wish to "save" these costs by choosing to build to create environments that will not create illness. This will normally be done through legislation, since Building Control exists to maintain the health and safety of the users of buildings.

The case for environmental pollution and its relation to changes in buildings is somewhat easier to trace. Barry Commoner looked at a wide range of causes of environmental pollution.[10] What he found in a sector-by-sector analysis of US production was that there had been considerable growth in certain sectors, but during the same period production of more "sustainable" technologies, such as returnable bottles, cotton and wool fibers, and soap had declined. He concluded that pollution was the result of the substitution of new technologies and products for existing ones, combined with a lack of foresight and concern on the part of those who were introducing the new products and technologies (non-returnable bottles, artificial fibers, detergents) without looking at the effects beyond their immediate purpose.

The effect that this idea had on buildings was to suggest that these new "wastes" could be re-used as building blocks. Thus research was undertaken into bottles which, rather than being discarded, could be used to make the walls of dwellings.[11] This resulted in the Heineken "wobo," a flat-sided beer bottle that could be used as a building block after the contents had been drunk, though only a few experimental structures were ever made using such material. Far more convincing were the settlements of Drop City in the USA, where abandoned cars had the roof panels cut out which were then used as panels in a timber geodesic framework to make permanent dome dwellings. At the same time, buildings were designed to make more use of traditional methods of disposing of wastes, such as composting, and those who lived in such buildings had to change their way of life to make this possible.

Barry Commoner refers briefly to another factor that influenced the critics of modern technology at this time.[12] This was the realization that certain minerals and ores extracted from the earth could never be replaced. The best-known expression of this problem, contemporary with Commoner's work, can be found in the Club of Rome's computer study. This extrapolated the then current demand rates for various resources and concluded that many important non-renewable resources would become prohibitively expensive in the next hundred years if demand continued to grow exponentially.[13]

From this period dates the renewed interest in vernacular building and renewable sources of energy.[14] Quite simply the search was on to find ways of making and operating buildings that did not rely on resources that were finite. Building techniques that were examined were the use of mud as a building material, the use of timber, since that was a renewable resource, finishes that could be made from simple materials, such as lime washes in the place of paint, and thatch and wool rather than mineral fibers for insulation purposes. The real converts were concerned with how to detail timber buildings without recourse to polluting substances such as timber preservatives. At the same time, the market also saw an opportunity in this concern for not using non-renewable resources. This interest in the traditional ways of doing things became manifest in mainstream society and resulted in publications such as *Your House: The Outside View*.[15] The Habitat chain of interior design shops also drew heavily on the vernacular and made links with the old-fashioned ways of doing things, especially through the kitchenware that was sold at this time.

In terms of the energy required to operate the building, the search was on for ways of using the "free" energy of the sun and wind, and even water power in some sites that were fortunate enough to have this potential. However, a paradox always existed between the availability of the technology to use these resources and the quest to use only renewable resources. Most of the equipment that made use of wind to generate electricity, for instance, made clear use of mainstream resources. From the wind generator made at home from an old bicycle wheel that could produce enough power to trickle charge a single battery it was a big leap to the manufactured machine of 5 kW that was just about sufficient to provide the electric power for a single dwelling.

A further argument existed between those who wanted renewable technology to be integrated into the building form and those who felt that it was possible to accept the technology for what it was: a generator set on top of a tall mast with a propeller that could be spun by the wind. Such a configuration was bound to produce vibrations and was probably best separated from the building. Others worked hard to produce designs, such as the Cambridge Autarkic House (which was never in fact constructed), which mounted the wind generator onto the building structure. Only in the collection of solar energy was it possible to produce design solutions that could be said to be based on renewable resources. However, the laws of thermodynamics are such that the energy available from the sun is not in a concentrated form such that it can immediately provide the kind of power levels normally found within a house. The use of solar energy in buildings is worth considering in some detail because it is the one renewable energy source that had an immediate effect on building form.

Solar Energy and Buildings

Vitruvius was probably the first to document ways of using solar heating in ordinary buildings.[16] What emerged from his work was the deliberate ordering of the orientation of spaces within buildings so that those that were required to be warm faced the sun. The development of geometry and its application by Socrates and others had offered a new way to view the world through the ability to measure it, and this approach became formalized through writings such as those of Vitruvius. The principle of orientation toward the sun was probably older than this formalization: in the underground cave dwellings of China the main room had been placed on the side that received sunlight, with latrines and store rooms on the side facing north. Overhangs were also known; however, these were sized according to tradition.

The "discovery" of passive solar design in the early 1970s was no more than a rediscovery and publicizing of these basic rules. Solar design had always been a part of the architectural vocabulary, as confirmed in many orangeries and glasshouses. However, the poor, who could have made best use of this "free" energy, did not have the means to exploit it, and the rich had enough money to indulge aesthetic whims without having to consider it. Without plenty of cheap glass, however, the exploitation of passive solar energy is not possible on a large scale. The Modern Movement worked with a new architecture of glass and it only took a side step to link this into passive solar design. Indeed, Le Corbusier was not ignorant of the power of sunlight within the dwelling. His "Manual of the Dwelling" suggests that the occupant should demand a bathroom facing south with a fully glazed wall leading to a balcony for sun bathing.[17] For Le Corbusier, the house was to be full of light and sun, and, providing additional sources of energy were available, this could be achieved, even with his single glazed windows.

The problem with passive solar design is when it ceases to be a substitute for other sources of energy and becomes the only source of energy for heating. To some extent, all houses that need heating are heated by the sun. Solar gain, whether it falls through windows, or onto roofs and walls, will add energy to the environmental comfort levels within the building, so less additional energy will be needed to maintain these. Le Corbusier's idea of facing the bathroom toward the sun has practical advantages: the resulting higher air temperatures could help to offset condensation problems and a sunny bathroom usually means dry towels. In a house that needs all its energy from the sun, however, the rooms that people spend the most time in are usually given a solar orientation; storage areas, bathrooms, and circulation zones tend to be placed on the side without sun. This arrangement can be found in many Arts and Crafts house designs, even though these were not specifically passive solar. "It must therefore be a question of calculating exactly how much sunshine to give each room according to its purpose from which a whole science of correct layout has evolved."[18]

The only way to achieve complete solar orientation is to produce a house design that is only one room thick, and this typology has underpinned many passive solar designs in the late twentieth century, a famous example being the 1961 St George's School, Wallasey.[19] The school at Wallasey also illustrates that passive solar design was being challenged to deliver far more than the partial warming of houses in Rome. Apart from orientation, the techniques of sufficient insulation and sufficient mass within the building also had to be correctly applied. This could have little effect on the form of the building, or it could be used to determine form, as in the earth-sheltered houses at Hockerton, near Nottingham. These have no form of heating apart from the occupants and the sun, yet the minimum recorded temperature in the UK winter has been 17 °C. The houses are made of concrete block with concrete beam and block ceilings, all sitting on a reinforced concrete slab. On the outer side of this mass is a 300 mm layer of expanded polystyrene. A waterproof layer is then applied and the earth is backfilled to cover the rear and roof of the houses on the north side. All rooms face into a conservatory space on the south side.

It could be argued that this discussion of passive solar design has little to do with the vernacular and much to do with finding the best techniques for using the sun without compromising a predetermined life-style. The ideas of Vitruvius would have been acknowledged throughout the Roman Empire, with additional design features, such as the hypocaust floor, being applied in colder climates. This is a significant move away from the vernacular where life-style was related to the environment that could be achieved within the building. The way of life of Rome was to be maintained throughout the empire and the resources were found to make sure that this was achieved. The more recent aggressively passive solar buildings, such as Wallasey School and the Hockerton houses, are also attempting to provide comfort conditions that would be recognized as normal by those living and working in buildings tempered by fossil fuels.

Solar energy can be used in buildings in two further ways. The first is to heat water and the second is to make electricity. Neither approach will be found in the vernacular tradition. The only secondary use of solar energy in the vernacular is the growing of biomass, especially wood, that can then be used as a renewable fuel. Some use was made of mass combined with the burning of wood. This is found in the presence of large chimney pieces of masonry that become warmed whilst the fire is alight and continue to give off heat into the space even when the fire is out.

The use of solar water heaters, where water is deliberately channeled over a surface exposed to the sun, so that it heats up, dates from the late nineteenth century.[20] Photovoltaic panels, which consist of layers of semi-conductors such as crystals of silicon, did not appear until the middle of the twentieth century and only began to have a possible application to buildings after the technique was developed and refined as a result of the space race. Both technologies have presented problems when related to buildings.

The only limitation to the positioning of a solar water heater is the need to face the collector panel to the south (in the northern hemisphere). There is often discussion as to whether it is better to orientate panels for optimal winter collection when the sun is low, or to have a flatter orienta-tion, optimal for higher-angle sunshine. Decisions can be related to the available pitch of the roof or they can be guided by sunshine hours. It is no good optimizing a collector for winter if there is insufficient sunshine available to heat the water. Photovoltaic panels also need to be optimized though some can be mounted on an adjustable frame that will track the sun, and this will increase the amount of electricity generated. Like a wind turbine, however, this tracking system would normally be separated from the building. The big design issue with both photovoltaic panels and solar collectors for hot water is whether or not they should be integrated into the fabric of the building, rather than being mounted onto a completed building. This in turn has raised further issues about the efficiency of the conversion system.

One approach favors systems that are not necessarily the most efficient in terms of energy conservation, but can be used in place of conventional elements. Thus it is possible to make a solar water heater that also serves as the roof of the building. In its simplest form this is a dark roof covering of corrugated metal sheeting with a top layer of glass. Between the two layers at the ridge of the roof a perforated pipe distributes water into each of the corrugations. The surface heats up and this heats up the water, which is collected in a gutter at the bottom and pumped to the hot water storage cylinder. However, there will be condensation on the underside of the glass and this will reduce the efficiency of energy transfer from the sun, through the glass, and into the water. This trickle-type solar water heater, which can also be the roof covering, is not, therefore, as efficient as a solar panel water heater, but it is much cheaper. A solar trickle-type roof might be 30 percent efficient in conversion of solar energy to heat, whereas a closed collector system might be 40 percent plus. However, the trickle-type might be half the cost per square meter of the panel type and would also form the roof covering, whereas the panels are generally mounted over an existing roof covering.

Photovoltaic panels have similar problems. Where they are mounted apart from the building, airflow around them can keep them cool and this will raise the efficiency of the operation of most panel types, as efficiency tends to drop with increasing temperature. Only the amorphous silicon type actually increase in efficiency with increasing temperature. This means that when most panels are used as building claddings, whether for roofs or walls, they do not produce as much power as if they were free standing. However, the fashion is to integrate such technologies despite this disadvantage. This is not in the vernacular tradition where expensive materials and components would be used optimally at all times. Another problem that can affect some photovoltaic panel types is overshadowing, as this can knock out an area of panel that might not even be in shade. Again, free-standing arrays can usually be arranged not to be overshadowed more easily than panels used to clad buildings.

Most solar strategies, as described above, are used in a decentralized way since solar energy is essentially a decentralized commodity. The problem comes in making sure that there is enough solar energy to do the job required. A roof area of about 4 m^2 will give hot water but to gain enough roof area to generate all the electricity required for a house will not be possible unless some conservation practices are undertaken. To gain all the energy required for its operation from the skin of a commercial building is probably impossible using current technology, without the application of stringent conservation measures. These statements, however, suggest that life-style dictates what happens rather than adapting to what is available. If people were to do the latter then large buildings would not be a viable part of a sustainable future. Buildings would be designed according to the energy they could collect and this would tend to produce small-scale buildings and decentralization.

There was another argument made in the 1970s for the selection of technology of a particular type, and this was the argument for control of the technology. Those who favored the decentralization discussed above saw that a little technology everywhere gave control of that technology back to the users. It is centralization that produces the experts who have control of a commodity. In this way the alternative approach to technology contained within it a huge social change. This change may also have to be part of any sustainable future. At present, very little of the technology in general use is also controlled by those who use it. When the washing machine breaks down an expert is called in to mend it. The car has to be regularly maintained by an expert to ensure that it will always go every time the key is turned in the ignition. Very few people, however, understand how the car works, or are even able to judge whether the "expert" has carried out the maintenance satisfactorily.

Murray Bookchin refers to changes in popular attitudes to technology that have occurred in the past few decades.[21] He suggests that the optimism of the 1920 and 1930s, when industrialization seemed the key to social progress, has been replaced by a more ambivalent attitude to technology, with people wanting its benefits but also fearing its consequences, including the environmental damage it causes.[22] These ideas – and others – led to the emergence of the "counter-culture" or "alternative" movement, not an organization, but a loosely defined and changing set of attitudes to life. David Dickson stresses the fact that alternative technology (which became known as AT) does not have a firm definition, but consists of a set of approaches to design and the use of technology.[23]

It seemed as if it were necessary to reject the whole idea of conventional technology and replace it with a new alternative. However, most of the alternatives were in themselves pieces of conventional technology, produced in a conventional way. AT, therefore, became a selection of existing technologies, epitomized by such publications as *The Whole Earth Catalogue*, which made the selection for the reader by offering in one place everything that was on the market. However, to make the selection it was necessary to have a vision of the way of life that was to be supported by this selection. Hence it was impossible to divorce AT from ideas about the organization of society. Moreover, because the technology was "alternative" this vision also had to be different and "alternative."

Thus AT was not just about using alternative energy sources, such as the sun or the wind, but about keeping people in control of the devices that achieved the conversions of sunlight or wind into electricity. The designs for houses that were produced by the AT movement were disparaged by architects for being boring and simplistic, designed as they were for the occupants to build or to maintain. In many ways, this brings those in search of more sustainable buildings closest to the vernacular. It was the do-it-yourself attitude of the 1970s and the hand-built aesthetic that had direct parallels with the vernacular. All that was lacking were the centuries of tradition that underpinned the latter. Given time, these could have emerged.

Renewables themselves were also appropriated by mainstream science so that solar thermal power stations were tested and wind machines of megawatt output were made and linked into the grid to replace fossil-fuel power stations rather than making a new approach to the use of resources. This meant looking for sites windy enough to make such large-scale technologies viable, whereas the AT approach was to accept that sites were non-ideal but because there was some wind it could be made use of. As sites were non-ideal, resources also had to be husbanded. Power was available but not unlimited power. This is behaving in an ecological manner, whereby the person becomes an integral part of a system and the regulation of that system.

The modern centralized approach treats renewables rather as fossil-fuel reserves are treated: their use becomes space-specific so that who owns the site owns the power. This is in direct contrast to the AT approach which acknowledged that renewables occurred everywhere and all could own their own small bit of power generation. The fact that the large-scale technologies are promoted in the name of efficiency also links them to the mainstream rather than the alternative.

This suggests two possible future paths for sustainability which may or may not be mutually compatible. One follows the path of the AT movement and attempts to put skills back in the hands of people. Life is simple and governed by immediate resources and the ability to use them. Buildings are owner built and designed by architects who call themselves "enablers" rather than designers. The materials used are ad hoc, not necessarily optimal, but there can still be a great delight in the way that things are put together. It is impossible to judge the results of those working in the field in the 1970s without an appreciation of this philosophical position.

The other approach is to accept that "science will find a way" and that there will be a replacement of existing fossil-fuel-based technologies with renewable technologies, the replacement being as seamless as possible. Houses may make use of photovoltaic panels and passive solar design but there will be back-up systems to make a seamless way of living. Power will still be in the hands of the main suppliers. This is a world where the power companies will rent out the photovoltaic system to the users. This is not the world of the vernacular but is the world of the consumer and provider, running on renewables.

The advantage of the AT approach is that it puts control back into the hands of the users. In fact, such a society would have a population far more skilled in the manipulation of technology than at present, even though current society is regarded as a technological one. Unlike the situation in Bacon's *New Atlantis*, where the regulation of invention and innovation was in the hands of the few, the AT approach makes all into Bacon's guardians.

The grip that technology appears to have on society may be due to the effects of industrialization and the Modernist Movement. Philip Steadman viewed the unconcern displayed by the Modernist philosophy toward energy conservation as inherent within that philosophy.[24] The belief that the machine was capable of changing the way people lived, and that a new architecture was therefore required to reflect this change, depended upon there always being the energy to run the machine. If that source of inexhaustible energy were to be questioned then the whole of Modernist philosophy must also be called into question.

The AT movement could not offer less physical work. It could offer the individual power but with power comes responsibility. This is where the recent history of sustainable buildings comes closest to the vernacular tradition. It seems, though, that this attempt has been dismissed apart from a few individuals. The emphasis is now upon making mainstream buildings sustainable, and if this cannot be totally achieved, then the move toward being a little bit more sustainable is deemed sufficient. It will be up to someone else to solve the problem of the energy gap; it will be left to the power companies to turn from fossil fuels to renewables.

The advantage of this stance is that it is business-as-usual as far as architecture is concerned. A building does not have to be zero energy and zero carbon dioxide emissions, it can still be a visual fancy with a bit of sustainability tacked on. Buildings today are no longer sustainable because the availability of resources, especially the resources of fossil fuels, has rendered this unnecessary. Those who dwelt in the vernacular had to live within their means and adapt a way of life to suit the buildings they could make. The alternative technology movement in the 1970s briefly saw that this attitude could be rediscovered in the need to make sustainable buildings, but the attempt was swamped and the buildings dismissed as non-architecture. Mainstream architecture refused to accept the challenge that was offered it. This may explain why so few truly sustainable buildings have been produced despite the pressing need for their creation.

Notes

1   K. Hudson, *Food, Clothes and Shelter* (London: John Baker, 1978).
2   David Pearson, *Earth to Spirit* (London: Gaia Books, 1994), p. 33.
3   Anthony Trollope, *The Warden* (1855, reprinted London: Robert Hayes, n.d.), pp. 209–10.
4   Paul Oliver (ed.), *Shelter in Africa* (London: Barrie and Jenkins, 1976), p. 46.
5   Paul Oliver (ed.), *Shelter and Society* (London: Barrie and Jenkins, 1976), p. 80.
6   Oliver, *Shelter in Africa*, p. 58.
7   S. R. Jones, *English Village Homes* (London: Batsford, 1936), pp. 4–5.
8   Rachel Carson, *Silent Spring* (Harmondsworth: Penguin, 1962), pp. 193–213.
9   *Indoor Air: An Integrated Approach*, ed. M. Maroni, L. Morawska, and N. Bofinger (Oxford: Elsevier Science, 1995), p. 835.
10   Barry Commoner, *The Closing Circle: Nature, Man and Technology* (New York: Alfred A. Knopf, 1972).
11   Martin Pawley, *Garbage Housing* (London: Architectural Press, 1975), pp. 26–34.
12   Commoner, *Closing Circle*, p. 121.
13   Donella H. Meadows et al., *Limits to Growth* (London: Earth Island, 1972), pp. 66–7.
14   *Radical Technology*, ed. G. Boyle and P. Harper (London Wildwood House, 1976).
15   John Prizeman, *Your House: The Outside View* (London: Hutchinson, 1975).
16   Vitruvius, *The Ten Books on Architecture*, trans. M. H. Morgan (1914, reprinted New York: Dover, 1960), pp. 180–1.
17   Le Corbusier, *Vers une architecture* (Paris: Crès, 1923), trans. F. Etchells, *Towards a New Architecture* (London: Architectural Press, 1987), p. 114.
18   Hermann Muthesius, *The English House* (1904), trans. J. Seligman (London: Lockwood Staples, 1979), p. 68.
19   Reyner Banham, *The Architecture of the Well-tempered Environment* (London: Architectural Press, 1984), pp. 280–4.
20   Ken Butti and John Perlin, *A Golden Thread* (New York: Van Nostrand Reinhold, 1980), p. 117.
21   Murray Bookchin, "Towards a Liberatory Technology" (1971), in *Post-scarcity Anarchism* (London: Wildwood House, 1974).
22   Ibid., p. 85.
23   David Dickson, *Alternative Technology and the Politics of Technical Change* (Glasgow: Fontana/Collins, 1974).
24   Philip Steadman, *Energy, Environment and Building* (Cambridge: Cambridge University Press, 1975), p. 16.

5

Gordon Matta-Clark's Building Dissections

Stephen Walker

Bataille on Sacrifice

> Concerning sacrifice, I can essentially say that, on the level of Hegel's philosophy, Man has, in a sense, revealed and founded human truth by sacrificing; in sacrifice he destroyed the animal in himself, allowing himself and the animal to survive only as that noncorporeal truth which Hegel describes and which makes of man – in Heidegger's words – a being unto death (*Sein zum Tode*), or – in the words of Kojève himself – "death which lives a human life."[1]

Sacrificing *in a sense*. In exactly what sense Georges Bataille read Hegel's sacrificing needs to be examined, as it indicates both the extent of a more general complaint and the promise that Bataille held out for sacrifice. For him, sacrifice could permit passage beyond the world of work, and was linked to religious ecstasy, to the basis of religion, *and* to the maintenance of the world of work; the ecstatic sensibility involved in this passage or transgression could, importantly, also be precipitated by works of art.[2]

This strong sacrifice contrasted with other, weak sacrificial moments where such transgression failed to occur, and where the sacrifice was diverted to other ends. In so far as it works to found and maintain human truth within his system, Hegel's "sacrifice" becomes useful, servile; *it does a job*. Although not against usefulness *per se*, Bataille was critical of systems within which usefulness or rationality gained a hegemonic position. The functional role that sacrifice was allocated within Hegel's system, where it worked to maintain the separation between natural world and non-corporeal truth, Bataille believed was misgiven, for within the system there was contained the means of its own collapse; namely, death. "[I]nsofar as he is Nature, Man is exposed to his own Negativity."[3]

For Bataille, the point was that the final moments or the ultimate logic of the Hegelian system remained there all along, it was just that Hegel had forgotten about them; equally, this would be his criticism of Darwinian evolution. At their furthest point, at their final moments – full evolution, absolute knowledge – these systems collapse into their opposites: animality, blindness.

Bataille advocated that such "final moments" should not be forgotten, and he advanced several strategies to this end. His notion of the *Pineal Eye*,[4] for example, figures a last stage to the evolutionary process that moves from quadruped, via *Homo erectus*, to some "final moment." He describes how at this final moment violent discharges of energy would blast through the top of the skull – which is where he locates the Pineal Eye – in a "magnificent but stinking ejaculation."[5] At this moment, the sun is seen and scrutinized (the "real" sun rather than its scientific or idealized representation), and in this instant of scrutiny the human being is annihilated:[6] at the end of evolution the system collapses, and this particular dialectic "fails" to reach a synthesis.

The complex movement of this notion, if it can be described as dialectical at all, inscribes the whole "system" within a drive to auto-mutilation. As soon as the highest stage is reached, the whole collapses upwards into the lowest. Implicit in this formulation is the criticism of both Darwinian evolution and Hegelian teleology just noted: for Bataille, neither of these systems goes far enough, neither reaches their inevitable end because both deny that "only orgasm and . . . simultaneous death . . . are at the endpoint of the human."[7] He believed, however, that by establishing a mythical movement to social existence, such "scientific" systems could be overcome by destabilizing their homogenizing tendencies and pushing them toward their "logical" conclusions.

Within his writings on the Pineal Eye, this socio-mythical dimension is generated by the sacrificial aspect of the operation: the moment of fall (when the Pineal Eye releases an orgasm of energy into the night of the sun) is experienced as a moment of sacrifice.[8] Although there are aspects of this sacrifice that can be read on an individual level (the disruption of the "whole" body image is something to which this chaper will return), the importance that Bataille holds out for this sacrifice (as opposed to the weak sacrifice that he observed in Hegel) is the role it can play in making a social body cohere. Such cohesion is illusory, at least if is taken to be total or permanent cohesion, because inscribed within this system is the demand for auto-mutilation and collapse just noted; here, social gain becomes sheer loss. Nevertheless, this cohesion would open out human experience far beyond the withered state it had taken on under the auspices of science, beyond what he described elsewhere as *the present banality of the world*.

Bataille on Art

> *Art was only art by virtue of ignoring what we see, what we are, in the interests of a theatrical imagination parading before the eye such ghosts of a bygone splendour as might console us for the present banality of the world.*[9]

Bataille's concern with the social, historical, and individual dimensions of sacrifice, and with the ways in which these were written into evolutionary systems, can be found in the (few) essays that he wrote on art. In his 1955 book on Manet, Bataille rejected the "gradual, regular evolution comparable to vegetable growth"[10] that Gautier used to describe the development of art over time. Rather than explicitly offering an alternative schema, his response tended to be more oblique, addressing instead particular moments of epochal change such as those associated with the work of Manet, or with the Paleolithic cave paintings of Lascaux which he identified with the *Birth of Art*.[11] The individual and historical importance of these events is acknowledged on several occasions, although Bataille is more than a little reluctant to explore their diachronic implications, and concentrates instead on investigating the synchronic aspects of the production and reception of the particular artworks under discussion.

In *Manet*, much of the book is spent examining the reception of Manet's work, which Bataille hoped would act as a means of reaffirming the importance of art in general. Where he did engage more with the paintings themselves, the close readings of Manet's work deployed and developed his notion of *altération*, which involved change rather than simple growth, and which had been expounded in his earlier review-cum-essay on Luquet's book *L'art primitif* (Primitive Art): this essay itself could be reasonably considered as a forerunner to both *Manet* and *Lascaux*.[12]

Although Bataille's reception of Luquet's ideas was on the whole favorable, he took issue with some aspects and consequences of the central hypothesis: it was in countering Luquet's binary argument (in which *l'art primitif* was opposed to *l'art classique des civilisés adultes*) that Bataille instead advocated a more base notion of art, one that could operate without recourse to such an opposition, and that could be "simply characterized by the alteration [*l'altération*] of the forms presented."[13]

Luquet's "knowledgeably expounded concepts" inadvertently worked to maintain the neat categories of art history, notwithstanding the fact that they did begin to address examples previously excluded from serious art-historical study, namely art produced by children and by "primitive" societies. For Bataille, this neatness was denied by the facts, and he used Luquet's own concepts to demonstrate that both categories, *l'art primitif* and *l'art classique*, coexisted even in examples that were used by Luquet himself.

The notion of *altération* side-stepped the contradiction of Luquet's classifications, but more importantly for Bataille, it inscribed both a base and a sacred dimension, a low and a high, within artistic production:

> The term *altération* has the double importance of expressing a partial decomposition analogous to that of a corpse, and at the same time the passage to a perfectly heterogeneous state that corresponds to what the protestant professor Otto called the totally other [*tout autre*], that is to say the sacred, which is found for example in a ghost.[14]

This simultaneous decomposition and transcendence echoes the operative aspect of the Pineal Eye, where the drive to auto-mutilation does not announce a straightforward collapse, but instead works to maintain as well as to destroy. This movement releases bursts of energy into the system, operating to ward off the establishment of a status quo or a teleological framework. Rather than developing or evolving (in a Darwinian sense) or synthesizing, *altération* offers the possibility that this system remains beyond any enduring synthesis.

Bataille acknowledged that such a notion could allow the development of meaning in representational art (which is what he read Luquet as doing) but what interested him more was the possibility that this *altération* could evacuate meaning, something that Luquet's categories could not contain or explain.[15] Without offering specific examples, Bataille claimed that the work of some contemporary artists demonstrated this aspect of *altération*, where baseness was revealed, and where "rotten" painting was the result. This art, "as art it unquestionably is, proceeds in this way [*sens*] through successive destructions. Inasmuch as it releases libidinal instincts, these instincts are sadistic."[16] During the operation that was "rotten" painting, this libidinal energy was released at the moments of destruction, which in a Pineal register could be equated to the moment of sacrifice.

Bataille makes this connection explicitly when writing on Manet, observing that it was the subject that was destroyed in Manet's painting: "To break up the subject and re-establish it on a different basis is not to neglect the subject; so it is in a sacrifice, which takes liberties with the victim and even kills it, but cannot be said to *neglect* it."[17] For Bataille, the importance of Manet's painting lay precisely in the depreciation it brought about. Manet attempted to paint what he saw, which short-circuited the *theatrical imagination* with all its attendant conventions of academic painting and reception. Bataille's criticism of these conventions was that they were moribund, that they belonged to a bygone era, and yet they were sustained by the bourgeoisie in their own interest.

Initial and indeed many subsequent reactions to Manet's *Olympia* were couched in terms of these conventions of form or of content, but for Bataille these responses all missed the point that Manet's approach had actually sacrificed painting, or at least sacrificed the established mores governing painterly production at that time; sacrificed them through the artist's indifference toward them. In their stead he was working to realize a "new world of forms" that would be relevant for contemporary society. Through what might be read as the *altération* of academic painting, Manet's work destroyed the received forms of painting, with the demise of these forms bringing about the decomposition of this painting and the passage to a more liberating form.[18]

Bataille described Manet as "a skilful practitioner [who] had radically cured painting of a centuries-old ailment: chronic eloquence."[19] By "curing" painting in this way, Manet's work frustrated the expectations of his audience by shifting importance away from any "meaningful" content and investing it instead in the operative aspect of painting itself.[20] These paintings exceeded the meaning that the bourgeoisie sought in them; instead of being useful on any terms they might acknowledge, Manet's work, for Bataille at least, was important because it overshot any such notion of use. Rather than giving spectators a reflection of their neat self-image, Manet's work fell short, provoking instead a release of base or animal energy: "the laughter that lay in wait for *Olympia* was something unprecedented; here was the first masterpiece before which the crowd fairly lost all control of itself."[21] Importantly, this laughter worked on both an individual and a social level, signaling as it did the destruction of both the assured self-image and of artistic conventions: the loss of control announced at least a degree of reciprocity between the artist (or the operative artistic act) and the audience, where an emergent energy might offer the prospect of a fuller experience of the human condition.

Human Form, Architecture

mankind cannot remain indifferent to its monsters.[22]

The conventions of academic painting worked to consolidate the whole-object quality of the human body that science demanded: furthermore, science itself worked to maintain and expand its authority by imposing what Bataille referred to on several occasions as the "common measure," a notion which he frequently discussed in the context of the human form.

> The composite image [formed by synthesizing all possible variations of a particular thing] would . . . give a kind of reality to the necessarily beautiful Platonic idea. At the same time, beauty would be at the mercy of a definition as classical as that of the common measure. But each individual form escapes from this common measure and is, to a certain degree, a monster.[23]

In *Figure humaine*, he remarks on the "stubborn efforts" made by conformists to suppress such an escape and to "finally recover a *human appearance* [*figure humaine*],"[24] criticizing the narrowness of this approach, this desire for homogenization. Instead, he argues that the actual absence of this ideal common measure between human beings is one aspect of the general lack of proportion between man and nature. A scientific sleight of hand (intimately linked to *the destruction of the animal in man*) is necessary to shore up this notion, proffering an explanation for the contradictions raised by individual instances of "escape." The aim of such a move is to subject nature to the rational order, a strategy that Bataille again traces back to Hegel, who similarly attempts to inscribe moments of contradiction into his own system by arguing that they are logically deducible.

For Bataille, however, such contradictions were not recoupable, and they would always exceed science's attempts to contain them. It was through his efforts to address the contradictions in Luquet's thesis that he developed the dualistic notion of *altération*: although Luquet's concept was still directed toward the establishment of meaning, his categories were read by Bataille as formalizations of a fuller, more interesting condition where contradiction existed, and which he hoped the process of *altération* would maintain.

The extent to which Bataille's own notion succeeds in remaining beyond any formalizing tendencies is somewhat ambiguous, though, and this has prompted conflicting readings. Georges Didi-Huberman, for example, states that *altération* is actually a dialectical system, *La dialectique de l'altération*, arguing that the moments of contradiction within this notion provide the motor for a dialectical development of art that was present at and has operated from the very moment of its birth.[25] However, this formulation is open to precisely the same criticism as that which Bataille raises against Hegel, namely the attempt to inscribe moments of contradiction into a dialectical oscillation, when in fact these moments are irrecuperable. Such a reading is predicated on the purely formal, tied as it is to representation or figuration; despite the fact that it might have been brought about by following Bataille down one of his own figurative paths, the danger is that it narrows the field within which the operation of *altération* can occur.

The promise of *altération* was that it could start to exceed science and thus reestablish a contact with nature, a concern that recurs in Bataille's criticisms of Hegel's weak sacrifice, of "common measure," and of the neat human form. In the context of his broader project, he believed that in the assault on the whole-object quality of the scientific human body, which he read in the artistic sacrifice of painters such as Manet, he could recognize an attack on architecture, a discipline which was even more dedicated to whole-object aesthetics, motivated by the impossible wish to last forever, or in his own words, "whose essence is the annulment of time."[26]

Although architecture was to prove one of Bataille's enduring targets, the links he made between its development and human evolution again reveal a tendency toward formalization: despite arguing that the very being of a society was expressed through its architecture, it was the physiognomy of architecture rather than architectural order that remained at the center of his critique. Similarly, the strategies that he developed to attack it did not really move beyond a formal affront: indeed, critics have noted more generally that his figurative conception of art resulted in fairly unambitious violations, and that his loss of interest in art as a possible weapon against homogenization had a similar cause.[27]

To take architecture as a purely formal notion is to launder it of the complexities that a fuller account might offer: Bataille could be accused of substituting a formal notion of architecture for this fuller version, despite his own criticisms of vicarious sacrifice, the "cowardly" substitution of animals for the human (part or whole). His objection to the latter would be that to sacrifice an animal instead of a human being demands that animals be considered in a qualitatively different way from humans, that a fundamental distinction already exists between the two prior to the sacrifice, which would deny the latter's fully transgressive possibilities. Similarly, by adopting a conception of architecture constrained in advance to the purely formal, Bataille's attempts at transgression would always be frustrated because the aspects of architecture that might actually respond to the approaches of his notion of *altération* were already separated from the Architecture that was to be his target. Both these instances of substitution would usher in a weak sacrifice, similar to the *sacrifice in a sense* that Bataille himself observed in Hegel's philosophy, where sacrifice did a job, was put to work, had a use.

The notion of use becomes more complex and has particular connotations within an architectural debate so frequently absorbed with form and function, and it is necessary to consider the extent to which and the mode in which architecture can respond to the remit of *altération*. Although not preventing the *altération* of architecture directly, the relationship that architecture has with use is involved in the possible short-circuit of the strong sacrificial aspirations of this notion, just as it is implicated in Bataille's frustration.

It could be suggested that his thinking on art – and architecture – became far more interesting when he was not thinking about art. The desublimatory aspects of *altération*, and the operative nature, continuing attack, sacrifice, and violation of the Pineal Eye, present possibilities that become more apparent when considered in connection with artworks that are not at the mercy of a figurative approach. Much of the work produced by Gordon Matta-Clark is interesting in this light, though in this specific context a range of his works that have become known as the building dissections warrant more careful attention. Although they can be taken in a figurative sense, where an inane observation might be that Matta-Clark "sacrifices buildings," these pieces, working as they do beyond figuration, can permit discussion in more operative terms.

Gordon Matta-Clark and "Operation"

Gordon Matta-Clark studied architecture at Cornell, spending a year at the Sorbonne before graduating in 1969. Rather than practicing as an architect, he began to work with artists such as Denis Oppenheim and Robert Smithson before setting up a studio in his own right in 1969. His artworks were produced in a period that was witness to various reactions to Minimalism and Pop, and it is somewhat easier to consider his *oeuvre* as a continuing experimentation that dealt as much with politics and with interpretation as it did with sculpture and architecture, than to attempt to define it in formal terms.

Matta-Clark worked in a wide variety of media, though common concerns can be traced across his work. Rather than trying to reveal a coherence between the various building dissections, it is the consequences of the operative approach both to making and interpreting these works that is of interest here.

The circumstances and the generators for the various building dissections were specific to each piece, though they can all demonstrate a certain preoccupation with issues architectural. The cuts that began the dissections themselves followed a progressively more complex geometry that is echoed in their titles, from early works such as *Splitting* (1974, figure 5.1), to *Conical Intersect* (1975), to the last dissections that Matta-Clark produced before his untimely death, such as *Office Baroque* (1977, figure 5.2) and *Circus-Caribbean Orange* (1978, figure 5.3).

Splitting inscribed a straight, planar cut located with an apparently symmetrical logic. This strict geometrical rationale to the incision recurs in the later dissections, though rather than addressing a formal notion of architecture they began to map geometrical considerations onto broader architectural concerns such as movement and space. *Conical Intersect*, for example, influenced by Anthony McCall's Expanded Cinema work *Line Describing a Cone*, used a geometry described by the path of a two-dimensional "object" to generate a multi-dimensional piece that foregrounded an opening movement through cellular architectural space. The title of *Office Baroque* itself suggests an engagement with a period of architecture that articulated a more self-conscious desire to manipulate space, though the sweeping circular cuts that make the dissection were widely used by Matta-Clark in other pieces. Beyond this obvious link, *Office Baroque* dealt with other Baroque motifs such as fragmentation, excessive detail, and with the infolding of utopian space and mundane space.

Figure 5.1   *Splitting*, 1974. Black and white photocollage, 101.5 × 76.2 cm.
© ARS, NY and DACS, London, 2003.

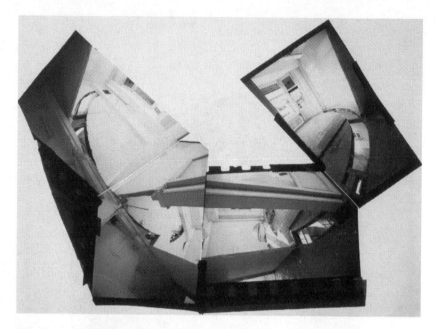

Figure 5.2   *Office Baroque*, 1977. Cibachrome, 101.5 × 76.2 cm. © ARS, NY and DACS, London, 2003.

However, here, as in the other dissections, the architectural conventions that might be referred to as part generators of the works were turned against architecture itself, forcing a juxtaposition of architectural "moments" that would usually remain apart, their separation policed by the institution of Architecture. The principles or norms of this Architecture would be expected to remain in the minds of the practitioners, rather than to fall into the hands of the users, in order that the usual diachronic relationship between these moments be sustained. With the building dissections, the manipulations of these architectural conventions exposed and altered this sequential development, promoting instead a synchronic event through which the institution of Architecture would be opened to challenge. This event may well have made the visitor feel awkward, yet this awkwardness announces the transgression of the architecture of Architecture.

This is not a situation that developed through an ignorance of Architecture, but one that arose through an indifference to the normative framework usually demanded. Elsewhere, in a discussion of Artaud's drawings,

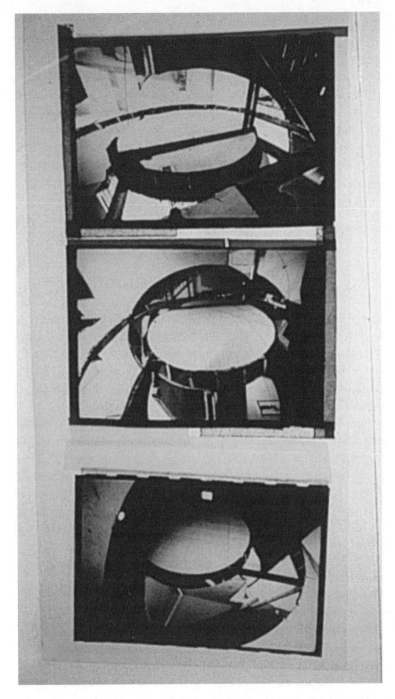

Figure 5.3 *Circus-Caribbean Orange*, 1978. Cibachrome, 101.6 × 50.8 cm.
© ARS, NY and DACS, London, 2003.

Derrida describes a similar condition as a "good awkwardness [which] would . . . consist of unlearning the 'drawing principle', ridding oneself of a nature too tractable with respect to norms only in existence because of a default . . . If [Artaud] 'abandoned' the 'principle of drawing' like that, then he must once have had it at his disposition."[28] Similarly, Bataille never suggested that Manet was ignorant of artistic conventions, merely that he was not constrained by them and would quite happily combine different genres of historical painting, mythological narrative and still life – and produce an "awkward" result in the process – if such a mix was wagered: "Conventions were meaningless . . . [in Manet's production of *Olympia*] since the subject, whose meaning was cancelled out, was no more than a pretext for the act – the *gamble* – of painting."[29]

Matta-Clark's building dissections operate in a parallel way to the *altération* that Bataille wanted to observe in Manet's work. The successive destructions that this notion involved could contribute to the development of meaningful figuration, or to the evacuation of meaning; what was of greater importance for Bataille was that the operation was sustained, rather than settle into a condition of stasis. He acknowledged that works of art could carry distinct meanings, as could particular sacrifices, but he drew a distinction between "mediocre works" where this particular meaning dominated and where the movement of *altération* faltered, and other stronger situations where a more general move to transgression was demonstrated, for here the structure of the profane world would be revealed with all its normative prohibitions.[30]

Matta-Clark's works undertook such a continuing transgression,[31] but, as already observed, this transgression was generated more by an *altération* of the norms of Architecture rather than by a simple "low blow" against building fabric. "It's true that the principal *altération* is not that undergone by the support of the drawing. Drawing itself develops and becomes richer in diverse ways, by accentuating the deformation of the object in all senses [*sens*]."[32]

The building dissections were not simply about cutting into buildings; their principal *altération* was not that undergone by the fabric itself, but more importantly they demanded that Architecture be deformed so as to reveal aspects of architectural practice that are hidden from the usual experience of architecture. The consideration that went into the cuts themselves has already been touched on and is not to be denied, as it again reminds us that if Matta-Clark could be said to have *abandoned the principle of Architecture, he must once have had it at his disposition. Splitting,* for example, involved dividing a derelict building in half by cutting a one-inch slice through all the structural surfaces, then tilting one half back through five degrees by chiseling out a wedge shape from the foundation and jacking the superstructure down onto its altered base. More important than the care of this actual removal were the demands this work made on the visitor; it could not be seen in a single view: "you have to walk." In addition to defying "that category of a sort of snapshot scenic work,"[33] this strategy began to abandon architectural principles, turning architectural convention back upon itself in an active and awkward alteration. Taking the static mapping of architectural space usually associated with its design and production, rather than with its "use," *Splitting* adopted the means of architectural convention – the section, or sectional drawing – and literally sectioned the building. And then with an equally literal follow-up tampered with the very foundations of architecture, removing a section of foundation to allow the building to be lowered onto its new base.

The experience of *Splitting* would change as the visitor moved around the dissected building, stepping over the split as the passage was made from room to room and from story to story. This movement through the building, horizontally and vertically, in plan and in section, would have been interrupted by the presence of the cut, the section, which would begin to call into question the tacit assumptions that architecture makes on our behalf, and to counter any claims that the architecture might make toward attaining a "whole-object" quality that can be understood once and for all. Rather than just being the "snapshot" work that Matta-Clark criticized, available for consumption from a single point of view, and rather than allowing observation "from nowhere" that the privileged Architectural system presumes, *Splitting* would demand an operative viewing.

Here, as with other dissections, this operative viewing would work to deny both the single view and the overview: the "whole" or recognizable building was held in balance. Conventional architectural space provided the surroundings for the viewer, but overlaid across this conventional space were the spaces opened up by the dissection cuts. These simultaneously suggest the total revelation that predicates the language of architecture, and its impossibility; the offer of the omnipresent view is both held out and withheld. Excessive concentration on the cut would also conflate the part for the whole, and the work of this fragmentation would overload and frustrate the expectations of the viewer, developing an architectural synecdoche that moved in two directions, two different registers, playing the game of partition, the divide and conquer that the institution itself deploys to maintain its hegemony. With the dissections, however, the normative framework that such hegemony usually hides away and denies is presented to the viewer. The spent architecture left by these works belongs both to the fragment and to the system. It could be said that it is simultaneously profane and sacred, as the transgression that occurs moves this system in two directions. The awkward position of the visitor, within and outside the system of architecture, is brought about through the denial of any assimilation to the system to which the works are "supposed" to belong, which leaves the visitor, or one might say the subject of architecture, in a position between support and collapse.

The cut offered the visitor an opening onto the omnipresence of architecture and to its limitation: as the revelation that underlies the Architectural principle was enjoyed through the cut, it would have been undermined by the insistence that there was something else to see, and that there always would be something else to see. As with Bataille's *altération*, a demand was set up for a continuing operation of destruction which would guard against stasis. It was not necessarily the fabric of the building that was offered for further dissection, but the subject of architecture. This insistence situated the subject within a dualism rather than a dialectical process; rather than moving toward architectural truth, the subject merely moved, had to maintain a movement that both grounded him/her within a world of architecture or of work, and made him/her aware of the conventions such a world demands for its own stability.

To this extent, the dissections did not mark the replacement of architecture with something else; they merely worked to reveal the presuppositions it makes. They offered a simultaneous experience of architectural space (the building itself), of a representation of that space (the cut), and of a denial of that representation (the synecdochal workings of the cut), an experience that would not reject the dominant tradition of architecture or replace it with an equivalent, but that would merely rehouse it. This experienced form of architecture would thus include the previous idealized Form of Architecture, and work in such a way as to open it to reformulation at every moment.

In addition to the effects that the vertiginous experience of these dissections had on the totalizing space of architecture, they also marked an attack on the whole-bodied individual subject of scientific and architectural language. In a marked parallel to the role that sacrifice plays in the Pineal systems, here the discrete subject would be fragmented by the spatial experience that the dissections set up.

The visitor effectively occupied two spaces simultaneously, and was moved on from these spaces by their conflictual demands, by the awkwardness noted earlier. The awareness of this superposition would open the visitor to the possibility of inscribing him or herself in the experience, of effectively seeing him or herself occupying another space, a situation linked to the structure of trauma where the individual realizes the presence of a loss, especially of (his/her own) death. The sadistic, or necrophilic, impulses that have been associated with the successive destructions of *altération* open the viewer to the prospect not only of their own mortality, but also and through this to the prospect that others might interpret the experience in a different way, or that they might be there after the viewer's own death. The temporality that such a perception begins to set up is more complex than that admitted by Hegel's system (at least the system as Bataille read it) as it re-admits a natural temporality into the process of human perception, which has the consequence of broadening it out to demand the inclusion of a social dimension.

In this respect the sacrifice of the individual in this work reminds us of Bataille's observations regarding sacrificial mutilation, which he read as attacking the "neat" boundary of the body, in order to set up a more ambiguous flesh in its place. As architecture both collapses and is sustained by these works, so the subject's own boundaries become blurred as a more visceral, fleshy, and socially determined body emerges. To this extent, the emergence of this body and the opening up of the principles of Architecture are inextricably linked, a point again emphasized by Derrida:

> And as the drawing principle supposes the "taking possession", the subjection to malevolent forces, the only way to dispose of the drawing principle is to put oneself passively at its disposition – and this is the normal cleverness of the draughtsman . . . [The drawing principle] would have tampered with our body, our eyes, and the limits of our vision, the "principle of our cranial box" (which commands the "principle of drawing"), our organic constitution in its general architecture.[34]

Rather than advocating a passive submission to the principles of Architecture, and to the attendant tampering with our organic constitution, the dissections can expose the general architecture of both and demand that they be taken up and used.

It is tempting to approach these works in formal terms, as the gestures themselves have a great formal seduction. However, the experience of the dissections produces a vertigo that parallels the final evolutionary moment that Bataille envisaged: the moment of fall or the moment of sacrifice. Matta-Clark's work here attacks an architecture that is the expression of the impossibly fixed and stable, and that has situated itself as the high point or ideal of evolution. These gestures cause architecture to collapse, and it falls upwards. To the extent that the totalizing space of architecture is allowed to remain isotropic, architecture adopts a specious naturality, and thus instigates a (weak) social cohesion that shuns change and espouses homogenization. By forcibly foregrounding perception of the parts, the building dissections bring about a deformation of this totalizing space, and in so doing they transgress the "language of architecture," demonstrating its contingency and denying its claims to be taken for nature.

In this operation, these are not merely works of spatial complexity, and their interest lies in the way that the consequences of the dissection move the piece beyond architecture. These works are no longer architectural, and yet they cannot be considered without acknowledging the machinations of architecture: paradoxically, they are wholly and impossibly architectural.

In a more Pineal register, they occur at the moment when the whole edifice of the architectural system falls, not into a dialectical synthesis, but into an opposition that demands the system remains beyond synthesis, *that it keeps going as an operation.* In other words, it is not a straight destruction, as this collapse works to sustain as well as to bring down architecture. (Following Bataille, we might say that it *takes liberties with the victim* – here, architecture – *and even kills it, but cannot be said to* neglect *it.*) At the high point of its evolution, architecture's attempts to annul time are revealed as illusory and its impermanence is demonstrated: it is not replaced, but *simply overshot, outdistanced.*[35]

Architecture and Sacrifice

Approached in this way, the relationship that can be set up between Bataille's thought and Gordon Matta-Clark's artwork reminds us of Bataille's description of the "evolution" of art, which has been discussed in terms of his notion of *altération.* Although the change that artistic practice has undergone exceeds Bataille's rather unambitious conception of art's possibilities, as an *operation* this movement picks up on many of his ideas.

Such links must be carefully made, though. Any argument to the effect that the meaning of Bataille's operation can only be understood when redeployed by such later practice would be problematic, inasmuch as it would pursue a "weak" evolutionary route that Bataille's project had as a target;[36] the "afterwards" would take on the task of explaining and recuperating the "before," *making sense of it*, and in some cases institutionalizing it in the process, rather than "altering" it as Bataille would advocate.

Equally problematic would be those who adopted Gordon Matta-Clark's artworks as a blueprint for architectural production. Within certain schools of architecture there have been minor industries generating projects to the Matta-Clark pattern, as well as occasions where more renowned practitioners have faced similar criticisms.

Such positions might attract subscribers by appearing to offer some kind of catharsis, alleviating any anxieties generated by Bataille's work and sweeping away the demands for continuous destruction and reformulation that the process of *altération* entails, and tendering instead the prospect of synthesis. However, whether used to describe artistic development or broader social "progress," this catharsis would only produce a weak form of social cohesion, linked to that generated by the totalizing language of architecture. On Bataille's Pineal model, though, this approach would begin to undo the cement that could *really* help society cohere by explaining away moments of contradiction or collapse or sacrifice. Indeed, it is the energy that these moments release that could allow society to develop a much fuller and more heterogeneous approach to life.

Conclusion

If we recall the point at which this chapter started – Hegel's "sacrifice in a sense" – where such an attempt at catharsis occurs through a "useful" or "weak" sacrifice (the sacrifice of the animal in us), it can be observed that this sacrifice has the intention of minimizing loss, rather than celebrating it. Indeed, this system would strive to produce a sacred that could represent and sanction homogenization and accumulation.

An architectural concept is available to serve such homogenizing systems, one that again endeavors to provide stability and permanence. As an obverse to the weak sacrifice of animality, this concept requires a similar move in order to "reveal" and to "found" an architectural conceit that would predicate such dictums as *Firmness, Commodity, and Delight*.

What is sacrificed here is "function," or at least the notion of function as an operation. This is not to suggest that architecture has no function, but rather that this conceit removes the operative aspect of function from the architectural concept: this architecture has *one* function, it is *that which had a use*. Inscribed in this way, "function" locks such architectural concepts into a teleology not dissimilar to Hegel's, while also forming the highest court of appeal in any judgments of architectural propriety. Coincident with this weak sacrifice of function is a naturalization of architecture. Apparently freed from any prospect of change, this architecture becomes a mere backdrop to our lives, we take it for nature rather than for an artifact or a product of culture.

There appears to be some strange accounting going on here: for human truth to fly high, animality or nature has to be written out of its economy, but coincident with this there occurs an attempt to naturalize architecture. In a system where accumulation is sacred, moments of sacrifice become increasingly weak and increasingly vicarious. Death is denied as thought attempts to attain hegemony, and function is denied as architecture attempts to last forever; however, both death and function remain as the Negativity within these systems.

When doing his own accounting, Bataille suggested that architecture could include aspects of what he termed *symbolic expenditure* – "representations of tragic loss (degradation and death)"[37] – which he considered to be close in meaning to sacrifice. He distinguished these cases from those where architecture comprised *real expenditure* – where it served utilitarian ends and permitted "useful" functions to be carried out.

The distinction for Bataille lay in the way that architecture was *used*; we might say that the choice was between a symbolic use and a real use. Paradoxically, in this attempt to categorize artistic production, he was not far from Hegel's hierarchy and a valorization of certain forms.[38] Despite this anomaly, the notion that the *use* to which architecture is put – its function, in other words – could somehow be linked to sacrifice in its strong sense warrants attention.

If it is actually possible to talk of architecture and sacrifice within these terms, then this notion must inscribe an excess of functions, in order to side-step the teleological implications that are attendants of weak sacrifice, and instead to become the description of an operation that could avoid a weak catharsis and produce a system that strives to fail. In this light, the importance of Gordon Matta-Clark's dissections, their closest position to Bataille's sacrifice, lies not in their material expenditure, the simple loss of architecture, but rather in the work they make the subject of architecture do: subject here in its broadest sense. Theirs is not a formal proximity, but one of use, where the use of architecture demands a distancing from and a reunion with nature.

Although Gordon Matta-Clark's works were not works of architecture, they can illustrate the possibilities of an architecture operating beyond teleology. Rather than being legible "once and for all," what they actually reveal is the coexistence, the juxtaposition, or superposition of several (possibly conflicting) readings or uses, partly productive of the vertigo discussed earlier. As artworks, they were conceived perhaps more for their *symbolic use* than for their *real use*, but it is the latter that we should explore more energetically when thinking of this notion of architecture and sacrifice. Rather than releasing real expenditure with a shrug, much as Bataille did, Matta-Clark's work can make us aware that once a figurative or purely formal concept of architecture is abandoned, the notion of function can be spent over and over, in order that the subject of architecture be put to work (rather than laundered of its energies by a weak sacrifice) and thus opened up to a fuller experience.

Notes

1 Georges Bataille, *Hegel, Death and Sacrifice*, trans. Jonathan Strauss, in *Yale French Studies*, 78 (1990): 18.

2 "La transgression que je désigne est la transgression religieuse, liée à la sensibilité extatique, qui est la source de l'extase et le fond de la religion. Elle se lie à la fête, dont le sacrifice est un moment de paroxysme . . . Une oeuvre d'art, un sacrifice, participent, si l'on m'entende, d'un esprit de fête débordant le monde du travail et, sinon la lettre, l'esprit des interdit nécessaires à la protection de ce monde." Georges Bataille, *Lascaux ou la naissance de l'art*, in *Oeuvres complètes de G. Bataille*, vol. 9 (Paris: Gallimard, 1993), pp. 40, 42.

3 "Human Negativity, Man's effective desire to negate Nature in destroying it – in reducing it to his own ends . . . – cannot stop at Man himself; insofar as he is Nature, Man is exposed to his own Negativity." Bataille, *Hegel, Death and Sacrifice*, p. 15.

4 In addition to the essay "The Pineal Eye," see in particular "The Jesuve," both of which are included in Georges Bataille, *Visions of Excess: Selected Writings, 1927–1939*, trans., ed. and intro. Allan Stoekl (Minnesota, MN: University of Minnesota Press, 1985).

5 Bataille, "The Jesuve," *Visions of Excess*, p. 77.

6   "In practice the scrutinised sun can be identified with a mental ejaculation, foam on the lips, and an epileptic crisis. In the same way that the preceding sun (the one not looked at) [and therefore given some elevated poetic or mathematical meaning or "spiritual elevation"] is perfectly beautiful, the one that is scrutinised can be considered horribly ugly." Bataille, "Rotten Sun," *Visions of Excess*, p. 57.

7   Allan Stoekl, in Bataille, *Visions of Excess*, p. xii.

8   And compare: "Such an action [as auto-mutilation or sacrifice] would be characterised by the fact that it would have the power to liberate heterogeneous elements and to break the habitual homogeneity of the individual, in the same way that vomiting would be opposed to its opposite, the communal eating of food . . . The one who sacrifices is free – . . . free to throw himself suddenly *outside of himself*, like a gall or an aissaouah." Bataille, "Sacrificial Mutilation and the Severed Ear of Vincent Van Gogh," *Visions of Excess*, p. 70.

9   Georges Bataille, *Manet*, trans. Austryn Wainhouse and James Emmons, *Manet: Biographical and Critical Survey* (Lausanne: Skira, 1955), p. 78.

10   Ibid., p. 63.

11   His book *Lascaux ou la naissance de l'art* was published in the same year as *Manet*.

12   Georges Bataille, *L'art primitif*, first published in *Documents*, no. 7, Deuxième Année, 1930, pp. 389–97. Reprinted in *Oeuvres complètes de G. Bataille*, vol. 1: *Premièrs écrits, 1922–1940* (Paris: Gallimard, 1970), pp. 247–54. Further references to this essay will be to the *Oeuvres complètes*.

13   "simplement charactérisé par *l'altération* des formes présentées," *Oeuvres complètes*, vol. 1, p. 251.

14   "Le terme *d'altération* a le double intérêt d'exprimer une décomposition partielle analogue à celle des cadavres et en même temps le passage à un état parfaitement hétérogène correspondant a ce que le professeur protestant Otto appelle le *tout autre*, c'est-à-dire le sacré, réalise par example dans un spectre." *Oeuvres complètes*, vol. 1, p. 251n.

15   Luquet also expressly excluded sculpture or three-dimensional work from his thesis for reasons that are beyond the scope of this chapter. Although Bataille remarks that it was regrettable that, by this move, Luquet had eliminated a question of no lesser importance than the one he actually developed a response to, his own notion of *altération* was not reliant upon the same issues; the consideration of three-dimensional work under the operation of *altération*, although complex, should not be taken to be doomed-in-advance because of Luquet's exclusion.

16   "L'art, puisque art il y a incontestablement, procède dans ce sens par destructions successives. Alors tant qu'il libère des instinct libidineux, ces instincts sont sadistiques." Bataille, "L'art primitive," in *Oeuvres complètes*,

vol. 1, p. 253. Hollier would insist that rather than being sadistic, these impulses are necrophilic: "Bataille's [Freud] is the post-war Freud, the theoretician of collective psychology and the death drive. For Bataille, however, the libido is fundamentally necrophilic, and it reveals itself without exception as the most insistent – if indirect – manifestation of the death drive: the love of death is the only thing stronger than death itself." Denis Hollier, "Bataille's Tomb," in *Absent Without Leave: French Literature under the Threat of War*, trans. Catherine Porter (Cambridge, MA: Harvard University Press, 1997), p. 47.

17 Bataille, *Manet*, p. 103. Compare also: "Manet wrung the last drop of meaning out of the subject. To suppress and destroy the subject is exactly what modern painting does, but this does not mean that the subject is altogether absent." *Manet*, pp. 51–2. Consider also Bataille, *Lascaux*, in *Oeuvres complètes*, vol. 9, p. 42.

18 "What inspired him as much as anything was the prospect, for him an act of grace, of entering a new world of forms which would deliver him, and with him *the others*, from the bondage, the monotony, the falsehood of art forms that had served their time." Bataille, *Manet*, p. 33.

19 Ibid., p. 52.

20 "We have seen how essential the destruction of the subject – at least of the meaning it conveyed – was to *The Execution of Maximilian*. It was even more essential to *Olympia* . . . Conventions were meaningless here since the subject, whose meaning was cancelled out, was no more than a pretext for the act – the *gamble* – of painting . . . [This] operation reached its climax in *Olympia* . . . [Malraux] fails to define what gives *Olympia* . . . its value *as an operation*." Bataille, *Manet*, pp. 61, 82, 86, 88.

21 Ibid., p. 17.

22 Bataille, "The Deviations of Nature," in *Visions of Excess*, p. 55.

23 Ibid., p. 55.

24 "les efforts les plus obstinés ont été poursuivis par le blanc et la blanche pour retrouver enfin *figure humaine*." Bataille, "Figure Humaine," in *Oeuvres complètes*, vol. 1, p. 184.

25 Georges Didi-Huberman, "Pensée par image, pensée dialectique, pensée altérante: L'enfance de l'art selon Georges Bataille," *Les Cahiers du Musée Nationale d'Art Moderne* (Winter 1994): 4–29. See especially p. 21ff. Didi-Huberman is not unaware of the problems that Bataille is attempting to engage with; regarding the differences between Bataille's and Hegel's dialectic, he remarks that, for Hegel, destruction is merely a point (antithesis) that the dialectic must pass through, whereas for Bataille, he argues, the dialectic must work to maintain these moments of destruction within their movement, and thinks this dialectical movement as the possibility of maintaining all the moments of the process present. Didi-Huberman, "Pensée par image," p. 11.

26   "L'harmonie, comme le projet, refette le temps au dehors; son principe est la répétition par laquelle tout possible s'eternise. L'idéal est l'architecture, ou la sculpture, immobilisant l'harmonie, garantissant la durée de motifs dont l'essence est l'annulation du temps." Georges Bataille, *L'expérience intérieure*, in *Oeuvres complètes*, vol. 5, p. 70. See also Georges Bataille, "Architecture," trans. Dominic Faccini, in *October*, 60 (Spring 1992): 26: "an attack on architecture . . . is necessarily, as it were, an attack on man."

27   See, for example, Yve-Alain Bois, "Threshole," in Yve-Alain Bois and Rosalind E. Krauss, *Formless: A User's Guide* (New York: Zone, 1997), pp. 185–91.

28   Jacques Derrida, "To Unsense the Subjectile," in Jacques Derrida and Paule Thévenin, *The Secret Art of Antonin Artaud*, trans. Mary Ann Caws (Cambridge, MA: MIT Press, 1998), p. 105.

29   Bataille, *Manet*, p. 82.

30   "Chaque oeuvre d'art isolément a un sens indépendant du désir de prodige qui lui est commun avec toutes les autres. Mais nous pouvons dire, à l'avance, qu'une oeuvre d'art où il est faible et joue à peine, est une oeuvre médiocre. De même, tout sacrifice a un sens précis, comme l'abondance des récoltes, l'expiation, ou tout autre but logique: il a répondu néanmoins de quelque manière à la recherche d'un instant sacré, dépassant le temps profane, où les interdit assurent la possibilité de la vie." Bataille, *Lascaux, Oeuvres complètes*, vol. 9, p. 42.

31   It is important at this point to draw attention to further *altérations* that the building dissections underwent as Matta-Clark recorded the actual cutting process and the results, which he subsequently reworked as filmic and particularly as photographic collages. In the particular context of this chapter, it is important to maintain the focus of the investigation on the building dissections themselves, because of the particular demands they placed on the visitor, rather than pursue the collages, which in their own way address architectural norms and the representation of architectural space.

32   Bataille, "L'art primitive," *Oeuvres complètes*, vol. 1, pp. 252–3. It is tempting to translate *le support du dessin* as the subjectile, as this would open a conversation with Derrida's essay on Artaud, mentioned above.

33   Gordon Matta-Clark: "you can't see *Splitting* [in a single view]. You have to walk – this is always one of the big issues which I've brought up before: the difference between a kind of anecdotal piece – I don't know how to classify it – and this sort of internal piece. There are certain kinds of pieces that can be summarized – or at least characterized – very quickly from a single view. And then there are other ones which interest me more, finally, which have a kind of internal complexity which doesn't allow for a single and overall view, which I think is a good thing. I like it for a number of reasons, one of which is that it does defy that category of a sort of snapshot scenic work. The other thing is that it also defies that whole object quality that is with all sculpture,

even with people who have escaped the so-called 'sculpture habit' by going into some sort of landscape, or extra-gallery, extra-museum type of territorial situation." Gordon Matta-Clark, interviewed by Judith Russi Kirshner, Museum of Contemporary Art, Chicago, February 13, 1978. Reproduced in *Gordon Matta-Clark*, ed. Maria Casanova (Valencia: IVAM Centro Julio Gonzàlez, 1993), p. 390. Pamela Lee's book on Matta-Clark, *Object to be Destroyed: The Work of Gordon Matta-Clark* (Cambridge, MA: MIT Press, 2000), covers several building dissections. On *Splitting*, in particular, see pp. x–xii and pp. 11–33; on *Circus . . .* , see pp. 137–61. Lee also acknowledges a debt to Bataille's influence in the overall economy of her work; see note 7, pp. 236–7.

34   Derrida, "To Unsense the Subjectile," p. 105.

35   Cf. Bataille, *Manet*, p. 103.

36   Some theories posit this *lag* in psychoanalytic terms, using a traumatic temporal structure to provide the theoretical underpinning for the argument. Thus a Freudian "afterwardsness" – a neo-avant-garde – explains an earlier (traumatic) event – the historical avant-garde.

37   Georges Bataille, "The Notion of Expenditure," in Bataille, *Visions of Excess*, p. 120.

38   More precisely, he was not far from the *doctrine of the types of art*, from the *Lectures on Aesthetics*. Nor was he too far from Kant: when discussing Manet's need for "official success," he argued that the desire for this recognition was a response to "the need to compensate for that cumbersome *hypertrophy of the ego* which is the artist's lot, and which sets him apart from the artisan." Bataille, *Manet*, p. 27. This is somewhat reminiscent of Kant's categorization in the *Third Critique* (see §43 *Art in General*) where a distinction is made between *art* and *handicraft* on the basis that only the latter is "labour, i.e. a business," an observation underlined by Bataille's next comment that artisans do it for the money but that artists do it for recognition (from their peers). Interestingly, Kant's distinction is the outcome of a desire to establish that "*art* is distinguished from *nature*."

6

Territoriality and Identity at RAF Menwith Hill

David Wood

Making Menwith

We are not yet accustomed to seeing late twentieth-century military establishments as architecture, even though they are among the most significant human constructions of the period. In contrast, we have no such blindness to castles and ramparts which, in disuse and decay, safely convey the romance of conflict long past. Military architecture, whether of the recent or distant past, is caught up in the symbolic landscapes and complexes of meaning that surround constructed forms, and is the visible element of vast networks of socio-technical power. This chapter examines a particular military base in this context, looking at the simultaneous construction of place and identity at RAF Menwith Hill in North Yorkshire, UK.

Built from 1955 on 562 acres of land bordering the main road between Harrogate and Skipton on the edge of the scenic moorland of Nidderdale, and officially opened in 1960, RAF Menwith Hill is one of the world's largest and most significant Signals Intelligence (SIGINT) bases.[1] Although its title is British, RAF Menwith Hill is controlled by the American Department of Defense, and most of its staff are either directly or indirectly employed by the National Security Agency (NSA), the US SIGINT organization.[2]

Despite its fairly isolated location, RAF Menwith Hill is very visible, and is subject to a multiplicity of interpretations. My own first impressions of the base were apocalyptic. Coming over the brow of a hill, the sky heavy and grey with an oncoming storm, the numerous white geodesic radomes seemed to grow from the moors like a great cluster of enormous mutant mushrooms transported from the fantastic imaginings of a 1950s' post-nuclear apocalypse movie. Others see it very differently. My companion on that first journey was more favorably impressed by the way in which the spherical forms of the radomes stood out starkly against the dark skies and bleak moorland landscape.

RAF Menwith Hill can be many things: beautiful, monumental, bizarre, ugly; symbolic of either the protection of the free world, or of an authoritarian new world order; a source of employment, or an economic threat; a blow to civil liberties; another area of beautiful English landscape lost to militarism or modernism; a sinister site of unexplained phenomena; or simply a continuing planning problem. One thing is certain: how these sites appear is connected to limited and imperfect knowledges of what happens behind the razor wire-topped steel fences. To focus on the immediately visible mushroom shapes of the radomes is to get an incomplete picture. Menwith Hill's arrays of sophisticated interception and communication technologies consist of far more than the satellite dishes concealed beneath.

Intelligence Sites as Military Land

Menwith Hill is officially a Royal Air Force (RAF) site, and therefore part of the "defence estate," the land owned and/or used by the Ministry of Defence (MoD). The history of military land use in Britain has seen only limited research, the most extensive work being John Childs's *The Military Use of Land: A History of the Defence Estate* (1998).[3] He shows that the Defence Estate reached its greatest extent during World War II when the Emergency Powers (Defence) Act of 1939 gave the state the ability forcibly to requisition land for defense purposes. By 1945, 20.5 percent of the land area of the UK was controlled by the War Office. Most, but not all, of this land was returned to the original owners within two years of the war's end.[4]

However, the number of requisitions began to increase again as NATO strategic plans for Cold War defense required bomber bases and communications, intelligence, and ballistic missile early warning sites in the UK,[5] as well as in other European countries, particularly Norway, Italy, and West Germany, which took the bulk of NATO ground forces. Duncan Campbell famously described Britain as America's "unsinkable aircraft carrier."[6] Menwith Hill dates from this "First Cold War" period, which is conventionally seen as following from the 1950 Anglo-American Agreement and the 1951 Status of Forces Agreement.[7] However, Campbell showed that much of the American air force returned in July 1948, the time of Stalin's blockade of Berlin and the US airlift of supplies into the city, and that a series of informal agreements and de facto decisions, including the secret UKUSA treaty on SIGINT thence governed the growth and maintenance of American bases in Britain.[8]

Official figures underestimated the number of US bases and facilities in Britain, and academic analysis has generally accepted the underestimates: Childs gives a figure of 75 American facilities in 1985 based on contemporary government figures;[9] however, Campbell's intensive research revealed a total of 135 facilities the previous year.[10]

Intelligence Sites as Iconic Landscapes

At the intersection of military lands and a wider consideration of landscape is a paper by Jackie Tivers. In examining Aldershot, a complex of barracks, HQs, military housing, and training lands in the south-east of England, which has grown into a "military town," she argued that "military defence landscapes are iconic in nature; that there exist specific icons which symbolize for us (or symbolized for our forebears) military defence and which have a meaning which goes much further than their overt presence."[11]

Drawing on Cosgrove and Daniels, Tivers outlines the way in which such landscapes can be read as texts containing "markers" which give particular meaning and identity to the landscape. Cosgrove and Daniels define iconography as "the theoretical and historical study of symbolic imagery,"[12] and trace its development from the Renaissance through the early twentieth-century Warburg school of art history. They note that it resonates strongly with Clifford Geertz's ethnographic approach in anthropology, with its call to read culture as a text, and its use of "thick" description.[13] Iconography is important as a means of enquiry because signs and symbols cannot be taken for granted: they shift and change. Indeed, Cosgrove and Daniels argue that, in a postmodern perspective, "landscape seems less like a palimpsest whose real or authentic meanings can somehow be recovered with the correct techniques, theories or ideologies, than a flickering text displayed on the word-processor screen whose meaning can be created, altered, elaborated and finally obliterated by the merest touch of a button."[14] The meaning of landscape thus can be contested. As

Cosgove had earlier argued, "the power of individual visual appropriation of the external world, once the preserve of the privileged few . . . is now open in large measure to anyone."[15] Tivers argues that these interpretations can be analyzed within a three-dimensional matrix of existential meaning made up of security/stress, stimulus/ennui, and status/stigma, based on Ley's work on urban landscapes.[16]

This iconography of military landscape resonates strongly with the way in which nationhood is constructed. Several authors, apart from Tivers, have contributed to this strand of research. This can take the form of examining obviously symbolic landscapes like military memorials and cemeteries, as Heffernan and Morris have done.[17] There have been exciting analyses like those of Rachel Woodward, who has tackled the question of the co-construction of landscape and gender in military training,[18] and Pyrs Gruffudd, who examines the tradition of the "RAF pastoral."[19] The latter outlines the linking of the symbolism of the wide open skies and supposedly distinctive light of southern England with Royal Air Force fighters like the Spitfire, particularly during and following the Battle of Britain during World War II. Gruffudd examines the way this was achieved through art and advertising, and, interestingly, concludes that this RAF pastoral is now well over, and with the advent of American bomber and later cruise missile bases, "the sky has been dispossessed of its Englishness, by American missiles and Soviet fallout . . . now the sky is anything but reassuring, and a whole new realm of symbolism is attached to it."[20]

Both these analyses are particularly interesting for a study of sites such as Menwith Hill, which has a widely varying and contradictory iconic significance, particularly when this symbolic presence is considered to be one of the functions of American military bases. The question of what is represented by such places, and how this changes over time, is crucial. British and American interpretations of landscape symbolism are also very different and brought to serve different purposes within a framework of the construction of national identity, as Daniels and Matless have shown.[21] In addition, Dodds has demonstrated how English landscape constructions were transposed to their "mirror image" of the Falklands, during the conflict of 1982.[22]

Intelligence Sites as Territories

Despite the possibility of egalitarian viewings, Cosgrove contextualizes the concept of landscape in Britain as a product of the nineteenth century, a nostalgic, bourgeois idea of an ideal Britain: "landscape is a restricted way of seeing that diminishes alternative modes of experiencing our relations with nature."[23] Whilst this may be true of the particular historic signifier "landscape," the idea of landscape in general has been appropriated and reinterpreted. Cosgrove notes that the discipline of geography itself had its roots in landscape, but also contains the seeds of very different ways of seeing. For example, Yi-Fu Tuan's classic study of fear is predicated on this very idea, that landscapes are both internal and external: " 'Landscape' as the term has been used since the seventeenth century is a construct of mind as well as a physical and measurable entity. 'Landscapes of Fear' refers both to psychological states and to tangible environments."[24]

It is therefore necessary to move beyond landscape and discuss the ways in which social relations construct space, place, and identity. Space can be conceptualized in many ways. There is a mundane view that it is simply the context in which things exist. This is what Michel Foucault famously referred to as "the dead, the fixed, the undialectical, the immobile."[25] This abstract idea of space will not be considered here since, by its very definition, it cannot be affected by action. Instead, space can be conceived of as something that is constructed; in other words: created, delimited, controlled, and defined by the interaction of humans and non-humans.

Henri Lefebvre was one of the first to argue that space was produced within capitalism. He pointed out the confused stance of modern philosophical use of the idea of "space":

> We are forever hearing about the space of this and/or the space of that: about literary space, ideological spaces, the space of the dream, psychoanalytic topographies, and so on, and so forth. Conspicuous by its absence from supposedly fundamental epistemological studies is not only the idea of "man" but also that of space – the fact that "space" is mentioned on every page notwithstanding.[26]

Mental or social space (to which Tuan refers above) was now admitted back into the arena of discussion but it seemed to represent everything and nothing. Lefebvre argued that "(social) space is a (social) product," but that this fact is hidden by the illusion that space is transparent or, alternatively, that "things" have more reality than does the subject. He developed a conceptual "triad" of spatial practice, including the production and reproduction of space; representations of space, which would include iconography and the ideal spaces of military planners; and representational spaces, which "tend towards more or less coherent systems of non-verbal symbols and signs," and which here include iconic landscapes.

However, spatial construction acts not only "outside" but is involved in a dialectical relationship with the "human;" spatial construction can also be seen as the act of constructing identity. Spatial construction is thus clearly connected with power. Human attempts to control space are directed and conscious and can be carried out with specific aims in mind. Acts creating specific places are, according to Doreen Massey, "attempts to stabilize the meaning of particular envelopes of space-time."[27] Robert Sack called this behavior "territoriality," which he further defines as "the attempt by an individual or group to affect, influence, or control people, phenomena, and relationships, by delimiting and asserting control over a geographic area."[28] This involves three basic processes: "classification," or defining an area by a system of categorization imposed by the powerful, the actor expressing the territorial behavior; "communication," the act of telling others that a space is a territory; and "enforcement," or at least "an attempt at influencing interactions" involving the territory.[29]

The concept of territoriality as power over space does not mean that all places are territories. Territories are particular places that must be established and constantly maintained. They do not necessarily have to be defended in the sense that the actor establishing the territory has to be inside the territory, "territory can be used to contain or restrain as well as to exclude,"[30] and proxies such as physical barriers or even legal and cultural ones, like signs forbidding entry or restricting behavior, are territorial devices. For example, the act of defining an area as "forbidden" creates a place that is spatially separate. It also defines, through this territoriality, what are expected human behaviors in relation to the place. This, of course, can be reinforced by technology (fences, security cameras, guns, and so on), by the exercise of power (e.g., force used by guards), and by law (arrest, courts, prisons, and so on). It effectively creates a regulated, controlled, and potentially "invisible" space. Sack calls this particular component of territoriality "the idea of socially *emptiable place.*"[31]

The creation of invisible spaces (and "emptiable places"), particularly in relation to technology, is similar to "black-boxing,"[32] an anthropological concept derived from the contrast between the visible and hidden aspects of complex modern technologies. Black-boxing is "the way science and technology is made invisible by its own success,"[33] but I would suggest that part of this success is the same process by which any space is constructed and defined as separate, by whatever method. The interplay of space, information, and power leads to black-boxing as a normalized and expected way of organizing society. Thus, for most of society it is not so much the fear of violence or punishment that prevents investigation of forbidden territories, but the common acceptance of their invisibility. In other words, people consent to these territorializations, whether they are based on coercive power or on technological expertise, and in doing so construct the space as socially empty, invisible, black-boxed. Territory can thus reflect hegemony, a condition described by Gramsci as the dominance of a social class through consensual methods.[34]

What results when many such places are connected as part of a network is an effectively "hidden geography," which, while it may possess a superficial coherence and visibility, is in fact effectively unknowable due to the character and intensity of its territorialization. Peter Gill produced a theory of how the liberal-democratic state relates to internal security and intelligence-gathering mechanisms,[35] which can easily be represented as a meta-territorial model of this kind. He presented a model of the state as a series of concentric circles of security, with the "secret state" of intelligence organizations at the center, moving progressively through the executive (government and bureaucracy), other state agencies (judiciary, parliament, and so on), and, finally, to the citizen or subject. The concentric circles mark what might crudely be called power, but which are characterized by degrees of autonomy and secrecy, increasing toward the center, and penetration, increasing outwards. This model is panoptic, where the intelligence agencies are seeing (and acting) without being seen (or acted upon).[36]

Military bases serve clear territorial and panoptic purposes. Joseph Gerson claims that six purposes are served by US bases in the post-World War II period: to project conventional military power, particularly in the Third World; to prepare for and launch nuclear war; to act as "tripwires" to guarantee US response to attack; to serve as symbols of US power; to ensure US economic access to foreign markets; and, finally, to influence and control the governments of the areas where the bases are situated.[37]

Territories that have been emptied of social meaning may well be subject to conflicting reinterpretations or attempts to fill the emptiness. Clearly, the actors who create and maintain the territory have an advantage here, in the case of intelligence sites, an enormous advantage; however, hegemony and panopticism are ideal conditions, their existence is always incomplete or in process; thus, even powerful territorializations can be challenged. In the case of US military installations, Gerson shows that resistance to US control of bases was more widespread in the twentieth century than is popularly believed, with particular struggles in Iceland, Guam, Puerto Rico, and the Philippines. The continued campaigns of protest groups at Menwith Hill are also evidence of the challenge to territorial constructions, as we shall see.

Making Menwith (1): Function

According to James Bamford, Menwith was chosen due to its isolated moorland location, which was "virtually free from urban electromagnetic interference."[38] Campbell and Melvern revealed the coevolution of the base and the nearby Hunter's Stones post office (now British Telecom) microwave relay tower, and indeed the whole of the British government's "backbone" microwave communications network, first proposed in a 1955 White Paper.[39] This was designed "to provide a strategic reserve communications system" and was originally intended to "enable a bomb-blasted Britain to carry on functioning throughout a prolonged nuclear war as an airbase and support base."[40] However, it had a peacetime function, which was to funnel international communications passing through the UK into Menwith. Thus from Hunter's Stones, which was one of the hubs of the system and which connected the original "backbone" (London–Birmingham–Manchester–Leeds), and their huge underground telephone exchanges, to the "northern backbone" section (to Dundee) completed in 1962, a special spur was constructed to Menwith.

In 1966 the NSA transferred its operations from Kirknewton in Scotland and took over command of the site. After the handover to the NSA, technological change at Menwith Hill was rapid. Increasing satellite communication and surveillance meant that interception of radar, radio, and cable-transmitted information was inadequate. The USA had launched its first surveillance satellite in 1959, two years after the first Soviet "sputnik" orbit, and by 1966 hundreds of public and secret launches had taken place.[41] Dish antennae to receive satellite transmissions were constructed at Menwith Hill in the late 1960s and the first two "radomes" were constructed during 1974; there were eight on the site by the end of the 1970s. The base now has twenty-eight radomes, and numerous aerials and masts for intercepting and transmitting on many different radio frequency types. According to FAS, Field Station F-83, as RAF Menwith Hill is known to the NSA, currently acts as a "regional SIGINT operations center" and is "the principal NATO theater ground segment node for high altitude signals intelligence satellites."[42]

Numerous satellite platforms have been shown to be linked with Menwith; for example: the Defense Support Program (DSP) (now replaced by the Space-based Infrared System (SBIRS), completed in 2001), which is part of complex networks of technologies that give early warning of military attack on the USA;[43] Communications Intelligence (COMINT) satellites "capable of sucking microwave signals from out of space like a vacuum-cleaner picking up specks of dust from a carpet";[44] real-time PHOTINT (Photographic Intelligence) platforms; and imaging radar systems, that overcome PHOTINT deficiencies by being able to "see" through clouds; as well as systems associated with weapons control functions; and many others.

Two planning notifications submitted in 1975 to the borough council were both for a primary electricity sub-station which suggests that more energy-demanding equipment was being installed,[45] and it seems that an improved cable link to Hunter's Stones was installed shortly afterwards in 1977. Campbell and Melvern estimated that, after this upgrade, the base could deal with 32,000 simultaneous telephone, telex, and other cable transmissions.[46] This suggests that the old functions of the base had not decreased with the increased emphasis on satellite SIGINT; instead, the base had expanded its capacity and range of activity. Several planning notifications were made during the 1980s of new masts and radomes, and there were at least two notifications in 1987 of one or more new electrical sub-stations, which suggests that, as in the mid-1970s, a substantial increase in capacity was being planned. This could have reflected the advent of another marked upgrading of Menwith Hill's earth-based COMINT capabilities. Campbell claimed that it was about this time that planning started for the P415 civilian communications monitoring and analysis network, otherwise known as ECHELON,[47] "a global network of computers that automatically search through millions of intercepted messages for pre-programmed keywords or fax, telex and e-mail addresses."[48]

ECHELON has been the main means by which Menwith has become known to the wider world, through Privacy International, Statewatch, and other campaigning groups and journalists, but in particular through the European Parliament. Its Scientific and Technological Options Assessment (STOA) sub-committee of the Civil Liberties Committee published a report, "An Appraisal of the Technologies of Political Control," which included a paragraph on ECHELON: "All e-mail, telephone and fax communications are routinely intercepted by the [NSA], transferring all target information from the European mainland via the strategic hub of London, then by satellite to Fort Meade in Maryland via the crucial hub at Menwith Hill in the . . . [United Kingdom]."[49] The latest information to emerge about ECHELON has again been via STOA and the European Parliament: to follow the original report, the parliament commissioned a series of four further reports, and has held an inquiry. The report on technology, "Interception Capabilities 2000," was written by Duncan Campbell, and concentrates on the COMINT aspect of SIGINT.[50]

Making Menwith (2): Form

The most obvious visible aspect of RAF Menwith Hill is its geodesic radomes. A radome – a contraction from "radar dome" – is merely a protective geodesic cover for satellite dishes and other sensitive equipment, usually made of Kevlar polycarbonate material; it protects equipment from both the weather and the prying eyes of the public, whilst allowing radio waves to pass through. However, radomes have particular architectural interest. The geodesic dome was first patented in 1947 by Richard Buckminster Fuller, who designed it as a structure with extraordinarily efficient load distribution and strength.[51]

It is ironic that Fuller's domes have a countercultural image, largely as a result of the Drop City commune project in Colorado in the mid-1960s, where they were seen as a practical way of making low-cost homes for radical living, composed of scrap materials including the disused shells of automobiles.[52] However, Fuller actually built his first geodesic domes for the USAF and US Marine Corps in 1949 and 1954, and saw US military innovations as part of an onward exponential trajectory of human progress toward a high-tech enabled common good.[53] The hippie communes were about as far from Fuller's ideal as could be imagined. The radomes used for satellite covers are in any case slightly different from Fuller's design, tending to be far more spherical, rather than hemispherical, and resting in a reinforced concrete collar.

The radomes result in much public confusion. Many people I have talked to, even those who live in North Yorkshire, confuse RAF Menwith Hill with another military site in the county, RAF Fylingdales Ballistic Missile Early Warning Station. This site also had three prominent radomes until 1996, when they were replaced by a giant pyramid, and indeed so well known were these essentially temporary and militarily contingent structures at Fylingdales that there were calls for them to be listed for their heritage value. In addition, there have been outlandish explanations for what was hidden beneath the domes at Menwith. For example, Campbell and Melvern report one example from the early 1970s: the then new radomes were breeding centers for killer flies.[54] It is a testimony to the power of rumor in the netherworld of conspiracy theorists that similar ideas emerged as a major part of the plot in the 1998 movie *The X-Files: Fight the Future*, a spin-off from the popular television series.

Apart from the radomes and aerials, there are several other architectural aspects of Menwith that are worth noting. The first is the security apparatus, which until the 1990s was surprisingly weak. This is not unusual at military bases. Leaked minutes of a meeting at the US Embassy in 1994 showed UK representatives politely suggesting to US officials that a barrier of some kind at the gate of the Lakenheath airbase might stop activists from entering. Even the most powerfully territorialized places are sometimes extraordinarily incomplete in this regard. However, a rolling program of security upgrades took place from 1993, a date which coincided with the showing of Duncan Campbell's *The Hill* on British television, and with the setting up of the Women's Peace Camp. These upgrades involved much stronger, apparently bolt-cutter resistant, steel fences topped by rolls of razor-wire, and new guard towers.

These facilities have not stopped incursions into the base, however. There have been several well-publicized examples, including activist-comedian Mark Thomas's televised balloon journey over the site, and the Greenpeace incursion in 2001 protesting against US National Missile Defense plans, as well as continuing incursions by activists from the Campaign for the Accountability of American Bases (CAAB) and the former WoMenwith Hill Wimmin's Peace Camp. The fencing has also caused some discomfort to the local authority, as it disturbs the ease with which it can present the base as a positive place, in particular as a source of employment.[55] The local councillors succeeded in persuading the Americans to plant trees to hide some of the most visible new security fences. There is certainly an element of what Thayer calls "landscape guilt," that is, the hiding of human structures considered necessary but aesthetically unappealing behind natural screens.[56] Menwith Hill, or at least the security fence, in this context *is* out of place in the Nidderdale landscape. The councillors would rather not see it despite the benefits the base brings their district in terms of employment and the perceived personal/national security benefits of the activity at Menwith. However, this becomes more complicated when the more dubious aspects of the espionage activities are mentioned. The base ceases to be named when these aspects are discussed, but becomes "it" and "up there" respectively, as if the "bad" activities are not really present in the same place as the "good" employment. The "bad" Menwith is presented almost as a kind of invisible, placeless shadow of its beneficial and visible twin; there seem to be two Menwiths, with differing characteristics and spatial qualities. However, the separation between the two Menwiths is difficult to maintain.

The second architectural aspect is the day-to-day facilities for on-site personnel. On-site accommodation had originally been what the USASA Historical Office describes as "surplus commodity housing;" in other words, old wartime prefabricated buildings, although the senior personnel eventually lived off-site in rather more salubrious detached houses in the nearby village of Darley. Now, there are far superior houses, an expanded school and nursery, larger shops, and better medical and leisure facilities, including an outdoor running track. These developments could be seen at least in part to be designed to reduce the frequency and length of time base personnel and their dependants spend outside the base, and to lower the risk of unplanned contact with the public and particularly those opposed to Menwith, now that far more of the general public have become aware of the base. This would be a continuance of a series of changes in rules on contact with foreigners and an order issued by the American military commander in 1994 that all personnel must from thenceforward wear military uniform when traveling into work. However, the RAF Base Commander insists that this is not the case: he points out that "over 1,000 US families" still live outside the base, and that many American service personnel from Menwith Hill are involved in local charitable and leisure activities.[57] According to the Commander, these activities have included donations totalling £18,000 to local good causes by the Menwith Hill Women's Club, as well as the rather more questionable benefits of MoD policing and civic receptions.[58]

The domestic architecture of the base is often used to try to project an image of normality. For example, when a peace camp was first set up at the site in 1983, the campaigners were invited by two American personnel to "tour" the base. According to a paper written by prominent local activist, Christine Dean, this resulted in a somewhat surreal meeting:

We watched a long, tedious slide show focusing on such important areas of the base as "two person facilities with matching curtains and counterpanes, the nearly new clothing facility and Uncle Sam's beefburger bar." We were told that the two armed guards on the base were solely to protect the liquor store and the postal facility. After the slides, we were invited to "mingle" and ask questions.[59]

It is almost as if the NSA expected either the tedium or the sheer ordinariness and reasonableness of the base as portrayed in the official presentation to overwhelm the protesters. Such a meeting never happened again, but it does show that the symbolic aspects of territorialization, in this case represented through interior design and architecture, can be used in place of, or alongside, physical constraint. Such domestic symbolism was common in local newspaper reports of and after the opening of the base, with stories about home-life, schools, weddings, and so on.[60]

Finally, there is the issue of underground buildings. In response to questions in the House of Commons, Ministers have always denied the existence of underground or even hardened concrete structures at RAF Menwith Hill. As is usual with ministerial answers, this is a partial truth. Many of the operational buildings, if not technically underground, are earth-sheltered to the extent that they are visible only as unusually regular excrescences in the gently sloping hillside. As with radomes, earth-sheltering is now often associated with progressive political causes, in this case the environmental movement; for example the "Earthships" of the US architect, Michael Reynolds. However, earth-sheltering is an ancient concept both domestic and defensive. At Menwith Hill, particularly around the major STEEPLEBUSH area under the largest radomes,[61] these bunkers are connected by outside walkways enveloped in transparent glass or plastic tubes, providing a strange juxtaposition of defensive strength and visible vulnerability. The denial of the existence of such obvious underground facilities adds to the perception of RAF Menwith Hill as sinister.

Making Menwith (3): Identity and Territory

At the start of this chapter it was noted that "RAF" Menwith Hill has very little to do with the Royal Air Force. Names are important: they are signs that designate territory, they also symbolically represent whole histories and sets of images. We saw earlier how Gruffudd's "RAF pastoral" presented the idea of the RAF as standing for safety and idealized rural English values. Other designations, such as "NSA Field Station F-83, Menwith Hill," do not have this protective and reassuringly English element. There are also legal implications in terms of land tenure and bylaws. This importance is not lost on the UK government, although it took them some time to realize it.

Several unpublished memoranda and letters between the 3rd USAF, its RAF liaison officer, the War Office (Lands Branch), and the Air Ministry dating from September 1957 refer to the site as "the US Army installation at Harrogate,"[62] or, in one case, the "US Army wireless station."[63] In 1958, Menwith Hill was officially designated the USASA 13th Field Station, and named Menwith Hill Station. When the NSA took over in 1966 no indication was given of its new designation, and it continued to be known as Menwith Hill Station. The public seemed unaware of the change in control: a 1969 newspaper report on a small demonstration still described the base as "the US Army Station."[64] "Menwith Hill Station" continued in use until December 1, 1995, when the site was only officially renamed "RAF Menwith Hill" and a token RAF "Base Commander" (he is, in fact, anything but, not even being allowed access to many areas of the base) was installed.

Why did this renaming happen? It seems likely that the official redesignation was an attempt to pre-empt any problems that might have arisen as a result of information about the site being forced into the public domain. This occurred, first, because of a revelatory television program, *The Hill*, made by Duncan Campbell,[65] and, secondly, because of a series of court cases in the 1990s brought by and against peace protesters. The cases involved many complex issues around the right of occupancy of the Americans, the local bylaws, access restrictions, and so on, but their main effect was that the security of tenure arrangements between the UK and the USA over Menwith Hill were revealed for the first time.

A letter from the Parliamentary Under-Secretary of State for Defence, Earl Howe, to the MP Keith Hampson in response to a parliamentary question early in 1996, explained the official position on renaming and the revised bylaws:

> The reason Menwith Hill Station was retitled RAF Menwith Hill was to bring it into line with other RAF sites made available by the Ministry of Defence to the United States Government. The introduction of the revised bylaws, which were introduced on 19 February 1996, provided the

opportunity to clarify the proper title of the Station, which is an RAF site that was made available to US forces in 1955 on the same basis as other US bases in the UK.[66]

Earl Howe makes no mention of the fact that the UK government had been legally obliged to change the bylaws, merely that this "provided the opportunity to clarify the proper title of the Station." The latter phrase is particularly interesting. In one sense it is totally dishonest: there is no evidence that Menwith Hill had ever been an RAF site; it was requisitioned by the War Office entirely for the purpose of becoming a US Army intelligence facility. The only reason that any Air Force personnel became involved was because of the official attachment for logistical purposes of USASA personnel to the 3rd USAF. This then meant that formal arrangements were dealt with by the UK Air Ministry.

This is particularly interesting because of the problems that the two governments have had over the years in attempting to define tenure of the land on which the base is sited. In 1976, letters concerning the renegotiation of the twenty-one year "security of tenure" arrangements show that no evidence of any formal arrangements, supposedly dating from 1951, could be found – they had apparently been lost. And no extant record exists of any such arrangements. Yet in 1997, just a year after the name change, the Secretariat of the Air Staff could claim that:

> There is . . . no requirement for the US authorities to seek renewal of the security of tenure arrangements to allow their continued use of RAF Menwith Hill, and I can confirm that no application has been made by the US authorities to renew them. RAF Menwith Hill will continue to be made available to the US authorities on the same basis as other RAF sites in the United Kingdom, the arrangements of which are confidential between the UK and US governments for the purpose of our common defence.[67]

Was the formal agreement merely a myth, or a mistaken reference to a 1951 agreement that related only to bomber bases and airfields, and not to intelligence sites like Menwith Hill? A letter in the Public Record Office indicates that there were negotiations for an agreement in late 1951 with regard to "the transfer of responsibility for the administration of certain Royal Air Force stations from the respective Royal Air Force commands to the United States Air Force."[68] However, Menwith Hill was not an existing RAF station. There is no extant general agreement upon which the security of tenure arrangement for Menwith Hill is based. Are the arrangements for Menwith Hill actually dependent on entirely different and genuinely secret agreements, like the UKUSA agreement, or simply on informal correspondence?

Thus, far from being a "clarification" of the situation, the renaming is an attempt to reterritorialize Menwith Hill. Effectively, the changed signifier and token RAF presence stand for an entirely different official history than had existed up until this point. It is an attempt to diffuse sinister interpretations of the place and imbue it with the kind of reassuring presence of protective Spitfires, handlebar moustaches, and friendly chit-chat in the Officer's Mess that are represented by the acronym "RAF." Legally, it resolved some of the complex issues of access and tenure that had so embarrassed the UK government in the 1990s, providing a superficial veneer of formal legality to a previously dubious situation.

Conclusion

This chapter has examined some aspects of the tectonic culture of a particular military base through the lens of cultural geography. Even this limited glance shows that the smallest aspects of such places can be filled with cultural significance: matching curtains and counterpanes can be symbols of domestic normality or surreal and sinister within the context of an escorted slide-show and the wider function of the base. These symbolic significances place an important role in making places: in constructing space as territory, and in controlling cultural meaning. I will end simply with a call to be alive to the real and symbolic power of places as territories, and not to neglect modern military sites. The buildings and landscapes may be mundane, depressing, or frightening, but with careful reading they can reveal more about the nature of social control within modern societies than we would normally care to acknowledge.

Notes

1   SIGINT is the interception, interpretation, and communication of any transmissions from or through technological systems, from missiles to e-mail. It is divided into Communications Intelligence (COMINT), Electronics Intelligence (ELINT), and Foreign Instrumentation Signals Intelligence (FISINT).

2   Other than SIGINT, the NSA is also responsible for internal US state Information Security (INFOSEC), the defensive aspect of "Information Warfare" (IW), military cryptology (code-making), and, through the Special Collection Service (SCS), run jointly with the CIA, a range of functions from simple surveillance of targets in foreign countries to "black-bag jobs" (surveillance-related burglary).

3   John Childs, *The Military Use of Land: A History of the Defence Estate* (Bern: Peter Lang, 1998). For an analysis of current UK military land-use policy and practice, see Rachel Woodward, "'It's a Man's Life!': Soldiers, Masculinity and the Countryside," *Gender, Place and Culture*, 5 (3) (1998): 277–300.

4   Patrick Wright has written a fascinating account of one area that was never returned, the village of Tyneham in Dorset, which became part of the Lulworth Gunnery School range. Patrick Wright, *The Village that Died for England: The Strange Story of Tyneham* (London: Vintage, 1996).

5   Simon Duke, *US Defence Bases in the United Kingdom: A Matter for Joint Decision?* (London: Macmillan, 1987).

6   Duncan Campbell, *The Unsinkable Aircraft Carrier: American Military Power in Britain* (London: Michael Joseph, 1984).

7   John Childs, *The Military Use of Land*, follows Duke, *US Defence Bases*, in accepting this.

8   Campbell, *Aircraft Carrier*. According to Jeffrey T. Richelson and Desmond Ball, *The Ties that Bind: Intelligence Cooperation between the UKUSA Countries* (London: Allen and Unwin, 1985), the UKUSA agreement, signed in 1947 or 1948 by the USA (the "first party") and Australia, Canada, New Zealand, and the UK (the "second parties"), but still publicly undocumented, relates to global division of SIGINT effort, information-sharing (allowing the USA access to intelligence from second parties, but not vice versa), standardization of code words, the development of technologically compatible or convergent systems, and the exchange of personnel, as well as to the placement of intelligence bases. The UKUSA agreement has now expanded to include other nations as "third parties," including Austria, Denmark, Germany, Greece, Italy, Japan, Norway, South Korea, Thailand, and Turkey. See Jeffrey Richelson, *The US Intelligence Community*, 4th edn (Boulder, CO: Westview Press, 1999). They provide some accommodation to NSA units, and are not given a status comparable to the second parties.

9   Childs, *The Military Use of Land*, p. 209.

10   Campbell, *Aircraft Carrier*, pp. 286–94. Some of the differences have to do with what counts as a "facility." Campbell included housing and fuel supply depots along with bases and airfields; however, even taking this into account, the UK government figures still understated the total.

11   Jacqueline Tivers, "'The Home of the British Army': The Iconic Construction of Military Defence Landscapes," *Landscape Research*, 24 (3) (1999): 303–19, p. 303.

12   Denis Cosgrove and Stephen Daniels, "Introduction: Iconography and Land-
     scape," in *The Iconography of Landscape*, ed. Denis Cosgrove and Stephen
     Daniels (Cambridge: Cambridge University Press, 1988), pp. 1–9, p. 1.

13   Clifford Geertz, *The Interpretation of Cultures* (London: Hutchinson, 1973).

14   Cosgrove and Daniels, *Iconography of Landscape*, p. 8.

15   Denis Cosgrove, *Social Formation and Symbolic Landscape* (Totowa, NJ: Barnes
     and Noble, 1985), p. 263.

16   D. Ley, *A Social Geography of the City* (New York: Harper and Row, 1983).

17   M. Heffernan, "For Ever England: The Western Front and the Politics of
     Remembrance in Britain," *Ecumene*, 2 (1995): 293–323; M. Morris, "Gardens
     'For Ever England': Landscape, Identity and the First World War Cemeteries
     on the Western Front," *Ecumene*, 4 (1997): 410–34.

18   Woodward, "It's a Man's Life!," pp. 277–300.

19   Pyrs Gruffudd, *Reach for the Sky: The Air and English Cultural Nationalism*,
     Department of Geography Working Paper no. 7, University of Nottingham,
     1990.

20   Ibid., p. 14.

21   Stephen Daniels, *Fields of Vision: Landscape Imagery and National Identity in
     England and the United States* (Cambridge: Polity Press, 1993); David Matless,
     Landscape and Englishness (London: Reaktion Books, 1998).

22   Klaus Dodds, "Enframing the Falklands: Identity, Landscape, and the 1982
     South Atlantic War," *Environment and Planning D: Society and Space*, 16
     (1998): 733–56.

23   Cosgrove, *Social Formation*, p. 269.

24   Yi-Fu Tuan, *Landscapes of Fear* (New York: Pantheon, 1979), p. 6.

25   Michel Foucault "Questions on Geography," in *Power/Knowledge: Selected
     Interviews and Other Writings 1972–77*, ed. Colin Gordon (New York: Pan-
     theon, 1980), pp. 63–77, p. 64.

26   Henri Lefebvre, *La Production de l'espace* (Paris: 1974), trans. D. Nicholson-
     Smith, *The Production of Space* (Oxford: Blackwell, 1991), p. 3.

27   Doreen Massey, *Space, Place and Gender* (Cambridge: Polity Press, 1994),
     p. 5.

28   Robert D. Sack, *Human Territoriality: Its Theory and History* (Cambridge:
     Cambridge University Press, 1986), p. 19.

29   Ibid., p. 22.

30   Ibid., p. 20.

31   Ibid., p. 33.

32   Michel Callon and Bruno Latour, "Unscrewing the Big Leviathan: How
     Actors Macrostructure Reality and How Sociologists Help Them to do So,"
     in *Advances in Social Theory and Methodology*, ed. K. Knorr-Cetina and
     A. V. Cicourel (London: Routledge and Kegan Paul, 1981).

33   Bruno Latour, *Pandora's Hope: Essays in the Reality of Science Studies* (Cam-
     bridge, MA: Harvard University Press, 1999), p. 304.

34   Roger Simon, *Gramsci's Political Thought: An Introduction*, rev. edn (London: Lawrence and Wishart, 1991).

35   Peter Gill, *Policing Politics: Security Intelligence Agencies and the Liberal Democratic State* (London: Frank Cass, 1994).

36   The modern concept of panopticism derives largely from Michel Foucault's observations of Jeremy Bentham's proposed prison architecture, and the way in which he saw such architectures reproduced symbolically and socially. Michel Foucault, *Surveiller et punir: Naissance de la prison* (Paris: Gallimard, 1975), trans. A. Sheridan, *Discipline and Punish: The Birth of the Prison* (New York: Vintage, 1977). See also Robin Evans, *The Fabrication of Virtue* (Cambridge: Cambridge University Press, 1982).

37   Joseph Gerson, "Introduction," in *The Sun Never Sets: Confronting the Network of Foreign US Military Bases*, ed. J. Gerson and B. Birchard (Boston, MA: South End Press/American Friends Service Committee, 1991), pp. 1–27.

38   James Bamford, *The Puzzle Palace: America's National Security Agency and its Special Relationship with Britain's GCHQ* (Harmondsworth: Penguin, 1982; repr. with new afterword, 1983), p. 269.

39   Duncan Campbell and Linda Melvern, "America's Big Ear on Europe," *New Statesman* (July 18, 1980): 10–14.

40   Campbell, *Aircraft Carrier*, p. 307.

41   W. Burrows, *Deep Black: Space Espionage and National Security* (New York: Random House, 1987).

42   FAS IRP (22/01/2002) *Menwith Hill Station, UK* (http://www.fas.org/irp/facility/menwith.htm).

43   Jeffrey Richelson, *America's Space Sentinels: DSP Satellites and National Security* (Kansas: University Press of Kansas, 1999).

44   Bamford, *Puzzle Palace*, p. 254.

45   Under the 1984 UK Department of the Environment Circular DoE 10/84, notification of building at military establishments has to be given to the local authority, but the local authority is not able to reject or alter them as it is with civilian planning applications. Before this, notification of work was submitted at the discretion of the military.

46   Campbell and Melvern, "America's Big Ear."

47   Duncan Campbell, "They've Got it Taped," *New Statesman* (August 12, 1988): 10–12.

48   FAS IRP (22/01/2002) *Echelon* (http://www.fas.org/irp/program/process/echelon.htm).

49   Steve Wright, *An Appraisal of the Technologies of Political Control: Interim STOA Report* (PE 166.499), Directorate General for Research, Directorate A, The STOA Programme (Luxembourg: European Parliament, 1998).

50   Duncan Campbell, *Development of Surveillance Technology and Risk of Abuse of Economic Information* (An Appraisal of Technologies of Political Control), vol. 2/5: the state of the art in Communications Intelligence (COMINT) of

automated processing for intelligence purposes of intercepted broadband multi-language leased or common carrier systems, and its applicability to COMINT targeting and selection, including speech recognition (also known as Interception Capabilities 2000), Directorate General for Research, Directorate A, The STOA Programme (Luxembourg: European Parliament, 1999).

51 Richard Buckminster Fuller, "Preview of Building" (1963), in *The Buckminster Fuller Reader*, ed. J. Meller (London: Jonathan Cape, 1970), pp. 273–96.

52 Anon, "Drop City: A Model Hippie Commune," *The Lay of the Land* (Spring 1996) (http://www.clui.org/clui_4_1/lotl/lotlsp96/drop.html), accessed June 13, 2002; T. Miller, "Roots of Communal Revival, 1962–1966," *The Farm* website (http://www.thefarm.org/lifestyle/root1.html), accessed June 13, 2002.

53 Fuller, "Preview of Building."

54 Campbell and Melvern, "America's Big Ear."

55 This section is based on several interviews with Councillor Les Ellington of Harrogate Borough Council, and officials of the council, conducted in 2000.

56 Richard Thayer, *Gray World, Green Heart: Technology, Nature and Sustainability in the Landscape* (New York: John Wiley, 1994).

57 Letter to the author from Squadron Leader H. J. C. Vincent, August 22, 2000.

58 Ibid.

59 Christine Dean, "Arguments against the Continued Use for Yorkshire Moorland as a Spy Base," unpublished paper, Archives of the Otley Peace Action Group (1986), p. 1 [hereinafter OPAG Archives].

60 *Harrogate Herald*, "People See How US Army Lives" (Wednesday, September 21, 1960); *Harrogate Herald*, "American School in Yorkshire Dale" (Wednesday, October 12, 1960); *Harrogate Herald*, "First Wedding in US Army Base" (Wednesday, November 16, 1960).

61 STEEPLEBUSH is an American intelligence community code name (always written in upper case). It is used here as a shorthand for both the groundstation of the MAGNUM/ORION satellite platform from the 1970s onwards, and the STEEPLEBUSH II groundstation for the TRUMPET/Advanced ORION satellite platform operational from the 1990s, which vastly extended the original STEEPLEBUSH area at Menwith.

62 Letter from Wing Commander C. T. W. Morgan for Director of Administrative Plans, Air Ministry to the Under-Secretary of State, War Office (Lands Branch), A251308/56/OP2 (November 6, 1957), OPAG Archives.

63 Memo from S. H. Bailey War Office, to HQ, 3rd USAF, 119/General/ 1065(LB(E)) (October 17, 1957), OPAG Archives.

64 *Harrogate Herald*, "Protesters at Menwith Hill" (Wednesday, July 23, 1969).

65 *The Hill*, directed by Duncan Campbell, October 6, 1993, in the *Dispatches* series.

66   Letter from Earl Howe, Parliamentary Under-Secretary of State for Defence, to Keith Hampson MP, March 27, 1996, D/USofS/FH0683/96/M, OPAG Archives.

67   Letter from Secretariat of the Air Staff to Lindis Percy (1997), OPAG Archives.

68   R. H. Melville, Letter from Air Ministry to the Commanding General, 3rd USAF, G.311026(a)/BR/11/51/60, unpublished papers, Public Record Office AIR 2/10997.

7

Domestic Space Transformed, 1850–2000

Elizabeth Cromley

The Architecture of American Houses and its Interpretation

This chapter surveys the architecture of American houses in three periods, linking the changes in house design and performance to shifts in the culture and economy of the United States. The first period, 1850–1900, was an era of industrialization, urbanization, and frontier settlement. Immigration swelled the population with new workers, while successful new industries created wealth and a self-conscious "upper class," newly preoccupied with conspicuous consumption. Most dwellings during this period were individually built by owners, masons, or carpenters, typically using lumber cut to size in sawmills, mass-produced brick, and factory-made nails. Their varied architectural styles gained picturesqueness from asymmetrical house plans, which led to a better match between the size and location of rooms and their functions.

The second period, 1900–1960, saw the expansion of a middle class, as the upper class dwindled after the introduction of income tax in 1916 and the Depression of the 1930s. A successful labor movement increased salaries and led workers to adopt dwellings with middle-class attributes. Towns and cities were transformed by suburbanization, the addition of automobiles to the landscape, and the baby-boom-driven demand for single-family houses. House production depended on factory-made, uniformly sized construction and finished elements – from 2×4 lumber through drywall to many types of windows. The small, free-standing house became the ideal – from bungalows to ranch and split-level houses to variations on the Cape-Cod cottage. Architectural styles ranged from the exotic details of bungalows, through historic Colonial, Tudor, and other revivals, to the radical simplicity of Modernist architecture.

The third period, 1960 to the present, saw large-scale, publicly subsidized housing for the poor, continued suburbanization, and the development of new middle-class domestic architectures based on working and living in the same space. New fortunes led to the production of "McMansions," very large houses for single families. Competition for space in the major cities led to exorbitant rents and property costs. Disparities in wealth between the richest and poorest increased, as did the disparities in the square footage of dwellings for those groups. Throughout these periods changes in the structure of families, the place of children, and the role of women had a continuing influence on the organization of and expectations for houses. House production was more automated with manufactured housing modules accounting for much of the lower-cost dwelling market, and prefabricated elements, such as roof trusses and window and door units, used even in upper-class houses.

Descriptions of some of the major architectural and social currents of each era will be organized by examining the middle-class norm, then the working-class and upper-class variations. At the end of each chronological section, I will consider some recent scholarly interpretations of that era's houses, identifying new issues and perspectives that have engaged architectural historians and other analysts of domestic architecture.

Houses 1850–1900

The range of American houses during the last half of the nineteenth century included enormous diversity: everything from modestly sized, wooden-framed houses in agricultural landscapes for farm families to ornamental cottages and villas inspired by architectural pattern books for the emerging middle class, workers' cottages in industrial cities and mill towns, log cabins for frontier settlers, enormous mansions for those with new fortunes, and the first working-class tenements and middle-class apartment houses in cities. For the top and the bottom of house values, consider these examples from the city of Buffalo in 1875: William Fargo, president of American Express, had a mansion costing $500,000, while John Madigan,

a laborer, had a house worth $50.¹ Industrialization transformed the organ-
ization of society. Immigrant and native workers drawn to new industrial
centers needed new types of housing. The modern form of the suburb was
established during this period at Llewellyn Park, NJ, and other locations,
with winding roads, collectively owned landscaped parks, and picturesquely
styled houses. Cities grew rapidly and required systems such as city water,
sewers, public transportation, and the creation of new streets on which to
build new dwellings. New milling shops, the mass production of nails, and
prefabrication technology transformed the possibilities for house construction, while settlers in the frontier areas still made their own log houses.
Mass production of furnishings and new services like electricity changed
the ways that houses could be inhabited.

Middle-class dwellings

A distinctive middle class came into being in mid-nineteenth-century
America, and dwellings – both houses and apartments – specifically
designed for middle-class clients were created to support middle-class
manners and codes of behavior. A prosperous middle-class family of 1880
would have a free-standing house on a landscaped lot in the suburbs, a
row-house (terraced house) on a residential street in a city, or an apartment (flat) in one of the newly developed urban apartment houses. The
dwelling (house or apartment) contained numerous separate rooms with
specialized functions, linked by a well-developed circulation system. Rooms
would be organized in three domestic zones: public reception, private
family, and service. Household technologies, such as central heating, fixed
bathtubs, or electricity and gas for lighting and kitchen ranges, were found
in middle-class houses, although the wealthiest sometimes substituted servants' labor for these conveniences.

   An example of a middle-class house can be found in one of the numerous pattern-books or style-books that were published during this period.
Oliver P. Smith published his *Domestic Architect* in 1854 with house designs
for rural settings.² His Italianate villa (plate 19) has a central entrance,
passage, and staircase on the main floor. On either side are disposed a
front parlor, a dining room, a sitting room, and a nursery in the main
block, while a kitchen extends into a rear ell. On the second floor are three
large and four smaller bedrooms, those over the kitchen intended for
servants. In Smith's design for a Gothic cottage (see figure 7.1) the main
floor has a parlor and dining room at the front, nursery, pantry, and

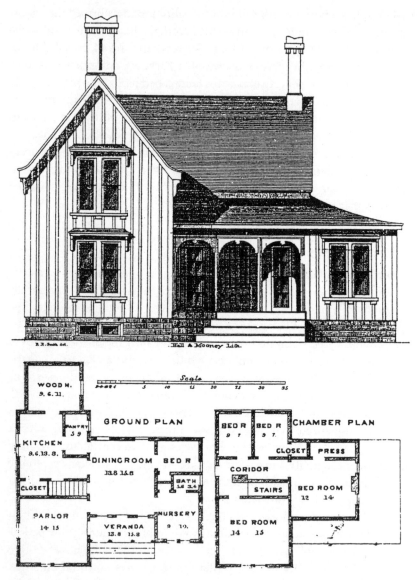

Figure 7.1   Oliver Smith's "Bracketed Style" Cottage, plate 25, from *The Domestic Architect*, 1854; reprinted as *Victorian Domestic Architect* (The American Life Foundation, 1978).

kitchen to the rear, and a ground-floor bedroom. On the second floor there are four more bedrooms and a library. The large number of rooms and their function-specific names manifest the later nineteenth century's interest in setting aside separate spaces for each domestic function. Typically, the exteriors of villas and cottages presented picturesque, ornamental faces to the public and were quite varied in style.

A new type of dwelling for the middle class that developed in the later nineteenth century is the apartment building. An example in New York City is the building called The Berkshire, built on the corner of Madison Avenue and 52nd Street. It was designed by architect Carl Pfeiffer and published in the journal *American Architect* in 1883 (figure 7.2). A family who rented an apartment in the Berkshire would get an entrance hall, a parlor, and a dining room looking out over the street; a kitchen, a servant's room, a pantry and a bathroom in the center of the unit; and three bedrooms in the rear. The apartments were served by both passenger elevators and service elevators, and there were separate stairs for the servants to get to the basement or the roof to take care of their housekeeping tasks. Apartment houses quite often had restaurants, a doorman, elaborate lobbies, and sometimes small shops, all of which provided extra convenience for the tenants.[3] Some buildings employed their own service staff so tenants were spared having to hire their own maids, cooks, and laundresses.

The most important room in the middle-class dwelling was a room called the parlor, which contained the best furniture and decorations kept in perfect order to receive guests. The behavior in a parlor was to be formal, not relaxed; it was a place where the family could present itself to the outside world and assert its claim to respectability. To sustain this impression, 1860s' families could buy matching suites of furniture upholstered in the latest satin, plush, or brocade, framed in cherry, mahogany, or walnut, and ornamented with carving. These were often arranged around a marble-topped center table. By the 1880s, the fashion for matching suites gave way to individual pieces still elaborately upholstered, and the center table was replaced by many small tables and shelves for bric-a-brac.[4] Gas lighting made evening entertaining possible. Strong deep colors for draperies, carpets, table coverings, and upholstery gave the Victorian parlor an appearance of richness. This palette of colors both asserted the family's good taste and helped to conceal the soot produced by gas lamps.

As the parlor was a "best behavior" room with everything arranged just so, it encouraged the development of another room for family relaxation. This complement to the parlor in middle-class dwellings was sometimes

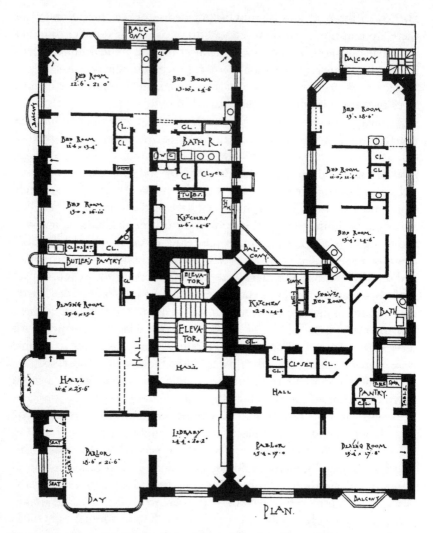

Figure 7.2   Plan of apartments (two units per floor) in The Berkshire, New York, from *American Architect and Building News* (August 4, 1883), no. 397, n.p.

called a sitting room, a back parlor, or even a "family room." The name "family room" occurs as early as 1875 in Charles Lakey's *Village and Country Houses.*[5] The sitting room, also called the "every-day room," was the place for comfort rather than beauty of decoration, according to *The Social Mirror* (1888). Such a room was wanted to allow the family a cozy place to gather together, not under the eye of guests. It was a room that could be allowed to collect piles of half-read books and the residue of children's activities, not constrained to achieve the perfect public neatness of the parlor. Furnishings would include a large catch-all table in the center, a divan with pillows, a rocking chair, an easy chair, a couple of light side chairs, and a small sewing chair near a work table. Card and game tables provided attractions. If the house had no library, the sitting room was the place for book cases. Dried grasses and leaves, a vase filled with plants, or peacock feathers were recommended to decorate the mantelpiece and the various picture frames. Lastly, a window garden with "an abundance of climbing or trailing plants" made this room a comfortable "living-room."[6] The idea of a room for relaxed family sociability lives on in the family room or "great room" of late twentieth-century American houses.

All prosperous households of the Victorian era had individual bedrooms for sleeping, and usually only one or two individuals were expected to sleep in any one room. This is in contrast to seventeenth- and eighteenth-century practices where many people shared a room, and several could be found in each bed. Mid-nineteenth-century bedrooms could be furnished with matching suites of wood furniture that included the bedstead, bureau, chiffonier, dressing table, mirrors, wardrobe, and washstand. If the family could afford more, there would likely be some upholstered chairs or a day-bed. The upper- and middle-class bedroom was private for the occupants and supported intimate family visits. All the furnishings were geared to sleeping, resting, dressing, and care of the body.

Victorian recommendations for bedroom decoration often put health concerns at the center: ventilation must be effective, draperies and hangings that harbored germs should be simplified, paint was cleaner than wallpaper, movable rugs cleaner than fixed carpet (figure 7.3). Health reformers also cautioned mothers against sleeping with their babies, or putting children to sleep with their grandparents. Everyone should have pure air, they believed, and sleeping in groups gave everyone used air. The frequency of cautions against this practice indicates that group sleeping was probably common at all income levels.

The shift from outhouses and chamber pots to indoor plumbing and bathroom fixtures was dramatic in its effect on household comfort. It was common for New York City dwellers to have fixed toilets and bathtubs installed in their 1840s' town houses, hooked up to a city water supply. But for country-dwellers this change was slow in coming: rural and small town families had to wait decades to enjoy the same conveniences. An inventory from an 1888 house in Albuquerque, New Mexico, shows the

Figure 7.3   A healthy Victorian-era bedroom with no draperies to catch the dust, from Clarence Cook, *The House is Beautiful* (1878).

contents of each bedroom to include a washstand, a bowl and pitcher, a soap dish, and a chamber pot. In the bathroom could be found a cuspidor and a pail. In the larger bedroom there was also a tin water bucket and a foot tub.[7] These movable pieces of washing equipment were common in all houses without fixed plumbing. Many householders worried that fixed plumbing would bring sewer gas and repellent smells into the house; it seemed healthier to segregate human wastes to outdoor privies.

By the mid-nineteenth century in upper- and middle-class houses there would have been numerous function-specific rooms. To get from room to room discreetly, separate circulation space was required in the shape of halls, corridors, foyers, vestibules, and stairs. It has always been the case that dedicated circulation space is expensive, so houses that have a fully articulated circulation system independent of the rooms in a house are few and costly. Often a house will have some dedicated circulation, and some circulation paths combined with room space, as when there is a separate entrance hall, yet one must walk through the dining room to get to the kitchen, there being no other way. The nineteenth century's fondness for creating specific-purpose spaces led even those without extra resources to include specific circulation elements where they could afford them.

Victorian houses used the front entrance vestibule and hall as an elaborated symbolic field on which to declare their social standing. Hall stands with marble and brass fittings held a card tray and served as a hat and coat rack. For architect Ralph Adams Cram, the hall of an upper-class city house should be a formal, restrained, and quiet space that protects the house from the street yet does not hint at domesticity.[8] Hard floor surfaces such as tile were recommended in Charles Eastlake's popular book *Hints on Household Taste* to preserve formality and restraint in social interactions until one was truly invited into the home.[9]

Working-class dwellings

At the mid-century workers lived in a variety of inexpensive or makeshift dwellings. Some had small cottages or built little shacks with found materials. Some occupied a room or two in an older house that had been subdivided to accommodate multiple families. Factories required concentrated labor, and labor required housing. Factory owners and real-estate investors built both workers' cottages and tenement houses, multi-story buildings holding several working-class households under one roof. Tenements provided few amenities to residents, and many had no indoor

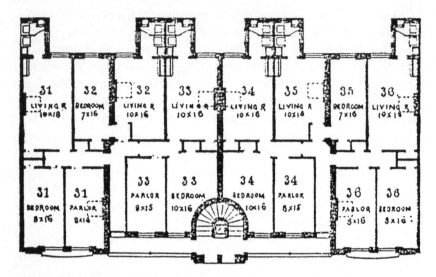

Figure 7.4   Alfred Tredway White's 1890 reform tenements, The Riverside Buildings, for workers, Brooklyn, NY, from a pamphlet "The Riverside Buildings" (New York, 1890).

water supply or toilet. Water was carried from a pump in the back yard, where an outdoor privy served all the residents. Bathtubs, considered a luxury, were rarely included. Overcrowding and lack of sunlight and fresh air seemed to exacerbate diseases and led to housing reform efforts in the last quarter of the nineteenth century.

A reform tenement designed and financed by philanthropist Alfred Tredway White in Brooklyn, NY, called the Riverside Buildings, was completed in 1890 (figure 7.4). The Field Brothers, architects, used relatively inexpensive brick to create a lively façade, its visual interest achieved with iron-work balconies, yet in no particular historic style. To secure light and air, White's building wrapped around a spacious courtyard. Apartment units were limited to three or four rooms each. All rooms faced the sunlight and fresh air of either the courtyard or the street; there were no dark rooms. Each family had its own indoor sink and toilet; in the basement those who wanted to take baths would find collective bathing facilities. Children could play in the courtyard, while their parents listened to band concerts there, provided by the management. Workers paid moderate rents in weekly installments. White encouraged his fellow capitalists to invest in reform housing designed to return 5 percent of investment annually – a much smaller return than avarice expected.

Commercial real-estate developers interested in greater profits were restricted by urban building codes such as the new tenement law passed in New York in 1879. Regulating the fresh air by requiring a window to the outdoors in every room, this law forced speculative tenement developers to attend to tenants' health. A typical tenement built under this law located four household units per floor in a five-story building. Family units contained three rooms per family – one "living room" with kitchen equipment, and two bedrooms – with a shared toilet for every two households in the common hall. No apartments were allowed in damp basements. Indoor staircases (no elevators) led to landings on which four front doors were located.

Entrepreneurs sometimes built whole workers' villages to assure that their employees lived close to their workplaces. The railroad sleeping-car manufacturer George Pullman built a town for his workers at the site of his factory outside Chicago in the 1880s, with buildings designed by architect Solon Beman. Dwellings for workers there included single-family, free-standing houses for managers; dormitories for single workers; row-houses with four rooms each for small families; apartment buildings; and a hotel for traveling salesmen.

The number and size of rooms in working-class dwellings were fewer and smaller than those of the middle class. The term "living room" first arose in working-class, not middle-class, interiors. In most early eighteenth-century American houses a single room had served as the all-purpose space where cooking, food storage, spinning or candle-making, dining, and entertaining visitors all took place. Such a common room continued as the central space in tenement apartments. In the reform tenements of the 1870s, a room called the "living room" was the central all-purpose room in the apartment unit in which cooking, eating, and socializing combined with income-producing work and even sleeping. The single-floor designs for "Cheap Houses for Mechanics" published by Charles Lakey in 1875 had three- and four-room plans. The main room was marked "living room," with a separate kitchen and one or two bedrooms.[10] The idea of comfort achieved by a relaxing of strict parlor manners led to adopting the name "living room" for middle-class houses after the turn of the century, an example of an architectural idea moving up in social status rather than "trickling down."

Bedrooms were labeled on tenement plans, but we know from dwellers' reports that all the rooms were used for sleeping in crowded households. In tenement units the numbers of people who needed beds depended on the size of the family and on whether there were boarders who supplemented the family income. When there was a large number of sleepers, not just bedrooms but also the living room or kitchen was enlisted as sleeping space. Kitchens were sometimes preferred over bedrooms for sleeping because they were the warmest rooms.

While tenement breadwinners often worked in factories or made money from other jobs outside the home, the working-class dwelling was also a site for income-producing work. Men brought the materials for cigar-making home and rolled cigars in their living rooms. Women picked up pre-cut clothing parts from factories and sewed them together at home. Thus workers' housing served as live–work space in the late nineteenth and early twentieth centuries, a trend later seen in middle-class dwellings at the turn of the twenty-first century.

Upper-class dwellings

Houses for the well-to-do were built in three kinds of locations in the late nineteenth century. In cities, specific districts developed into habitats of the wealthy, such as New York's Fifth Avenue. Chicago's architects published their designs for well-to-do families' houses like the S. Leonard Boyce House in the journal *Inland Architect* (figure 7.5). There were also well-to-do suburbs that developed during this time such as Tuxedo Park, NY. Houses for the wealthy could also be found in resorts: for example, the mountains of North Carolina or the sea coast town of Newport, Rhode Island.

Houses for the upper class during this period were made of costlier materials than their middle-class counterparts, housed more servants, displayed more costly furniture and textiles, and typically had carriage houses to store family vehicles. Houses for the wealthiest families contained multiple rooms in each of the three domestic zones – reception, private family, and service – in architecturally stylish forms.

The Chicago house designed in 1885 by architect Henry Hobson Richardson for the Glessner family is an example of a well-to-do family's urban mansion. The house, located on a street corner in the wealthy neighborhood of Prairie Avenue, presented two architecturally strong Romanesque-style facades made of cut stone. There were several reception rooms – an entrance hall, a library, a parlor or drawing room, a dining room – and a master-bedroom suite with a fitted dressing room. Several additional bedrooms for children and guests occupied the second floor. The main-floor service area comprised a kitchen, pantries, a walk-in refrigerator, and servants' hall; above this area were several servants'

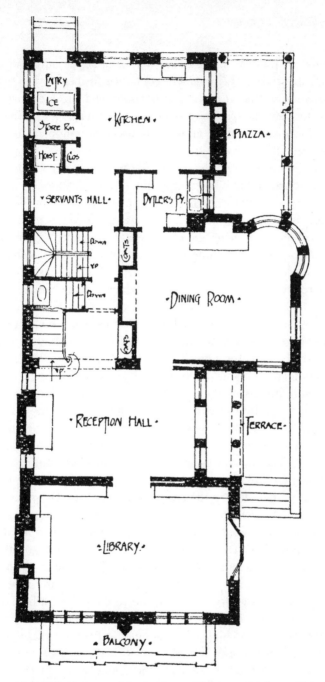

Figure 7.5 Plan of the S. Leonard Boyce House, Chicago, 1893, by architect Francis M. Whitehouse, with the array of reception rooms expected by an elite family, from *Inland Architect* 21, plates for no. 3 (April 1893).

bedrooms. At the rear of the house were a carriage house and an apartment for the driver. The basement contained further service and storage rooms. In the summer, the Glessner family and some of their servants traveled to New Hampshire to their summer house, in keeping with the pattern for many wealthy families; households migrated to enjoy the seasonal benefits of diverse locations.

The 255-room house called Biltmore for the wealthy family of George Washington Vanderbilt is an example of a very grand house. It was designed in the 1890s by Richard Morris Hunt near Asheville, North Carolina, with the grounds landscaped by Frederick Law Olmsted's firm. The number and type of rooms in such a grand house were expanded well beyond those of normal mansions to include a vestibule, an entrance hall, a staircase hall, a winter garden, a billiard room, a banquet hall, a breakfast room, a salon, a music room, a gallery for paintings, a library, and a chamber in the style of Louis XVI, all on the main floor. On the second floor are numerous bedrooms, family sitting rooms, dressing rooms, and rooms for maids. On the third floor are numerous additional bedrooms and bathrooms. Downstairs in the basement is a bowling alley, sitting rooms, dressing rooms, a gymnasium, and servants' bedrooms. The basement kitchen was supplemented with special rooms for pastry-making, a rotisserie, walk-in refrigerators, several pantries, several laundry rooms, and servants' quarters.

A formal dining room was the sine qua non of proper upper-class Victorian houses, but was a relatively recent arrival on the scene. Grand houses in the eighteenth century had had rooms called dining rooms, but daily dining took place in many parts of the house including the parlor, the sitting room, and even the chamber or bedroom. Dining in a specific room used exclusively for the purpose is a mark of Victorian manners.[11] Such a room and its furnishings and equipment gave families an opportunity to show that they had the knowledge, the leisure, and the money to perform dining rituals and thus assert their social status. The furniture for a Victorian dining room included a dining table and several chairs, a buffet that was used to display decorated china, and a high sideboard with shelves and racks to store glass and china. Victorian dining-room furniture came in matching suites, popular in the Civil War period, or in individual pieces more in keeping with the aesthetic of *c.*1890. Natural objects were also used to decorate the dining room of the 1870s and 1880s, such things as stuffed birds or deer heads, tropical plants, or a fern display.[12] The middle class followed these dining practices, and dining rooms became common even in relatively low-cost houses.

Representing an aestheticized and elite point of view, the architect Ralph Adams Cram observed in 1886 that eating with others was gross, a bodily function elevated to a public occasion. He regretted that eating together had become *the* principal way to mark any occasion. Cram hoped that one day people would recognize that eating, like sleeping, ought to be done in private. But until that day, dining-room decoration ought to try to stress the mental and intellectual reasons for conviviality, to downplay the bodily functions and the sensuous. Refined objects of decorative art can help, he said, but "vulgar" stuffed animals, or indeed anything that suggested food in the carving or decoration, should be avoided.[13]

The dining room, of course, depends upon the kitchen and its work; and the attitude toward who executes housework is one of the biggest differences between the Victorian era and the present. For the Victorian upper classes, as well as the middle classes, no house ran without servants. Many of the machines and inventions that execute tasks for us today were just being developed in the Victorian period and had not been disseminated; these tasks were done by servants. Well-to-do families often employed many servants – cook, kitchen maid, parlor maid, nurse, groom, butler, and so on – but even in the lower reaches of the middle class a servant was expected. A simple farm household had resident housework help, perhaps in the form of the neighbors' older daughters. The Victorian kitchen was home to the servants, not to the mistress of the household. Mid-nineteenth-century advice books constantly reminded householders that the kitchen should be decorated cheerfully, have a sunny window, some plants and pictures, and a comfortable chair for the servant to use. These reminders suggest that the kitchen was habitually furnished with the dreariest objects and received the least attention because it was only the servant's domain.

Interpretations

Traditional architectural history has focused on architectural styles and aesthetic or formal refinement. Professor Vincent Scully's 1955 book *The Shingle Style* is a good example of this approach.[14] He examined examples of resort and suburban architecture designed in the 1870s and 1880s in a simplified style using wood shingles, with large enveloping roofs, porches, and verandahs. He praised architects for achieving a truly American style by avoiding the eclecticism or revivals of historic styles favored in the mid-nineteenth century. By focusing on stylistic issues, traditional historians have often reinforced architects' own interest in form, as well as their neglect of social, cultural, or functional aspects of architecture in favor of its visual aspects.

Recent interpreters of later nineteenth century dwellings have approached their readings from a social or cultural point of view, giving credit for design initiatives to builders and dwellers as much as to trained designers. For example, Catherine Bishir's 1981 article on Carolina builder Jacob Holt shows how he used local traditions of house design and combined them with fashionable ideas that he gleaned from his travels and from reading architectural pattern books.[15] A traditional architectural historian would find Holt's work inferior because he did not employ correct interpretations of historic styles or develop an original formal vocabulary of his own. Bishir, however, finds praiseworthy Holt's method of merging national fashion and regional tradition. By incorporating local dwelling arrangements and familiar materials with details rendered in nationally recognized architectural styles, Holt made houses that better suited his clients' practical and symbolic needs. By resisting the pressures to be fashionable with up-to-date national styles, Holt produced houses that better fitted into their Carolina contexts.

Historian Lizabeth Cohen utilizes a similar shift in point of view in her article "Embellishing a Life of Labor," in which she analyzes the separate standards of differing social levels.[16] She reports on the clash between workers' furnishing ideas for their tenement apartments and the furnishing ideals of visiting social workers. Social workers of the turn of the century wanted to see tenement dwellers decorate their dwellings with simple, unornamented furniture that was inexpensive and easy to clean. The social workers' taste represented mainstream, educated, middle-class taste, which was reinforced by shelter magazine articles of the period praising the simplicity of decoration produced by the Arts and Crafts Movement. However, immigrant tenement dwellers desired ornate furniture that conveyed valued sentiments and preserved homeland traditions. Embroidered linens, velvet upholstery, or very large beds all preserved values from the home country and preserved memories of the family homes that immigrants had left behind. Being able to afford elaborate furniture also showed immigrants' successes in the New World and their access to mass-produced American goods. Cohen shows how taste in interior decoration carries deeper meanings than just being in style.

These two scholars show the shortfalls in assuming that architectural ideas "trickle down" from elites to lower classes. By shifting viewpoints from that of the elite critic to that of the client, Bishir identifies ways to value Holt's buildings for their suitability to their context and purpose rather than for their approximation to abstract ideals of "good design." Cohen shows us how to assess stylistic choices for their emotional and cultural meanings and not just for their formal value.

Conclusion

In the nineteenth century all families beyond the working class lived in a dwelling formed to present the family to the public, which housed many ceremonious spaces and activities to accomplish this end. The house, in its formality, did not place as much emphasis on the individuals within the family, and their expressive needs as persons, as it did on the group. Thus, bedrooms were assigned to batches of children, and the sitting room was conceived for all the family to gather in together. In the twentieth century a stronger emphasis on the individual's wants led to architectural emphasis on private spaces, self-expression in decor, and fewer public reception rooms. Working-class housing, always small and cheaply built, provided a counterpoint and a lesson to contemporaries about what should be avoided in middle-class dwellings. The inadequacy of working-class housing led to a reform movement which had a sweeping affect on building codes and zoning laws.

The House of 1900–1960

New dwelling forms were added to the American repertoire in the early twentieth century in the form of simpler and smaller houses for the middle class, inexpensive free-standing houses and garden apartments for prospering workers, and elite apartment houses as well as mansions for wealthy families. New manufactured materials made their appearance during this era, including drywall or Sheetrock, concrete block, linoleum, Thermopane windows, and aluminum siding. The role of women changed during this era as they got the vote and began to consider themselves properly part of the public world as well as part of the domestic. Central heating, electricity, and indoor plumbing became standard in urban and suburban dwellings, gradually expanding into rural areas by World War II. Architects continued to design mansions for the elite with the historic array of servants' rooms, but, for the rest of society, servants gave way to household machines and electricity.

The early twentieth century is the era of reform in American political life. Urban zoning laws, starting in 1916, limited the kinds of function allowed in the several districts of cities, codifying practices that had begun in nineteenth-century middle-class residential enclaves like Gramercy Park in New York. Urban districts were to be purified of mixed uses so that single-family houses could occupy one area, multiple dwellings (apartment houses) another, manufacturing and commercial establishments yet another. Cities were to be comprised of many "rooms" each with its own function, much like an elaborate house of the later nineteenth century.

Middle-class dwellings

One common early twentieth-century house form was the bungalow, one story or a story-and-a-half, made of wood with porches and simple wood trim. While this house type can be found in elite, middle-class, and working-class sizes, with materials and budgets to fit, it was very popular with the middle class. Bungalows were perhaps the first national style of house, sold through catalogs or produced by developers in all parts of the United States. The typical bungalow had two or three bedrooms, a living room, a dining room, and a compact kitchen, with simplified interior finishes and built-in furniture.

Domestic-advice columnist Martha Bruere emphasized in 1914 that a modern house must be conceived as fulfilling two kinds of functions: collective enjoyment and individual development. In a modern house, the stress shifted to providing each person with his or her own spaces, such as separate rooms for sons and daughters or a den for the husband. Now, not the family's reputation but individuals' development and happiness were the primary purpose of the house. The bungalow replaced the ceremony of Victorian living with a new concept: efficiency. The modern homemaker was called a "manager" and her home equated with a factory which ought to be laid out as efficiently as any other business.[17] The housekeeper in the new era had responsibilities to serve her community as well as keep her husband and children happy. She needed an efficiently run operation so she could "pay her debt to society" in her own activities outside the home.[18]

By the turn of the twentieth century, the formal parlor as the principal reception room was disappearing, to be replaced by the title "living room" for the middle class as well as the working class (figure 7.6). Bungalow living rooms were characteristically modest in size and well-lit by windows. Lighter colors of paints and painted or natural woodwork complemented

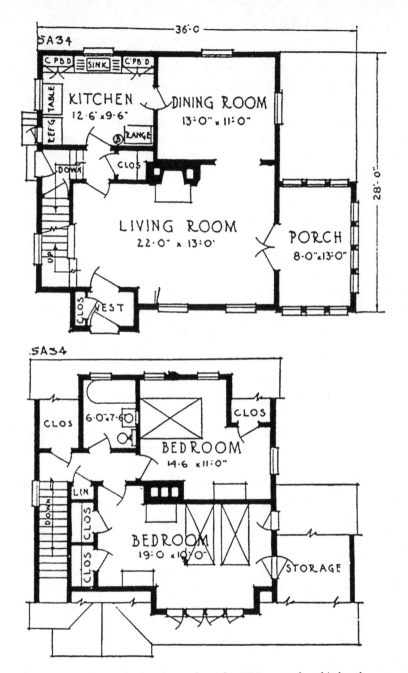

Figure 7.6 Plan for a suburban house from the 1920s; a modern kitchen has an ice-box that can be iced from the back porch. From *Small Homes of Architectural Distinction . . . by the Architects' Small House Service Bureau* (New York: Harper and Brothers, 1929); reprinted as *Authentic Small Houses of the Twenties* (New York: Dover, 1987), p. 43.

much simplified furniture styles. A leather and oak sofa designed by Gustave Stickley, for example, contrasts with a Victorian tufted and carved parlor suite. Overly decorated parlors became an object of concern in the household-advice columns of 1910s' magazines because they were believed to drive the children out of the house. A parlor "for company only," a bedroom kept "irksomely neat" provided nothing for a boy to do and nowhere to do his favorite things comfortably. A house that was just a showcase for possessions is "quite unadapted to the family need of having a good time."[19] The Victorian parlor had had the principal job of presenting the family to the public – a public made up of visitors paying formal calls. The bungalow era placed its emphasis much more on the family members' own comfort and amusement. A Victorian parlor kept everyone, parents and children, on their best stiff behavior, while the modern living room allowed relaxation and promoted family togetherness.

The simplicity in dining rooms that Ralph Adams Cram had desired was achieved in the first decade of the twentieth century. In order to unclutter life, storage pieces were often built into the architecture of the room. In parlors and sitting rooms, not much beyond a book shelf, inglenook seats, or a display shelf could be built in, but the dining room with its need for china, glass, linen and silver storage, was the ideal place for which to design built-in pieces. If not built-in, furniture of the early twentieth century was lightened in both weight and color. It was simplified by stripping away ornament and emphasizing surface textures and the natural colors of materials.

In keeping with the modern trend toward simplification, an argument for eliminating the dining room altogether began to be mounted in the 1910s, was actively pursued in the 1920s (figure 7.7), and became standard in the post-World War II era.[20] Advice writers asserted that a dining room was wasted, since it was only used 2–3 hours a day for meals. The rest of the time, dining rooms were vacant. Martha Bruere recommended in 1914 a living room that was generously dimensioned and that absorbed both the hall and the dining room, with a dining table at one end. Having a separate dining room allows the illusion of a magically appearing meal, she said, "but as in fifteen out of sixteen American homes the hand that sets the table is the hand of 'mother', that is not a hardy illusion anyway."[21] Simplifying the number of separate rooms in the house follows upon reducing the number of hands doing the housework.

By 1910, a major change had begun in the relation of servants to the middle class. Servants themselves observed that social mobility in the United

Figure 7.7 A scheme for getting rid of the dining room and using one end of the living room for (disguised) dining storage and kitchen access. From Edward Bok, "Abolish the Dining Room," *Colliers*, 79 (January 15, 1927): 10.

States would allow them to become educated and independent, and acted on that observation. The supply of serving labor decreased dramatically at the end of the nineteenth and beginning of the twentieth centuries. At the same time, household conveniences became more accessible than ever. By 1920, hot and cold running water, flush toilets and fixed bathtubs, kitchen sinks and laundry tubs, central heating, telephones, and even electric light all became commonplace in newly constructed houses. Bungalows for even very modest income families had such housekeeping aids in many parts of the United States, which only a generation earlier had been beyond the reach of poorer households. By about 1920 small electric motors began to appear in household tools such as vacuum cleaners and washing machines, disseminating conveniences that had in the Victorian era only been available at commercial scale or to wealthy families.

The assumption that the householder rather than a servant would use the kitchen altered the concept of the kitchen, its location, fittings, and decoration. The kitchen of a model farmhouse published in 1916 and sponsored by the US Department of Agriculture was described as excellent in light, ventilation, and location. It had the best view in the house, morning sun, was cooled by breezes, and had a screened porch. These pleasant features would be too expensive if the kitchen were intended for a servant, but when the housewife spent her day in the kitchen, it is reconceived. Not only was the new kitchen to be light and clean, but it also had to be designed for efficiency, like a machine. The 1914 kitchen recommended in *Good Housekeeping* was called a "laboratory," flooded with sunlight and always clean. Its stove, sink, and storage cabinets were called the "apparatus" – as befits a lab. This desire for efficiency arose from the study of efficient labor practices in factories, carried into domestic life by trained home economists and "efficiency experts."

As individuality and self-expression replaced group presentation as the goal of the early twentieth-century house, bedrooms came to be defined as individual spaces. New bedroom housekeeping principles for young home-makers were articulated by Christine Herrick in 1911. The new practice was to think of each bed as sleeping just one person. Both comfort and health will be improved, she wrote, if two people are put into two single beds rather than one double.[22] Ann Wentworth described to a *House Beautiful* audience how she fixed up sleeping accommodations for seven people in her new house. Each had his or her own room, and selected his or her own bedstead and appointments.[23] This era concretized the idea of individuality in bedrooms, especially for children. In the mid-nineteenth century, children were considered generically, bundled together in shared rooms, and not really allowed to express themselves, rather to be seen and not heard. In the 1910s, however, children's needs got more attention. "It is a happier time than it ever was for children," wrote Birdaline Bowdoin in a 1913 *Good Housekeeping*, speaking of 6–10-year-olds. "Their best qualities are given a loving chance to grow and expand" through rooms decorated especially for them.[24] Even relatively modest households tried to provide a room for each child, or, failing that, separate rooms for the male and female children. Bedroom decor asserted "masculinity" or "femininity" by the types of fabrics and furnishings deemed appropriate to each gender. For girls, ruffles and dolls, sweetly painted furniture, and a dressing table for primping; for boys, American Indian objects or cowboy decorations, chunky wooden furniture, and a workshop space in which to pursue hobbies.

The modern decorator of a bedroom in 1911 should still be especially concerned with hygiene, reported *Good Housekeeping*. Sleeping porches provided healthful outdoor bedrooms for the wealthy as well as the middle-class sleeper. As a counter to tuberculosis, doctors recommended sleeping in the fresh air year round. In California the Greene brothers designed the 1908 Gamble house with three sleeping porches as addition to second-floor bedrooms, integrated into the design of the house. Home-owners added such porches to existing houses. Christine Herrick assumed that there may still be a washstand, pitcher, and bowl in the 1910s' bedroom and cautioned the housekeeper to cleanse them thoroughly.[25] She also observed that bugs may lodge in the crevices of wooden bedframes and must be routed with deadly poisons; metal bedsteads, although less hand-some, did not harbor insects.[26]

Storage, always at a premium in small-house bedrooms, could be created in the low-budget bungalow by built-in storage. A built-in chest of drawers and closet could absorb the functions of a wardrobe, bureau, or chiffonier, leaving only the dressing table from the traditional array of bedroom furniture. The advantage is that the bedroom freed from this furniture can take on the atmosphere of a private sitting room and owners can find room for a desk, a couch, a sewing table, or a bookcase.[27] With clever furnishings, such as a roll-away bed that spends the day in a closet, each member of the family can have a private sitting room during daylight hours, asserted Martha Bruere in 1914.[28] The same argument that applied to the dining room was made about the bedroom: it was only used for a few hours a day, and thus was a waste of precious household space. In grander houses, of course, more generously dimensioned bedrooms allowed more function-specific furniture, and wealthy families built bed-room suites with a group of linked, function-specific rooms such as a sleeping chamber, a dressing room, a boudoir or sitting room, and a bathroom.

Plumbing and fixtures both improved rapidly in the later nineteenth century as health reformers pushed for more sanitary awareness. Better traps controlled sewer gas – that blight of the Victorian house. Plumbing facilities at the expensive end of construction included choices about the location of washing equipment. In a new seven-bedroom house of 1911, the owner described three fully equipped bathrooms, but also reported that each bedroom had its own washstand. She attributed this to the fact that the inhabitants were "old-fashioned" or "English" in their taste.[29] At the turn of the century advanced plumbing techniques used exposed piping so any problems could be easily repaired; then by the 1920s a new taste for containing most plumbing within walls made possible the sleeker appearance of the modern bathroom. In an elite apartment or house of the later nineteenth century, there might be only a single bathroom. By the 1930s experts recommended that every upper-class bedroom have its own bathroom. Middle-class houses got indoor bathrooms in the 1910s replacing outhouses, and among the middle class two or even three bathrooms became common after World War II.

By the end of World War II, small one-floor ranch houses proliferated for newly formed families, and automobile garages and new kitchen appliances became expected features in houses at all social levels. A new suburb, Radburn, New Jersey, of 1929, had been designed around the automobile. Each house had a one-car garage, while the map of the town reflected separate circulation routes for cars and pedestrians. New families forming at the end of World War II led to a huge demand for small houses with garages in suburban enclaves, met by independent entrepreneurs like Fritz Burns whose company "built several thousand houses in Los Angeles area," in 1945–6. Experimental houses of the 1940s made use of the latest in new manufactured materials such as Thermopane windows, new spatial ideas such as a kitchen breakfast bar with stools, or a duplicate outdoor kitchen for patio entertaining, sprinklers built into the lawn, air conditioning, and a carport ("built for two cars or perhaps, later, one car and a helicopter").[30]

Breaking down barriers between formerly separated kitchen and dining room, dining room and living room, opened the plan up to create continuous open space, a hallmark of modern design. Architect Marcel Breuer designed a house as a demonstration of modern architecture for the Museum of Modern Art, which was erected in its Manhattan garden in 1946. The house presented a kitchen that was half open to a dining area, itself part of a living room. The openness of the kitchen – of what was formerly servants' space – to the social space of the house signaled architects' recognition that the era of servants was over for middle-class dwellers, and that the housewife, once segregated like a servant in her efficient workroom of a kitchen, was now incorporated into the social life of the house.

In the 1940s the wide availability of electrical appliances led manufacturers to research kitchen improvements. In addition to efficient traffic patterns, they determined that "the modern kitchen should be the nerve center and workshop of the home, and should therefore include office facilities or hobby equipment for the housewife . . . child care or lounging equipment." They recommended kitchens with specific personalities such as the "teenage" kitchen with room for snacks and games, and the "indoor–outdoor" kitchen with links to porches and lawns.[31] Laundries were also targeted as a domestic space in need of design. The washing-machine industry hired home economists to propose efficient laundry rooms; architect L. Morgan Yost declared "The laundry – whether on the first floor, the second floor or the basement – is planned just like a factory. Soiled clothes and linen come in one end and pass through the production line, coming out the other end, fresh, clean and ready to use." The language of factory efficiency was applied to kitchen and laundry alike, encouraging housewives to demand better work spaces, while lubricating the demand for new appliances.[32]

Working-class dwellings

In the first and second decades of the twentieth century, reformers in cities wrote new building codes to assure improvements in workers' housing where legislation of the previous era had fallen short. New housing laws were designed to provide enhanced light, fresh air, and indoor plumbing in workers' housing, and specified minimum dimensions for rooms. The federal government sponsored house designs to help upgrade the general standard. Some well-known architects interested themselves in the problem of designing a better working-class house. For example, in the first two decades of the twentieth century Frank Lloyd Wright designed houses for the Larkin Company workers in Buffalo, NY, and prefabricated houses for locations in Milwaukee, WI. Continuing a nineteenth-century trend, the owners of factories often erected whole towns of workers' housing, such as those at Copperton, Utah, for the Anaconda Copper company, to make sure that workers and their families would have clean and safe dwellings, as well as assuring that workers behaved themselves and arrived at work on time.

At the low-budget end of twentieth-century bungalows is an "Inexpensive House for a Farmer or Tenant" sponsored by the Department of Agriculture and published in *Country Life in America* in 1916.[33] The house has only one door to the outside, located near the kitchen, which was designed to serve as both "front" door and service door, in order to save on floor and wall space that would have to be sacrificed if another door were introduced. Omitting fixed plumbing was a common way to keep costs down. In this small house of 1916, indoor plumbing was omitted and the sponsors estimated that it would increase the cost of the house by 50 percent to include running water, sinks, a toilet, and a tub. In 1917 one reformer stated that bathtubs were luxury goods that the poor should do without – after all, they could go to the city-run public baths if they wanted to bathe.

In working-class dwellings of the nineteenth century a separate dining room had never been affordable, and the general-purpose living room had always been the location for meals. Workers' cottages and bungalows in the early twentieth century did sometimes have rooms labeled "dining room" on architectural plans, but it is unlikely that dining was the only use, since large families needed to use all their space efficiently. In cheaper houses of the bungalow era the dining room was sometimes supplanted by a built-in table and seats in a corner of the kitchen. Higher up the social scale, dining rooms slowly disappeared as separate rooms to be replaced by utilizing a corner of the living room as a dining area. The tendency to eliminate dining rooms as separate spaces finally caught up with stylish Modernist architects during the period between the wars.

By the late 1940s a new generation of houses built for working-class home-owners replaced bungalows with even greater simplicity. Houses such as those built by the Levitt Brothers on Long Island, in New Jersey and Pennsylvania in the late 1940s and 1950s included the latest kitchen ranges and refrigerators, continuous counters with metal cabinets, and convenient layouts for maximum efficiency for the housewife. In the 1910s the kitchen had been an especially conveniently arranged work room, an ideal continued in the Levitt and related post-war houses, but by the 1940s in more "modern" middle-class houses, the kitchen becomes a social space integrated with the reception rooms in which the housewife's work becomes one of the family activities.

Upper-class dwellings

In the early twentieth century enormous mansions continued to be built by wealthy families in both urban and country locations. On Long Island, New York, for example, there are numerous mansions from the 1910s and 1920s, typically done in historic-revival styles, which include a large number of public reception rooms and house extensive staffs of servants.[34] However, after the institution of income tax and the Depression of the 1930s such large estates declined in number. Houses of this size that still survive are often converted to use by institutions. For example, a number of mansions built by various architects in the first three decades of the twentieth century in Newport, Rhode Island, which once housed wealthy families for summer vacations, were taken over by Salve Regina College in the 1980s and adapted for use as offices, classrooms, and dormitories.

Some well-to-do families rejected historic-revival styled and grand modes in favor of the simplified aesthetic promoted by the Arts and Crafts Movement. An interesting example of an upper-class house is the 1908 Gamble House built as a very large bungalow by the architects Greene and Greene in Pasadena, California. The house was very expensive to construct, being made of hand-carved redwood, with custom-made stained glass, leather, and bronze fittings. It had very large living areas on the ground floor, with a piano carved to match the wall paneling. Three of the bedrooms on the second floor had attached sleeping porches. Nonetheless, because it appeared to hug the ground and displayed "natural materials," the Gamble House presented itself as a modest building with a relaxed tone, fitting the definition of a bungalow. This wealthy family enjoyed the aesthetic of simplicity made costly by superb workmanship.

Interpretations

Interpretations of early twentieth-century houses have recently focused on issues of gender. Feminists have been interested in the ways in which houses as "machines for living" (Le Corbusier's ideal) worked for homemakers. Ann Marie Adams studied California developer Eichler's houses to see how a modern open-plan house design was actually used by a family. How did Modernist open space work for the jobs of raising children and serving meals? Adams found that the fully glazed walls that Eichler provided to bring transparency to walls and light into the interior were in practice usually covered with curtains to preserve privacy. The open-plan kitchen-entertaining area, which Eichler envisioned for cocktail buffets as well as for family meals, was adapted to accommodate a desk as well as a table for family meals. The designer's Modernist forms were subverted to better accommodate individual families' needs.

The family home is typically gendered feminine in opposition to the masculine workplace, but the bachelor pad has both quiet, domestic areas and places for work within it. Decoding the ways in which masculinity is figured in bachelor apartments, Steven Cohan analyzed Rock Hudson's *Pillow Talk* apartment and its furnishings as a typical "bachelor pad."[35] He observed that, unlike a family home with its distinct public and private zones, the bachelor pad has spaces fluidly open to each other. The typically quiet, private zone of a dwelling, the bedroom, was used in this film for active purposes such as business telephoning and other work-related activity, while the bed itself is the command center of the pad: its controls can operate the door locks, the hi-fi, kitchen appliances, the drapes, and the lights. Normally public, the living room became the site for private seduction scenes on the automated, hide-a-bed couch. Bachelor dwellings, having only one occupant, are free to question typical boundaries between public and private to suit the resident, but in so doing they serve to heighten our awareness of the force of those boundaries in our conceptual map of the proper family home.

Architectural historian Alice Friedman's study of Dr Edith Farnsworth's 1940s' bachelor abode in Plano, Illinois, points up the divergence between a client's and an architect's view of such boundaries. Ludwig Mies van der Rohe, Farnsworth's architect, fixed upon an open plan with all-glass walls for Farnsworth's weekend house. Mies, Friedman writes, was an architect "for whom theoretical and formal considerations always came before practical ones."[36] Although Farnsworth approved of the original designs, after living in the house she commented that she could not keep her garbage can in a convenient location because it would ruin the aesthetic impact of the kitchen, all too visible from outdoors through the glass walls. Farnsworth complained that she was often being looked at by others both inside and outside her home: Mies wanted 5-foot tall interior partitions for formal reasons, while Farnsworth, 6 feet tall herself, wanted tall enough partitions between spaces to shield her activities. She wanted distinct bedrooms to preserve some privacy, but Mies had designed her house with sleeping areas, not enclosed rooms. Friedman's analysis points up divergences between an architect's pure, formal vision for a bachelor house, and the bachelor-occupant's disappointing experiences of daily life in that house. That is, a formalist analysis may find admirable qualities in a house while a social-cultural analysis finds lapses and failures, or vice versa.

Conclusion

The period from 1900 to 1960 is an era of consolidation. Household inventions, such as refrigerators or washing machines, became widespread in houses of the middle and upper classes. Electricity, which had first been available in apartment houses and hotels, now became widespread in dwellings of all classes. The rationalization of rooms according to function, which had been a big part of the nineteenth-century's upper-middle-class house, spread to working-class houses in the early twentieth century. Conversely, the multi-use space found in tenement living rooms percolated upward to become the living-dining-kitchen areas of Modernist post-World War II houses for higher-income residents.

Housing after 1960

The standards for American house comforts had been established in the early twentieth century and were well distributed among all classes by the 1960s. It is remarkable how quickly domestic conveniences spread to all classes. In 1880, for example, there was no plumbing available for the working class and little for the middle class. But, from 1960, houses throughout the economic spectrum would almost always have either gas or electricity (or both), hot and cold water, central heating, and modern kitchens. The fully applianced kitchen, dependent on good plumbing and electricity, and sometimes gas, was already conceptualized and marketed in its paradigmatic form by the 1930s: it contained the stove, sink, refrigerator, cabinets, and a continuous counter. Added to this array of appliances in the later twentieth century were dishwashers and microwave ovens. Washing machines and clothes dryers, first available in the later nineteenth century, became an expected part of the post-war house, sometimes located in the kitchen but more often in a laundry room in the basement or adjoining the kitchen, sharing a utility room with the furnace and water heater, or later located with the bedrooms following a logic of bodily care. Differentiated reception rooms for entertaining guests shrank as private spaces grew, since entertaining was done less formally than before in the combined kitchen–great room or outdoors.

Middle-class dwellings

Houses have been produced in very large numbers for the middle class and in a wide range of costs in the period from 1960. These houses were produced by architects, builders, and developers, while house owners could buy houses in kits or mail away for house plans from catalogs. An example of mail-order house plans from a company called Home Planners Inc. was published in a book of multilevel plans in 1982. Design no. 42173 is a low, spreading house with one end having two levels. On the main level are an entrance hall, a living room, and a dining room, all of which look out over

Figure 7.8 View of two "McMansions," large houses for the upper-middle class of the 1990s, York, Maine (photo: E. C. Cromley).

the front lawn; in the back are a family room and a room called "nook" which could be a breakfast room, and next to it are a kitchen and a service room with laundry facilities. This service room opens into a two-car garage. At the opposite end of the house is a two-level section with a master bedroom, its own bath and dressing room, and three other smaller bedrooms with two baths on the upper level. On the lower level, there are a recreation room, a snack room, a bar, a utility room, a room called "maid's room," another bathroom, and a storage room. This house is quite lavish with 2,290 square feet on the main level and 1,600 square feet on the top and again on the bottom of the bi-level portion. Although the house has a maid's room, it would be unusual to find a live-in maid. The expanded square footage of a house like this foreshadows the enormous "McMansions" of the 1990s at 10,000 or 12,000 square feet (figure 7.8).

Since the 1960s there has been a shift in the space allocated to kitchens and to bodily care. Kitchens went from being purely workrooms in 1920 to being the center of family social life in 1990. Ideally, one of the smallest rooms for home economists in the 1910s following scientific efficiency studies, kitchens have now become one of the largest rooms, incorporating the "family room" and outfitted with dining furniture, television, a computer, and equipment for other leisure activities. In the 1980s and 1990s in expensive dwellings, kitchens turned into theaters in which guests were entertained with cooking events, and appliances grew to restaurant proportions and quality. In receptive climates well-to-do homeowners built duplicate outdoor kitchens for entertaining on the deck or patio. Existing houses got additions of "great rooms," high-ceilinged family room–kitchen combinations where a crowd of family or guests could gather. Kitchens acquired upholstered seating furniture and nostalgic fireplaces once found in living rooms, sentimentally associated with idealized "farm kitchens" of the eighteenth and nineteenth centuries.

An architect-designed upper-middle-class house of 1966 is the house for Mr and Mrs Gordon Bunshaft in East Hampton, NY. The architect Gordon Bunshaft designed the house for himself and his wife out of concrete, with travertine facings and glass exterior walls. The house was to provide a weekend retreat for the architect and his wife, and a setting for their art collection. At one end of the plan are the couple's bedroom, the utility room, and bath. At the opposite end are a studio and another bedroom. In the center of the plan are the kitchen and bathroom adjacent to a large living-dining room which opens out onto a terrace. The glass walls incorporate views of the landscape and a pond.

A similar stark, modern style was used for a 1966 development house for a lower-income family. This house was designed by architects Keys, Lethbridge, and Condon, for a site in Bethesda, Maryland. The house has a two-level plan; on the upper level is a long dining–living space adjacent to a kitchen. A family room and a study are located at the other side of the kitchen. Three bedrooms and two bathrooms complete this level. On the lower level is another bedroom with bath, along with a recreation room and a utility room. The house materials were designed for factory fabrication and a reasonably low construction cost of $42,000.[37] While materials differ, these two houses have remarkably similar room conceptions and Modernist architectural styles, even though the Bunshaft house is designed for an elite family's weekend hideaway and the other is designed for an ordinary middle-class family's daily life. Modern materials, services, and appliances led to less obvious differences between the classes in this era.

In the recent period, middle- and upper-middle-class residents have been returning to live in cities to partake of the intensity of culture there. One effect has been the reclamation of disused building stock for the new use of dwellings. Historic buildings such as churches and schools, no longer in demand for their original uses, serve as apartments or condominiums for such city-dwellers. Abandoned factories in older downtowns have been renovated into loft apartments, first for artists who needed open space, and then for bourgeois families. An example of a loft renovation is the top story of the old chocolate factory bought by a French couple in New York City. They gutted the space and built a new roof 2 feet higher than the old one to give their apartment high ceilings. On the main floor are the living room and a massive kitchen in which they have their only dining table. The floors were made of broad planks salvaged from the sides of Massachusetts barns. The couple inserted the bathroom under an old water tower on the roof of the factory building.[38] Loft renovations participate in a general move toward recycling: abandoned factory space is recycled into a dwelling; used barn wood becomes a new floor. Rare or imported materials are recycled to give character to expensive lofts, but artists with low budgets do the same with local, found materials.

An important feature of recent middle-class house use is the fact of working at home. At the end of the nineteenth century it was common for tenant dwellers to work at home, making cigars or sewing piecework, but reformers of the early twentieth century worked to segregate paid work from home life. Now there is a trend to make earning a living something that can be done from home. The 1990 census showed that 3 percent of employed Americans named their home as their primary workplace; in 1980 only 2.3 percent worked at home. (The numbers are probably higher, but for legal and tax reasons many people are reluctant to talk about their home offices.) Employers even encourage people to work at home because it saves them the expense of leasing space, and people who do not commute to work save money on cars or trains and contribute indirectly to a cleaner environment. Most people who work at home belong in the category of "symbolic analysts," including architects, lawyers, brokers, engineers, and the like.

In many suburbs, zoning codes have made working at home illegal, but common practice is forcing some changes in these laws. The city of Boston has had a zoning law since 1964 that defined acceptable home-based professions, and in July of 1993 their list of professions was expanded to include specialists such as computer-related workers, consultants, and writers. Since "conventional single-family homes do not allow for an effective combination of home and office," some architects have devised solutions that will keep the domestic and the professional securely separated. For example, the architectural firm Abacus in Boston designed a free-standing outbuilding that one could erect in a back yard; it provides a minimal work place with a closet and a bath.[39]

The recent past has seen a significant increase in the square footage of upper-middle-class houses, whether on small or large lots of land. Houses of 10,000 square feet with three- or four-car garages and indoor swimming pools have become familiar in American suburbs. In some of the largest mansions, nineteenth-century room types, such as billiard rooms, are again included, along with newer room types such as an indoor lap-pool, or a media room for listening to the latest sound system and watching movies at home. Architectural styles that recall the past give these mansions picturesque outlines or symmetrical grandeur even as their interior machinery is computerized state-of-the-art. The shift in allocation of space from reception and social rooms to private space, evident in the mid-twentieth century, continues in recent interiors. Dressing rooms and bathrooms are provided for every bedroom; bedrooms are large enough to include television and seating areas. In master bedrooms some couples prefer "his-and-her master bath suites," which may have double sinks or larger shower stalls, or saunas and exercise equipment. Busy parents "want a place where they can think, where they won't be bothered. And there aren't a lot of places where that can happen," said the research director of the National Association of Home Builders.[40] Bathrooms become refuges, the only place in the house to get away from daily demands and distractions.

Working-class dwellings

For many low-income families in the United States manufactured housing provided a way to own their own home. Manufactured modules, carried from factory to prepared site on trucks, cost much less than custom-built houses and have been popular especially in warmer climates. Manufactured houses have had their reputations damaged because, due to lightweight construction, they are easily ruined by floods, hurricanes, and tornadoes, but recent construction innovations and permanent foundations for these houses have made them much more durable. Furthermore, new construction techniques have allowed housing modules to be stacked and used in innovative configurations to create houses with significantly more space and exterior variety.[41]

Manufactured housing, once limited in form to the mobile home, is now an industry creating housing modules that can be used for all kinds of house designs. New technologies are changing the way houses are produced in the United States and internationally. Now computer-aided design programs allow housing production to proceed from the design through the prototype to the robotically fabricated building. New kinds of computerized mass production will allow more houses to be created, and will make it easier to insert resource-efficient practices into housing construction.[42]

In the 1950s and 1960s the federal government took a special interest in slum clearance or "urban renewal." Old houses were to be cleared out of older downtowns and replaced by up-to-date housing for low-income households. At the working-class end of the housing spectrum, apartments in tall towers constructed with federal money in the 1960s provided the same array of rooms long favored by the middle class. The Pruitt-Igoe houses in St Louis, Missouri, are examples of federally subsidized housing of this period. Applianced kitchens, living rooms, individual bedrooms for each family member where possible, housed the working poor, and increasingly the unemployed. Similar apartment towers in New York, Chicago, and Boston increasingly segregated the poorest city residents.

The high level of services that made such high-rise, subsidized apartments work required a high level of maintenance not included in the public budget; among other causes, disrepair led to the collapse of habitability in Pruitt-Igoe and other public housing projects. More recent subsidized housing for low-income residents has taken the form of low-rise and sometimes single-family dwellings, and renters are encouraged to become purchasers of their housing to secure their interest in maintaining the property. Federal subsidies to the poor for housing take the form of low-interest mortgages and low-priced units.

In the late twentieth century, more attention was paid to the people who were to live in subsidized housing. Instead of just consulting experts, as had been done in the 1950s and 1960s, housing agencies consulted future tenants to discover what their needs were. As a consequence, some house plans for the poor reflect different values in space allocation from middle- and upper-middle-class house plans. For example, in Boston, Massachusetts, subsidized housing units of the 1990s, in the form of single-family houses or two-family semi-detached houses, have a contained kitchen and a separate "dining room," unlike their upper-middle-class counterparts with their multi-functional great-room–kitchens. This is not because poor people want formal dining, but because low-income families with several children want to be able to separate their rooms from each other to give privacy for competing activities. Sometimes the separate "dining room" will really serve as a homework room, or a place to iron and fold clean clothes, an extra bedroom, or some other use that needs its own space. Surveys of the clients for subsidized housing conducted by the Boston housing authority revealed these desires.

Interpretation of recent domestic architecture

Recent interpretations of later twentieth-century architecture continue a gendered analysis, apply social-history insights, and consider the roles that new technologies and politics play in the construction of dwellings. Pervasive computerization has led some architects to think of the dwelling as a "node within fully connected networks in which living and working now coexist under the same roof. The house is becoming, more than ever, an infrastructure or interface for the 'appliances' of everyday culture, linking our every act to the outside world."[43] The effect of new technology on house concepts parallels that of a century ago when the introduction of the telephone, gas, and electric light linked houses into networks serviced by utilities companies.

Lawrence Vale asks how politics, among other factors, has influenced the form of houses.[44] He focuses on Boston's public housing, comparing the ways in which this city has provided housing for its poorest at various times since the seventeenth century. By developing a history of cultural attitudes toward the poor, and accounting for changing attitudes about the responsibility of others to provide housing for the poor, Vale enables us to understand dwellings as politically charged elements in the architectural field.

Alice Friedman, in *Women and the Making of the Modern House*, continues the focus on gendered readings of dwellings by studying contemporary women clients' houses. She analyzes Ann Bergren's 1985 California house by architects Thom Mayne and Michael Rotondi of the architectural firm Morphosis. Friedman's text helps us see how completely the formal decisions made here are informed by the emotional, social, and cultural life of the client. Bergren worked with the architects to establish ordering devices – paths of movement which link to and diverge from visual paths. "Visual axes intersect with organizational and processional axes, creating a series of overlapping movements, vistas, paths, and rest points," framing both family and individuals, integrating mind and body.[45] Friedman in turn integrates the possible explanations of a work of architecture, showing how the architectural shapes and spatial relationships instantiate a narrative of Bergren's daily life as a single mother, a scholar and writer, and a breadwinner.

Conclusion

The production of dwellings in the United States has largely been a matter of private enterprise. Although production is decentralized, however, there have been strong themes of agreement among house builders and house dwellers as to what constitutes a suitable dwelling. In the latter half of the nineteenth century there were dramatic differences between the dwellings of working-class, middle-class, and upper-class residents. These were differences of dwelling size, methods of construction, array of rooms, provision for privacy, and material finishes. The first half of the twentieth century saw major improvements in the dwellings available to the working-class and something of a leveling out of materials due to the wide availability of industrially produced building products. At the beginning of the twenty-first century, although there are enormous size disparities between houses for the rich and poor, the availability of utilities, appliances, and mass-produced furnishings has made a convenient dwelling accessible to most Americans.

Notes

1   Lee Soltow, "Wealth and Income Distribution," in *Encyclopedia of American Social History*, ed. Mary Kupiec Cayton, Elliott J. Gorn, and Peter W. Williams (New York: Charles Scribner's Sons, 1993), vol. 2, p. 1525.

2   Oliver P. Smith, *The Domestic Architect* (Buffalo, NY: 1854; facsimile edn Watkins Glen, NY: The American Life Foundation, 1978).

3   Elizabeth Cromley, *Alone Together: New York's Early Apartments* (Ithaca, NY: Cornell University Press, 1990), pp. 138–9.

4   Rose Cleveland, "Introduction," in *The Social Mirror: A Complete Treatise on the Laws, Rules, and Usages that Govern our Most Refined Homes and Social Circles* (St Louis, MO: L. W. Dickerson, 1888), p. 347.

5   Charles D. Lakey, *Lakey's Village and Country Houses* (New York: American Builder, 1875), plates 35, 40, 47, 56.

6   Cleveland, *Social Mirror*, pp. 353–4.

7   Byron A. Johnson, "Probate Inventory: A Guide to Nineteenth-century Material Culture," *Curator*, 21 (3) (September 1978): 188–90.

8   Ralph A. Cram, "The Decoration of City Houses: Second Part – The Entrance Hall," *The Decorator and Furnisher*, 7 (December 1885): 90; Kenneth Ames, "Meaning in Artifacts: Hall Furnishings in Victorian America," *Journal of Interdisciplinary History*, 9 (Summer, 1978): 19–46.

9   Charles Eastlake, *Hints on Household Taste in Furniture, Upholstery, and Other Details* (London: Longmans, Green, 1869).

10   Lakey, *Village*, "Cheap Houses for Mechanics," designs 45 and 46, plate 59.

11   Clifford Clark, "The Vision of the Dining Room: Plan Book Dreams and Middle-class Realities," in *Dining in America*, ed. Kathryn Grover (Amherst, MA: University of Massachusetts Press, 1987), pp. 142–72.

12   Cleveland, *Social Mirror*, pp. 357–8.

13   Ralph A. Cram, "The Decoration of City Houses: Part Three – The Dining Room," *The Decorator and Furnisher*, 7 (February 1886): 150.

14   Vincent J. Scully, *The Shingle Style, Architectural Theory and Design from Richardson to the Origins of Wright* (New Haven, CT: Yale University Press, 1955).

15   Catherine Bishir, "Jacob W. Holt: An American Builder," in *Winterthur Portfolio* (Spring 1981), reprinted in *Common Places*, ed. Dell Upton and John Michael Vlach (Athens, GA: University of Georgia Press, 1986), pp. 447–81.

16   Lizabeth Cohen, "Embellishing a Life of Labor: An Interpretation of the Material Culture of American Working-class Homes, 1885–1915," *Journal of American Culture* (Winter 1980), reprinted in *Common Places*, ed. Upton and Vlach, pp. 261–80.

17   Una Nixon Hopkins, "The House of Efficiency," *Good Housekeeping* (April 1914): 513.

18   Martha Bensley Bruere, "The House that Jill Built," *Good Housekeeping* (April 1914): 510.

19   Ibid., pp. 509–10.

20   Ibid.

21   Ibid., p. 511.

22   Christine Terhune Herrick, "First Principles: A Department for Young House-keepers," *Woman's Home Companion* (March 1911): 47.

23   Ann Wentworth, "Modern Bedsteads," *House Beautiful* (November 1911): 185.

24   Birdaline Bowdoin, "Children's Rooms," *Good Housekeeping* (April 1913): 157–8.

25   Herrick, "First Principles," p. 47.

26   Ibid.

27   Antoinette Rehmann Perrett, "Model Bedrooms," *Good Housekeeping* (June 1911): 728–32.

28   Bruere, "House that Jill Built," p. 512.

29   Wentworth, "Modern Bedsteads," p. 185.

30   "The Fritz B. Burns $75,000 Postwar Research House," *American Builder*, 68 (April 1946): 76–86.

31   "Manufacturer's Research Assures Effective Kitchens," *American Builder*, 68 (February 1946): 112; the results of this research were based on having real housewives spend many hours in test kitchens whose designs were then corrected in response to comments from users.

32   "Home Laundries, How and Where to Plan Them for Utmost Economy and Labor-saving Efficiency," *American Builder*, 68 (March 1946): 87.

33   E. L. D. Seymour, "Inexpensive House for a Farmer or Tenant," *Country Life in America* (October 1916): 78–9.

34   See Donald Sclare, *Beaux Arts Estates: The Architecture of Long Island* (New York: Viking, 1980).

35   Steven Cohan, "So Functional for its Purposes: The Bachelor Apartment in *Pillow Talk*," in *Stud: Architectures of Masculinity*, ed. Joel Sanders (New York: Princeton Architectural Press, 1996), pp. 28–41.

36   Alice Friedman, *Women and the Making of the Modern House* (New York: Harry Abrams, 1998), p. 134.

37   "Bunshaft Residence, East Hampton, New York," *Architectural Record*, 139 (May 1966), pp. 41–3; "Development House, Bethesda, Maryland," *Architectural Record*, 139 (May 1966): 50–1.

38   "French Dressing, Met Home of the Month," *Metropolitan Home*, 27 (September–October 1995): 119–25.

39   "Cities Zone for Working at Home," *Metropolis*, 13 (October 1993): 120–1.

40   "Builders' Winning Play: A Royal Flush," Real Estate Section H, *The Washington Post* (24 November 2001): 4.

41 Bradley Grogan, "Curb Appeal," *Urban Land*, 58 (March 1999) special section on manufactured housing, pp. 70–83.

42 Association of Collegiate Schools of Architecture, *ACSA News*, 31 (3) (November 2001): 2.

43 Ibid.

44 Lawrence Vale, *From the Puritans to the Projects: Public Housing and Public Neighbors* (Cambridge, MA: Harvard University Press, 2000).

45 Friedman, *Women and the Making of the Modern House*, p. 221.

8

English Townscape as Cultural and Symbolic Capital

Andrew Law

Architectural Conservation and Englishness

Discussions of the architectural conservation movement in the architectural press have often located its historical developments within a language of Englishness.[1] Here, the development of the movement has been met with various criticisms of its descriptions of urban landscapes and the normative assumptions of English ethnicity, which seem to lie in their symbolic narratives. On the one hand, from the late nineteenth and early twentieth centuries, the architectural conservation movement has been related to an "anti-urbanism," which results in the application of a rural imaginary to urban form.[2] Moreover, with the development of what was seen to be "urban sprawl" in the early twentieth century, the architectural conservation movement has been associated with a progressive "English" valorization of the hiatus between the urban and the rural.[3]

From an alternative perspective, however, I argue that the architectural conservation movement has been involved in the construction of a regional discourse of Englishness, which has had a significant part to play in the construction of a language of the *urban landscape*. I argue that attention should be turned to the work of Catherine Brace to describe the way in which the architectural conservation movement has perpetuated notions of "landscape individuality" and "citizenship." However, rather than a focus on Englishness alone, I argue that the construction of a regional discourse of Englishness must be read through the lens of a class discourse. In this respect, I argue that the notion of townscape is transformed into a cultural and symbolic capital with the aim of constructing a new elite identity. However, against traditional notions of the idea of cultural and symbolic capital, I argue that the notion of townscape is understood through a populist language which is crucial to the development of the ideas of "squirearchy" and a more self-reflexive understanding of social class.

Ruralizing the City

Englishness has often been conceived as emerging from resistance to the processes of urbanization.[4] Discussions of Englishness and the urban landscape have found a central place in critical analysis of the garden-city movement associated with Ebenezer Howard.[5] Standish Meacham's *Regaining Paradise, Englishness and the Early Garden-City Movement* outlines the development of a suburban discourse, arguing that the construction of Englishness is not something which can be linked to the work of Howard himself. In focusing on the narratives of pioneering industrialists, such as Joseph Rowntree and George Cadbury, Meacham argues that the construction of Englishness was something that developed in the interpretation of Howard's work. Other commentators on the discourse of the garden-city and Englishness have included Rogers and Power, who have examined the development of a particularly anti-urban suburban discourse. For them, anti-urbanism is depicted in the development of new towns, urban villages, and middle-class gardens.[6]

However, while these writers and others develop a particular understanding of the urban, some general criticisms may be made. First, while Samuel and Meacham acknowledge the presence of an anti-urban discourse, this position ignores the range of popularity that living in the urban environment has enjoyed.[7] This theory of Englishness may explain to a certain extent an interest in the popularity of gardens and parks, but it still does not explain the reasons why actors have increasingly developed a nostalgia for urban places. As the "gentrification" model demonstrated, the landscapes of cities have been defined through new nostalgias for urban industrial solidarities, which docklands or disused warehouses represent.

Moreover, the urban landscape has often been defined through a variety of languages, which are multi-textual and multi-thematic. With the development of so many different landscapes, it is hard to see how a discourse of Englishness may be translated to all urban environments. Indeed, rather than a particular trend, Rogers and Power note the rich variety of different forms and styles of city which have developed over the course of English urbanization. Rather than a garden-city, they point to England as a collection of medieval, Renaissance, and industrial cities.[8] The way in which these different forms of "landscapes" are experienced and understood is therefore not addressed by an approach that gives weight to an inherent anti-urbanism.

Working with Modernism and Afterwards

Another key commentator on the notion of landscapes and Englishness has been David Matless. Despite a focus on the rural, his work can be associated with an understanding of the urban landscape and Englishness. His work may be viewed as an extension of the narratives of architectural conservation developed by Williams, Daniels, and Meacham.[9] In the first place, Matless argues that, rather than a simple anti-urbanism, notions of the urban landscape in discourse have developed alongside Modernism.

Matless turns to "planner-preservationist" discourse to demonstrate the way in which ideas of progress and the urban were tied to a language of Englishness and the rural. Here the concern for planners and preservationists was not that the urban would destroy the soul of the "English," but that the spread of the urban into the countryside would result in the destruction of the English landscape and the essence of Englishness. In the first place, then, Matless suggests that, rather than a program to ruralize the urban, the mission of planners and preservationists has been to construct an image of the urban landscape based on the idea that urban territory is small, compact, and can be contained. Matless argues that many of the propagators of this new Englishness deplored the development of garden-cities and suburbs since this would result in the "overspill" of the urban into the rural. In discussing post-war development in Modernism, Matless draws attention to the way in which visionaries wanted to eradicate the suburbs and develop green belts. For Matless, Patrick Abercrombie's Greater London plan is therefore the epitome of these movements where:

> the planner appears as a regional gardener, planting New Towns, trimming pre-war housing sites: "[Abercrombie:] these slabs of housing should be

welded into real communities, their ragged edges rounded off, social and shopping centres properly planned, and local green belts provided." For Abercrombie this regionalism went hand in hand with his CPRE ruralism, for good agricultural land was to be maintained, and pleasant and lively country living and recreation provided. Regional planning and rural Englishness are interwoven.[10]

However, despite these narratives of the Modern, Matless is also aware of the limits of his theory of the landscape and Englishness. In an early article, he concedes that his own discussion of landscapes and Englishness may not describe recent developments in discourses of Englishness.[11] Since his analysis more or less ends in the 1950s, Matless argues that the link between Modernism and Englishness has more recently been severed, with a growing disregard for the "authority of the architect and the planner."[12] He argues that the perception of the individual is crucial to the renewed development of the aesthetic and the vernacular, where the heart of Englishness lies in the idea of a "deep or vague England."[13] In this respect, rather than heritage or the landscape as a whole, individual landscapes of diversity and peculiarity are essential to the idea of defending a deep, local England. However, despite these definitions, Matless acknowledges the "preliminary nature" of these ideas, and therefore the potential for more research.[14] Given the absence of more indicative approaches to these ideas, the following explores these notions in further detail.

The Development of a Regional Englishness: Landscape Individuality and Citizenship

From an alternative perspective, it might be argued that a discourse of a regional Englishness has had a part to play in the construction of the architectural conservation movement. Catherine Brace has argued that a regional discourse of Englishness has developed since the late nineteenth century, and might be associated with the idea that England has been held together through regions. In this respect, the strength of a discourse of a regional Englishness is captured in the idea that, through its differences, physically, existentially, and socially, England and Englishness can be understood as a patchwork quilt of contrasts which are held together.

One major theme of this Englishness might be understood through the notions of landscape individuality, which are reflected upon in the non-fictional rural writing of early 1920s' writers such as H. J. Massingham (1888–1952) and can be understood through the idea that regional spaces are seen to be spaces of diversity. As Brace comments, this narrative of individuality therefore contributes to the idea of a regional Englishness since it suggests that the English landscape and its peoples are a whole despite the differences between them: "the variety of the English country-side offered itself in a 'series of packets' – Little Englands. Each time one came upon a view, one may say every time, and truthfully 'Here is England'. And fifteen miles beyond lies another tight little packet which also is England."[15]

However, while pointing to explicit narratives surrounding the idea of a regional Englishness, Brace also argues that this Englishness has been constructed through wider discursive influences. In particular, notions of a regional Englishness are also held together by what she describes as "outlook geography." In pointing to the work of the geographer Patrick Geddes and the urban designer Sir Lawrence Dudley Stamp, Brace suggests that a regional discourse of Englishness is wrapped up in the techniques of outlook geography, which pointed to the importance of recognizing local distinctiveness through the idea of the regional survey.[16] Particularly in the work of Patrick Geddes, the regional survey has a crucial place and is a technique of geographical analysis where an observer from a physical high point can chart the various natural and social features of a region. However, as Geddes was to argue, as well as being a tool of analysis, the regional survey was also focused on encouraging the viewer to take an interest in his or her surroundings both physically and spiritually. Therefore, for Geddes, such an interest was crucial to the way in which he, as an educator and citizen, could find meaning in the relation between himself and the nation. In recognizing these complex connections, Brace argues that, as well as encouraging a local appreciation of place, the "geographers involved in the regional survey were aware of the broader culture of landscape and played an important part in forming and guiding this culture."[17]

The Urban Townscape

In what follows, I argue that, rather than being abstract notions which have been confined to a rural imaginary, these narratives can be understood in relation to the development of an imaginary of the urban landscape.

As a starting-point, I turn to the development of the idea of "townscape" in the *Architectural Review* by various writers to chart the way in which notions of a regional Englishness have developed.

Commentators have usually pointed to the *Architectural Review* and its early editor, Hubert de Croning Hastings, as having an essential role in the construction of the notion of "townscape."[18] Hastings has been credited with applying a distinctly picturesque approach to the notion of the urban landscape. In discussing his work, Jacobs and Baucom have argued that Hastings aimed to develop notions of urban architecture and space through a methodology inspired by eighteenth-century English landscape painters. The development of the picturesque was based on the idea that painting somehow captured the intrinsic qualities of rural landscapes which, despite their variousness, have intrinsic local qualities. In developing a philosophy of the picturesque, according to Jacobs and Baucom, this approach was central to Hastings's idea that townscapes were also spaces where invisible frames could be placed around an area and be understood as a place. In such a philosophy, Jacobs and Baucom argue, the application of this aesthetic not only helped to produce an approach to town planning but rather a language of Englishness that reproduced the symbolic "survival power" of the idea of the rural landscape:

> The object of urban planning, de Cronin Hastings and his followers on the Corporation of London and in the conservation movement argued, should be to recapture in built space the distinctively English aesthetic of the rural locale, to enshrine in painterly architectural arrays the genius loci of place, the intrinsic, indigenous qualities of the locale.[19]

Read in another perspective, Hastings's picturesque style attaches a certain "natural" and "organic" quality to the idea of the urban landscape. Thus, in his discussion of the English city, Hastings argued that it is characterized by its "infinite variety," and it is therefore the task of the architect and planner to bring to light the "irregular" and "incongruous" features of the urban environment. In this respect, his approach aimed to recognize the townscape as being sporadic and growing in variety, as with natural plants and animals. Thus, in one statement, Hastings can be found to argue that in many ways urban architecture resembles the growth of natural forms from the earth:

> So does the lively earth go on pushing up a host of highly incompatible trees. Great men, our forefathers of the eighteenth century made a virtue of

that very incompatibility. They encouraged trees to be themselves, combed jungles for rugged individualists. Not a shape so unlikely but it could gain membership of this unplanned democracy of trees. It remains for this generation to apply this principle to the urban scene.[20]

However, Hastings's work was not just a philosophy that rested in a visual imagination, it was taken further by a variety of writers who called for a new way of looking at development in cities. Here it was not enough simply to discuss the re-planning of cities; rather, the problem for architects and planners was to create new manifestos of action and creation. The artist John Piper was a central figure in the creation of a new philosophy of architecture and planning. In particular, in his polemical text, *Buildings and Prospects* (1948), he explicitly saw problems with what he described as a new Modernist approach to the development of post-war planning. In his discussion of inland and seaside buildings the tensions between these philosophies are consequently illustrated:

> It is an inland ideal to attempt to make buildings "harmonize" with their surroundings – an inland attempt at superior sensibility . . . You cannot harmonize with the sea, when it is calm and blue one day and dark grey and dangerous the next. What you can do is make a virtue of not harmonizing. People think of the contrast among others when they say "I'm going to the sea for a change," or "for a breath of fresh air."[21]

In these small statements, then, it might be argued that Hastings's philosophy of nature and the organic began to take shape. For Piper, rather than a new philosophy of harmony as advocated by the new uniform aesthetics of development, the aesthetic of place must be seen through the notion of not harmonizing. While these initial ideas were unclear, it might be argued that Hastings's colleagues and predecessors in the *Architectural Review* sought to develop these narratives even further. The major figure in this work was Gordon Cullen whose regular features on townscape in the journal inspired a development of Hastings's original philosophy. Cullen called for the importance of recognizing an architectural aesthetic of individuality. The true calling of urban places was to avoid the uniformity and lack of idiosyncrasy provided by the new towns. In discussing the idea of individuality, Cullen can be found to emphasize the importance of juxta-position (and irregularity) as an opposition to the uniformity of the new town. Here the approach to townscape is one that recognizes the utter desolation of individuality by the Modern, which is said to reproduce the monotonous by the production of buildings that are congruous:

> If I were asked to define Townscape I would say that one building is architecture but two buildings is Townscape. For as soon as two buildings are juxtaposed the art of Townscape is released . . . But looking at the kind of towns and housing estates built by speculators or local authorities one is to conclude that this conception of the townscape has not been considered (to put it very mildly). We are still in the individual stage when the individual building is the be-all and end-all of planning. If buildings are the letters of the alphabet they are not used to make coherent words but to utter the desolate cries of AAAAA! Or OOOOOO![22]

As well as addressing the importance of juxtaposition, Cullen can also be found to encourage the importance of recognizing the real place of things. In his discussion of the townscape, he therefore calls upon the reader to acknowledge the importance of the rural as a "rule of thumb" for the urban landscape. In describing the "qualities" of the English village, Cullen suggests that, as opposed to many modern villages, the urban landscape does not fit well in relation to its surroundings. For Cullen, the future of cities and the well-being of citizens lie in acknowledging the natural differences that emerge in the places between the village and the countryside in the rural landscape. As opposed to the urban, the village fits into the wider landscape by its juxtaposition. Cullen therefore highlights the importance of recognizing a real or a natural order to the townscape, which comfortably fits into the wider landscape. Again, while Cullen does not offer an explicit philosophy, the attraction to an organic idea of the townscape is again evident:

> The unequivocal character of both [village and countryside] is brought sharply together; there is no fluffing. On the one side the wind soughs through the trees and on the other the hollow tread of boots resounds on a stone pavement. Hollow is an appropriate word. The town [on the other hand] turns in upon itself; it is enclosed and hollow in contrast to the exposure of nature . . .[23]

Cullen's discussion of the modern townscape recognizes the inadequacy of its relationship to the surrounding landscape. The expression of difference as represented in the "natural village" is therefore at the heart of a true sense of the landscape in which things are naturally different and juxtaposed to one another. In discussing the rural landscape paintings of Camille Corot (1796–1875), Cullen therefore stresses this point in arguing that it is only when we juxtapose the objects within "places" that these places become truly themselves:

> It is a matter of observation that in a successful contrast of colours not only do we experience the harmony released but also, equally the colours become more truly themselves. In a large landscape by Corot, I forget its name, a landscape of sombre greens almost monochrome, there is a small figure in red. It is probably the reddest thing I have ever seen.[24]

Rather than being an élite discourse, the *Architectural Review*'s reaction to Modernism was regarded as being "uniquely influential in the general British intelligentsia" and the development of further influences in practical architecture as a whole.[25]

At this point I turn to the work of Thomas Sharp, another advocate of the townscape approach. Cullen painted a particularly aesthetic appreciation of the townscape, but Sharp's attentions were more with the role of planning in the construction of urban place. It was clear that the aesthetic discourse of the "townscape" approach developed in the *Architectural Review* had a resounding effect on Sharp's attitudes to planning, as explained in *Oxford Replanned* (1948). While Cullen deals with the micro-aspects of the townscape aesthetic, Sharp wanted to place the individuality of buildings into the individuality of the town and city itself as a macro-actor. So Sharp argues that, as well as a philosophy of buildings, the individuality of buildings must be understood in relation to cities as a whole: "Oxford is Oxford; and despite anything that the old and the new industrial revolutions have been able to do, it has maintained its individuality more truly than any other city in England. That is why people feel more personally about Oxford than about Birmingham or Manchester, which also have universities."[26]

Sharp's links between the building, the townscape, and the town itself seem to be more explicitly worked out in his later texts. For example, in *Town and Townscape* (1968), Sharp's philosophy can be seen in the opening chapters, which are concerned with "unity in variety." In one aside, Sharp argues that what is important is to maintain the variety of "variousness" in towns since this ultimately adds up to the wider urban landscape of the nation:

That is the variety of contrast. And there is besides that, and more common than it, the variety in the buildings within the streets and the places themselves, variety that is not so much of contrast but variety within the same kind, variety within an established rhythm, variety (one almost might say) within similarity, within a broad unity of character.

It is that that is the quintessence of the physical generality of the older towns of England. Their character is established in variousness.[27]

The Narrative of Citizenship and a Visualization of a Broader National Landscape

Two other contributors to a discourse of individuality and idiosyncrasy in the urban landscape are Ian Nairn and Sir John Betjeman, contemporaries of Hastings and Cullen. They can be seen to produce a more explicit social philosophy of the relationship *between people and places*. Again, as with Hastings, Piper, Cullen, and Sharp, the development of this social philosophy is related to a rejection of Modernism, with recognition of an authentic distinctive landscape. However, rather than just the "natural" order of the physical landscape, Nairn and Betjeman stress the importance of recognizing the relationship between the English peoples and these landscapes. Thus, in a polemical issue of the *Architectural Review* "Outrage," Nairn can be found advocating the protection of "distinctive places" as important to the survival of a "distinctive English consciousness." Again, like Cullen, the force of this attack is against the mediocrity produced when the inspiring ideals of the Modern Movement were translated into real environments by less-than-inspired development processes. Nairn's name for this environment, "Subtopia," alludes to the degree to which the nondescript suburbs and new towns fell below the utopian ideal, and seemed to have no real identity: "Subtopia is an annihilation of the site, the steamrollering of all individuality of place to one uniform and mediocre pattern . . . But Subtopia has already gone so far that it is possible to present scenes that are indistinguishable, and to classify the causes which have made them look alike . . ."[28]

Furthermore, at the end of the "Outrage" issue, Nairn stresses the importance of recognizing the role of individuals in places by developing a strategic political plan for the everyday citizen. As well as the notion of individuality, the idea that people themselves have an individual relationship to their local place is also expressed in these sentiments felt in response to the urban landscape. Likewise, an emphasis on the notion of citizenship also replicates many of the ideas expressed by Brace, and a politics of the local was advocated, which was seen as essential to the recovery of the real evolutionary course of cities. Here, as with Brace's discussion of rhetorical reaction, the focus of Nairn's rhetoric is a resistance to the voice of the "planner" and a valorization of the relationship of individuals to "places":

> The first thing is to be able to see and feel. If you have come with us this far, you can; that is the premise we make in our call to arms.
> Then to know your local area inside out, whether it is a Surrey suburb, the middle of Swansea or the Yorkshire Wolds.
> Then to reach your decision on a change or a projected change. Your *own* decision, not ours; not blurred by sentiment or social or economic pressure. A matter that is between you and the site, without any pressure . . .
> In trying to keep intact the identity of your environment you will maintain your own as well.[29]

The work of Sir John Betjeman may also be said to reaffirm the nature of this social relationship between an observer and the landscape. In *First and Last Loves* (1952), Betjeman acknowledges the importance of the layman, and the need to encourage a local and an organic understanding of place. In trying to establish an anti-Modernist approach to the appreciation of the city, Betjeman argues that we "have ceased to use our eyes because we are so worried about money and illness. Beauty is invisible to us."[30] In opposition to the suburban *zeitgeist*, for Betjeman the spirit of urban landscaping can only be achieved if we lift our "eyes from the pavement to see the old windows and uneven roofs, or go so far down the beaten track as to wander down a side-alley and see the backs of houses and their neglected . . . [local] . . . craftsmanship."[31]

However, rather than just providing an appreciation of the local, Betjeman seems to supply a more conscious rendering of this approach to a wider spirit of community and national consciousness. Thus, while he condemns the average (Modernist-inspired) man as unpatriotic, Betjeman's discourse promotes the importance of recognizing the distinctiveness of urban peoples in their places. In this respect, the discussion of places and peoples seems to tie an entire philosophy of the urban landscape together. In the first respect, Betjeman suggests that, while urban landscapes are distinctive, this distinctiveness can be understood through the distinctiveness of the individuals who are composed by them. In his discussion of Leeds, Betjeman advances these connections through a textual poetics of place. He argues that, as well as being an intrinsically Victorian city, "secondly [Leeds] is parochial." Thus, Betjeman wishes to reify the naturalness of this physicality by a discussion of the peoples of Leeds as intrinsic "Yorkshire people," "loyal and parochial." Betjeman argues that, as well as being remarkable people, it is the essential "Victorianness," and the compact nature of the place, that allow Leeds people to have a shared consciousness.[32] However, it is clear later in this text that Betjeman does not wish to relay a theory of space; rather, it is the actual presence of physical places that determines the varying personalities of peoples. In discussing the varying chapel architectures of urban Britain, Betjeman argues that "the chapel architecture of the nineteenth century is not denominational but racial . . . the buildings are essentially local and vary with the districts."[33]

In relaying a theory of the urban landscape, Betjeman also appears to be constructing a national imaginary of Englishness where regional places are characterized by regional peoples. In resisting the advances of Modernism, Betjeman argues that the reader should be aware of the collapse of distinctive organic communities with the rise of suburbanization. In these discourses the loss of distinction is also about the loss of regional rivalries and a sense of the consciousness of people in districts. "Nationalised or not yet nationalised, the gradual suburbanisation of enterprise continues, the killing of local communities, the stamping out of local rivalries and the supplying of everything by lorry from industrial towns."[34]

Tied into a narrative of protest at the abhorrent standardization of the national railway service in the late 1940s is the sense that people are also tied to a national consciousness of the landscape. The rejection of Modernism is linked to what is seen to be the Englishman's understanding of the "true colors" of place, characterized by the building materials. Remembering the days when the railway service was in private ownership, Betjeman calls upon a common understanding of the "natural" colors of the various trains and their accompanying districts. The overlap between the physical, the social, and a wider discourse of the nation – and Englishness – is therefore complete in these textual poetics:

> Those colours by which we were wont to know the part of England we were in – red for Midland, brown for Great Western, grained Oak for East Anglia, green for Southern – have disappeared. For the convenience of suburbanites who like everything uniform and call it Administration, the trains are one of two colours.[35]

The Cultural Capital of Architectural Conservation and Symbolic Inversions

While the post-war architectural conservation movement might be seen to be steeped in a nostalgia for a regional Englishness, my argument is that this discourse must be viewed through the lens of a relational and symbolic class analysis. In this respect, and turning back to the architectural conservation movement's descriptions of "the individual landscape" and the importance of "citizenship and vision," I argue that the development of these notions from the post-war era shares a relationship to Pierre Bourdieu's analysis of social class. In particular, I argue that the notions of the individual landscape and the "citizen of vision" must be viewed in terms of Bourdieu's notion that actors compete with cultural and symbolic capital (signifiers of taste) to legitimate the dominance of their own power in social relations.[36] However, in turning back to the work of Brace and others on the development of rural conservation, I argue that a theory of cultural and symbolic capital must take in the possibility of the contradictory identity positions of power. In this respect, while I argue that the architectural conservation movement has used cultural and symbolic capitals to construct its own elite identities, the construction of these identities has been achieved through a contradictory power position. In short, I argue that while the architectural conservation movement has constructed itself as an elite, this elitism works within a tradition of non-elite, anti-professionalism. To direct a focus on Brace's work, I argue that this narrative can be understood through the metaphor of the "squirearchy" where identities are constructed through the idea that the elite is at one with the consciousness of the people.

Cultural and symbolic capital

The keys to Bourdieu's work on the notion of power (in a simplified overview) are his concepts of cultural and symbolic capital. "Cultural capital" is made up of knowledge and skills acquired in early socialization or education. The possession of cultural capital is therefore symbolized by formal educational qualifications. However, the notion of cultural capital refers to a whole host of activities and practices that might be considered as being symbolic of taste or the capacity of the actor to demonstrate taste. Bourdieu gives examples of cultural capital acquired through activities and practices such as going to the opera, listening to classical music, or having an interest in painting. "Symbolic capital" is the symbolic representation of cultural capital (and other forms of capital) to the extent that they become normalized and signal the status and authority of the user or definer of taste. In the words of Bourdieu, symbolic capital is "the form that the various species of capital assume when they are perceived and recognised as legitimate."[37]

Much of the discussion of the role of cultural and symbolic capital is developed in Bourdieu's critical research on social class in France. In *Distinction* (1984), rather than finding class traditionally based on economic, political, or ideological power, Bourdieu suggests that class distinctions may also be based on cultural and symbolic capital. In this way he argues that class boundaries are forged from cultural and symbolic goods, which have their own economy. Bourdieu finds that classes seek to reinforce their own boundaries by reifying the importance of their own *habitus* – their symbolic goods, their tastes, and life-styles. Therefore, as well as the limits of economy and social power, class reproduces itself according to cultural and socially transmitted ways of understanding. In this way culture and education can become as important as money and wealth in struggles for social dominance and power.

Theories of cultural and symbolic capital

The notion of cultural and symbolic capital has a range of applications. However, while Bourdieu's theory is useful, it links class back to a series of material relations which are built on the idea of an elite which is engaged in the processes of constructing both exhibitionistic and professional identities. Indeed, although such an approach accounts for traditional notions of power, new understandings of the construction of categories have emphasized the more self-reflexive processes that are involved in the construction of elite identities. Writers of various persuasions have pointed to the way in which categorical processes have been constructed through the idea of a backlash, where the populist perspective is seen to be more conscious of the processes of social oppression. However, rather than emancipation, the upshot of these new self-reflexive processes is a re-inscribing of power relations in such a way as to suggest that the elite perspective has now become oppressed.[38]

The construction of class identities might be read in a similar way. With the rise of loft living and the desire of upper-middle-class actors to adopt working-class symbols and new populist forms of sentiment, new structures of class power might operate from changing self-conscious positions. In particular, Savage et al. have documented one specific instance of this, which is related to new forms of middle-class individualism. Rather than rejecting working-class community, Savage has pointed to the way in which the new middle classes wish to encourage the idea of "working classness." However, as Savage argues, this is not an adoption of working-class culture, but an enactment of ideas of the working class with the intention of separating the middle-class actor from the culture in question. Working-class culture is constructed in this way in order to demonstrate a down-to-earth middle-class identity, which at the same time leads to the reproduction of its power to name and label, and therefore distance itself from working-class oppression.[39]

The Narrative of Townscape Individuality and Variousness

While a narrative of "variousness" has been connected to a wider regional Englishness, it might be argued that this discourse may be further understood through elite notions of taste. Indeed, while arguing for the importance of the organic, Hastings also suggests that this understanding of the landscape has become hidden in the present. The target of his criticisms is therefore the pre- and post-war town-planning movement with its eyes fixed firmly on the notion of community rather than aesthetics. Hastings argues that the obsession with modernizing has meant that the "organic" aesthetic has been lost and is now only available to "foreigners or historians" who have the capacity to view England as outsiders: "We think most town-planners are themselves puzzled and embarrassed by their lack of realistic vision, their inability to *reconcile visually* in the mind's eye what appear to be irreconcilable elements in any town plan: quaint bits, new bits, monuments, traffic, tall buildings, short buildings, flat blocks, individual cottages, etc., etc."[40]

These comments are a critical reflection on the more functional approach to architecture in the pre- and post-war development process, and the structuring of this text also serves to reflect on the capacity of the author to make social statements. Indeed, the positioning of town planners as visually unsophisticated is related to a populist narrative of English people being in tune with their surroundings. However, rather than advocating a nationalist sentiment of place alone, the object of these discourses is to construct Hastings as the "real" commentator on the art of "the people." The criticism of the "Modernist" therefore serves to elevate the status of Hastings as a "non-professional" authority who understands the hidden aesthetic of the people. Thus, Hastings argues that:

> There is nothing new, we are all aware, in what has been said. The fact remains that the approach natural to the English temperament has not yet been put to work on the urban scene. Any time he so desires the modern town-planner is free to pick up Picturesque theory at the point before its corruption by the Gothic revival; pick up the theory, rediscover the prophets, and apply the principles.[41]

Piper and Cullen entwine these notions in further narratives. Piper seeks to present the potency of individuality, and this narrative is combined with a resistance to a new aesthetic of functionality. In his chapter "Pleasing Decay," Piper therefore discusses an alternative to the Modernist aesthetic described through the idea of buildings which look "at one" with their natural surroundings. In the spirit of Hastings's notions of the picturesque, Piper therefore argues that the merits of new development must lie with an understanding of the hidden beauty of "English places." Again, the distinction between not-knowing and knowing is crucial to the construction of this narrative since Piper points to the hidden amenities – or artifacts and places of beauty – within a town which can become lost or forgotten in pure self-interest.[42] Here, as with an understanding of the English psyche, the "non-expertness" of the discourse is heightened by Piper's suggestion that he has the capacity to know what he is looking "for" in a place in a practical sense.

However, the distinction between the town planner as vandal and the author as "down to earth" or "messenger of the people" is also found in Cullen's work in the *Architectural Review*. The distinction between a functionalist aesthetic and the "non-professional" authority of the populist is emphasized by an almost "realist" approach to the aesthetic urban text. Here, while Cullen underlines the subjectivity of an artistic approach, the absence of the "I" in the text allows the author to employ a rhetorical device. In the early *Architectural Review* work, this is most explicitly expressed in the discussion of Subtopia, which is understood as a nowhere-place. In the statement that follows, Cullen's approach to Subtopia is therefore one of self-evident confidence where "I" becomes "we" and the author is leveled with the wider public. In fact, the use of "we" has an almost calming and understanding tone, which makes the narratives of the author feel more realistic. Moreover, as can be seen in the quotations that follow, the construction of social understandings of place are also made without any reference to an external view or views of the author. Indeed, as can be seen below, Cullen discusses the rise of what he sees as a cult of "ebbiness" or isolation, for which he provides little social evidence of its rise or future, and thus these whimsical references become sealed in the language of his populist and paternal "authority":

> One of the essential qualities of a town is that it is a gathering together of people and utilities for the generation of civic warmth . . . Where has it got to in the new towns? . . . We see no sign of it here. Instead we see the growth of a new ideal at work which might be described as ebbiness – the ebb tide: the cult of isolationism.[43]

In his later text, *Townscape* (1961), this view is elevated to a more philosophical level, where Cullen compares the town planner to an unimaginative scientist. Here, in these codes, the notion of the scientist is played off against an imaginary academic "other," who is therefore understood to be the popular artist, and the authenticity of Cullen's "non-professional" position as the aesthete is consequently reproduced. In opposition to the attempt to be scientific, it might be argued that Cullen's adoption of a popular and traditional stereotype of the un-aesthetic scientist simply serves to position Cullen as "knower." However, as well as rejecting a scientific approach to the urban townscape, the replacement of this approach with one based on feelings and subjectivity is constructed as more real. Cullen discusses the way in which humans communicate with each other on a first encounter, by making a comparison of the relationship between science and art. In this analogy, the scientist is viewed as a conformist, while the more relaxed tone of the later conversation is viewed as representing the heart of the aesthete:

> Let us approach by a simile. Let us suppose a party in a private house, where are gathered together half a dozen people who are strangers to each other. The early part of the evening is passed in polite conversation on general subjects such as the weather and the current news. Cigarettes are passed and lights offered punctiliously. In fact it is all an exhibition of manners, of how one ought to behave. It is also very boring. This is conformity. However, later on the ice begins to break and out of the straitjacket of orthodox manners and conformity *real human beings* begin to emerge.[44]

In this text the aesthete is constructed as "risky" and "radical" and more at "one" with "real human beings." The construction of Cullen's aesthetic status is also played through the idea of a radical or someone who is willing to break with conformity to pursue a hidden agenda. In these narratives and others like it, one might almost compare these discussions of a populist discourse of the people with an activist willing to speak for and reveal the hidden voice of "real human beings." This language also speaks to the idea that technical people are also far removed from the will and real power of people who are grounded in much more down-to-earth and practical knowledge. This view also points to an understanding of ordinary people as lacking abstraction and favoring a more real or everyday world, such as that outlined in Savage's discussion of the use of working-class motifs in the contemporary construction of the middle-class self.[45] Cullen argues that a real appreciation of the townscape must begin with our bracketing out what he describes as scientific and mathematical prejudice:

> Firstly we have to rid ourselves of the thought that the excitement and drama that we seek can be born automatically out of the scientific research and solutions arrived at by the technical man (or the technical half of the brain). We naturally accept these solutions, but are not entirely bound by them . . . statistics are abstracts: when they are plucked out of the completeness of life and converted into plans and the plans into buildings they will be lifeless.[46]

If the discourse of individuality and a regional Englishness is constructed through a realist and an English aesthetic, it might also be argued that the role of an impressionistic narrative has a part to play in the construction of this Englishness. Indeed, it might be argued that Thomas Sharp, while employing the realist strategies of Hastings, Piper, and Cullen, manages to enforce these textual tropes through a populist and "impressionistic style."[47] Here, then, it might be argued that, beyond the position of the "knower" of English life and the aesthete of the urban landscape, Sharp positions himself as a moral guardian of the landscape.

> It is through the architects and their clients that the influence of mere fashion has had, and is having, its effect . . . in tower-buildings that are wholly out of scale and character with the towns over which they exert tyranny. In these new buildings all previous acceptance of something like a collective discipline has been rejected. It has been rejected through an

architectural arrogance in which the general character of the town or street is considered of no importance compared with the intoxication of self-assertion and self-advertisement.[48]

It is this move in Sharp's work that sets up a new perception of the logic of individuality as a discussion of moral aesthetics. In the statement above, the speaker can be seen as the actor who has taken up arms against a hidden tyranny of architectural arrogance, on account of which the speaker deserves our respect. The construction of the town planner in this melodramatic language simply overlooks the constraints placed on the architect, and therefore Sharp can place himself as a moral authority. The impressionistic discursive binary of the tyrannous and the moral might therefore be further seen in the claims which follow, where, like a political leader at the point of war, the author can be viewed as the guardian of the "English character," nation, and "civilization":

And now that many architects themselves seem to have abandoned an interest in them [towns], these critical times for our towns, are likely, unless there is a rapid change of attitude, to mean the end of something in which we in England once showed a natural genius – the genius of creating towns that nearly always have had a whole character.

How a town looks is no less important than how it works; and if in making a town work we destroy its looks we destroy a large part of its intrinsic value to civilisation.[49]

Citizenship, Local Identity, and the Nation

While a narrative linking the citizen and the landscape has been connected to a wider regional Englishness, this discourse may be further understood through elite notions of taste. In the first place, Nairn's "Outrage" can be seen as a central component of this discourse. Although he focuses on an aspect of regional Englishness, like Sharp, Nairn creates an impressionistic vision of the future, through a trope of rhetorical authority. However, in Nairn's writings, the tyrannical figure of the town planner is developed into a wider language of the English self through a middle-class discourse. Nairn's witch-hunt is extended to what he sees as a growing consciousness in the everyday language of the English psyche. The target of Nairn's critique is the developing language of Subtopia, which has developed as a social disease:

But buildings affect people, and Subtopia produces Subtopians ... It's not just aesthetics and art-work: *Our whole existence as individuals is at stake*, just as much as it has ever been from political dictatorship whether left or right; in this case the attack is not clearly defined and coming from the other side of the globe, but a miasma rising from the heart of our collective self.[50]

This text produces a clear construction of a new form of identity which it sees as being related to the creation of a new "identityless" individual: a Subtopian. However, while one cannot ignore the critique of the built environment in this text, the idea that people have to change in order to have a sense of individuality reflects the author's elitism. A rhetorical trope of the landscape becomes converted into an attack on the lack of individuality of certain people, and therefore highlights the position of the author as an actor with the knowledge to understand which people have individuality.

Betjeman's work also develops these narratives. Betjeman has often been called "the poet of the suburbs, where most people now live, and had a deep sympathetic insight into the minds of suburbanites; he stands for the small, the local and the kindly, an ethos appealing to the English mentality."[51] However, in his valorization of suburban life, it would appear that Betjeman's critique was aimed at Edwardian suburban life, rather than the Subtopia that sprang from a low-grade Modernist vision. In *First and Last Loves* (1952), he describes an original pre-war suburban life where the landscape was "lovely ... with freckled tennis girls and youths in club blazers."[52] However, where Nairn taps into a new crass Modernism in the suburban mind, Betjeman takes this narrative further to suggest that the rise of development has produced a new kind of middle class – a new "common man." Here, in an extension of Nairn's critiques, Betjeman argues that:

We are told we live in the age of the common man. He would be better described as the suburban man ... He is not vulgar. He is not the common man but the average man, which is far worse.

He is our ruler and he rules by committees. He gives us what most people want, and he believes that what is popular is best ...

His indifference to the look of things is catching. We discover it in our attitude to the horrors with which the delicate variety of our landscape has been afflicted ... He is a crank. He is unpatriotic and is prepared to sell the country for an invisible asset.[53]

Having sketched a picture of the new suburbanite, Betjeman develops further the aesthetic problems that this new breed of urban dweller has "mindlessly" ignored. Indeed, as with Nairn's critique of the spread of Subtopia, Betjeman argues that this new class has allowed the rise of "Acres of unimaginative modern housing . . . of thick-necked brutes with flashy cars, elderly blondes and television sets – those modernistic, Egyptian, beaux-arts and other facades of the new factories outside every large town."[54]

These suggestions amount to a presentation of the suburbanite as a member of a new class of the "new rich." While Nairn's narratives are dressed in a concern for architecture, Betjeman's resistance to the "common man" is explicit and unashamedly elitist. As well as complaining about the problem of the urban landscape on the construction of Subtopia, Betjeman's target is the Subtopian, who, *en masse*, is presented as the cause of Subtopia. Betjeman takes further Nairn's impressionistic discourse, elevating his own moral righteousness and aesthetic tastes, by attacking not only a style but also a group of people. The daring with which this text moves from the physical to the social may be read as the powerful way in which Betjeman consolidates his populist status: moving an analysis of power from aesthetics to the social. An attack on the Subtopian environment, then, is not simply a protection of the nation's physical fabric; rather, it is an attack on a certain part of the population, which is critical in the protection of national identity. Betjeman's idea of Englishness is grounded in an aesthetic elitism of individuality, and he suggests that the populist appeal to the suburban common man should be placed against a "higher" scale of values: an understanding of the senses.[55]

Conclusion

The architectural conservation movement has sought to develop a regional discourse of Englishness since the post-war era through the notion of "townscape." The discussions of Hastings, Piper, Cullen, and Sharp of the character of an authentic urban landscape are crucial to the idea that authentic and "natural" urban landscapes are those that demonstrate a certain "variousness" of place. It is the notion of "variousness," reflected in Catherine Brace's discussion of a patchwork of "unique" landscapes, that has great resonance. In particular, Sharp's discussion of "variousness" in relation to the nation highlights the striking relationship between ideas of the townscape as a series of little packets and a wider regional English-ness found in Brace.

The townscape movement encouraged a certain rhetorical approach to the conception of the individual and place. Nairn and Betjeman's suggestion that individuals should be aware of their surroundings and their place in physical landscapes is a form of resistance to the suburban. Again, as with the notions of variousness and uniqueness, the call to citizenship has a parallel in Brace's discussion of "outlook geography" and the location of the individual in the regional landscape. In pointing to Betjeman's discussion of Leeds, it is suggested that he sought to extend a narrative of individual and place to the idea of regionality, as in Brace's notion of regional characteristics.

A regional Englishness cannot be understood without recourse to a discourse of social class, and architectural conservationists have constructed a regional Englishness with the intention of developing cultural and symbolic capital, but they do so by using a populist language of identity. Hastings, Cullen, and Sharp between them constructed an organic aesthetic of variousness, by presenting the author as non-technical, populist, and moral. Hastings and Cullen presented themselves as authorities by setting up a polarity between the abstract and the down to earth. In Sharp's work, a discourse of authority was further elaborated in the idea of the author as moral guardian of the people. In Nairn and Betjeman's work an organic aesthetic of citizenship and the geography of vision were translated through a construction of the author as a spokesperson of the people and a social activist. Nairn and Betjeman claimed authority for themselves, not only by rejecting the scientist, but also by rejecting the social spirit of the "common man." Their attack on the "common man" therefore constructs Nairn and Betjeman as figures who understand not just the aesthetics of the physical environment, but the entire social spirit and dislikes of the people. The specific focus on the common man extends beyond a mere critique of the physical landscape and serves to elevate the status of the writer.

It is in these figures that the implicit nostalgia for traditional class boundaries of upper and working class are revealed. The construction of a discourse of the Subtopian also has certain class overtones, making an appeal to a working-class "other" in order to reject a new populist middle class. If, however, these narratives are implicit, the writing of John Betjeman might be said to elaborate and enforce an understanding of these discourses in a more explicit manner. In his discussion of post-war suburbia,

Betjeman's narratives reflect a dislike of new development and the new rich, who have been seen to have set aside traditional notions of identity. However, given the sharp and elitist tones within which these narratives are constructed, it might be argued that Betjeman also serves to enforce a dislike of new forms of social identity, which have displaced traditional class boundaries. It is therefore the argument of this chapter that, in these small asides, the work of Nairn and Betjeman demonstrates a hidden narrative of the "organic" aesthetic as an agent of a new inverted class snobbery, which resides with the suggestions of Savage et al.[56] Furthermore, it is the reassertion of traditional class boundaries within their texts that might be read through Savage's idea to propose that the new middle-class elite has sought to position itself as belonging to the working class through an inverted populism.

Notes

1   Peter Hall, *Cities of Tomorrow* (Oxford: Blackwell, 1988); Denis Hardy, *From Garden Cities to New Towns* (London: Spon, 1991); David Matless, *Landscape and Englishness* (London: Reaktion, 1998); Standish Meacham, *Regaining Paradise: Englishness and the Early Garden-City Movement* (New Haven, CT: Yale University Press, 1999).

2   Robert Fishman, *Urban Utopias in the Twentieth Century: Ebenezer Howard, Frank Lloyd Wright, and Le Corbusier* (New York: Basic Books, 1977); Hall, *Cities of Tomorrow*; Meacham, *Regaining Paradise*.

3   Matless, *Landscape and Englishness*.

4   Raymond Williams, *The Country and the City* (New York: Oxford University Press, 1973); Franco Bianchini and Hermann Schwengel, "Re-imagining the City," in *Enterprise and Heritage: Crosscurrents of National Culture*, ed. John Corner and Sylvia Harvey (London: Routledge, 1991), pp. 212–36; Stephen Daniels, *Fields of Vision: Landscape Imagery and National Identity in England and the United States* (Cambridge: Polity Press, 1993).

5   Hardy, *Garden Cities*.

6   Richard Rogers and Anne Power, *Cities for a Small Country* (London: Faber, 2000). See also Fishman, *Urban Utopias*; Hall, *Cities of Tomorrow*; Hardy, *Garden Cities*.

7   Raphael Samuel "Introduction: Exciting to be English," in Raphael Samuel, *Patriotism: The Making and Unmaking of British Identity* (London: Routledge, 1988), pp. xviii–lxvii; Meacham, *Regaining Paradise*.

8   Rogers and Power, *Cities for a Small Country*.

9   Williams, *The Country and the City*; Daniels, *Fields of Vision*; Meacham, *Regaining Paradise*.

10 Matless, *Landscape and Englishness*, p. 205.

11 David Matless, "Definitions of England, 1928–89: Preservation, Modernism and the Nature of the Nation," *Built Environment*, 16 (3) (1990): 179–91.

12 Ibid., p. 189.

13 Ibid, p. 187, on Patrick Wright, *On Living in an Old Country* (London: Verso, 1985); Patrick Wright, "An Encroachment too Far," in *Town and Country*, ed. Anthony Barnett and Roger Scruton (London: Jonathan Cape. 1998), pp. 18–33.

14 Matless, *Landscape and Englishness*, p. 187.

15 C. Brace (on Burke) "Finding England Everywhere: Regional Identity and the Construction of National Identity, 1890–1940," *Ecumene*, 6 (11) (1999): 103.

16 Ibid., p. 104.

17 Ibid., p. 103.

18 Nan Ellin, *Postmodern Urbanism* (New York: Princeton Architectural Press, 1996).

19 Ian Baucom, *Out of Place: Englishness, Empire and the Locations of Identity* (Princeton, NJ: Princeton University Press, 1999), p. 175; see also J. M. Jacobs, *Edge of Empire: Postcolonialism and the City* (London: Routledge, 1996).

20 H. D. C. Hastings, "Exterior Furnishings or Sharawaggi: The Art of Making an Urban Landscape," *Architectural Review* (January 1944): 8.

21 John Piper, *Buildings and Prospects* (London: Architectural Press, 1948), p. 12.

22 Gordon Cullen, "Prairie Planning in the New Towns," *Architectural Review* (July 1953): 33.

23 Gordon Cullen, *Townscape* (London: The Architectural Press, 1961), p. 60.

24 Ibid., p. 14.

25 Hall, *Cities of Tomorrow*, p. 222; Ellin, *Postmodern Urbanism*.

26 Thomas Sharp, *Oxford Replanned* (London: John Murray, 1948), p. 13.

27 Thomas Sharp, *Town and Townscape* (London: John Murray, 1968), p. 13.

28 Again, the suggestion that the suburbs have no identity is based on the notion that they represent the blur between urban and rural and so they are not naturally occurring environments. Ian Nairn, "Outrage," *Architectural Review* (June 1955): 372.

29 Ibid., p. 452.

30 John Betjeman, *First and Last Loves* (London: John Murray, 1952), p. 2.

31 Ibid., p. 3.

32 Ibid., p. 35.

33 Ibid., p. 115.

34 Ibid., p. 4.

35 Ibid.

36   Pierre Bourdieu, *La Distinction: critique sociale du jugement* (Paris: Les Éditions de Minuit, 1979), trans. R. Nice, *Distinction: A Social Critique of the Judgement of Taste* (London: Routledge and Kegan Paul, 1984).

37   Pierre Bourdieu, "Social Space and Symbolic Power," *Sociological Theory*, 7 (1) (1989): 14–25, p. 17.

38   Anoop Nayak, "White English Ethnicities: Racism, Anti-racism and Student Perspectives," *Race, Ethnicity and Education*, 2 (2) (1999): 177–202.

39   Mike Savage, *Renewing Class Analysis* (Oxford: Blackwell, 2000); Mike Savage, Gaynor Bagnall, and Brian Longhurst, "Ordinary, Ambivalent and Defensive: Class Identities in the Northwest of England," *Sociology*, 35 (4) (2001): 875–92.

40   Hastings, "Exterior Furnishings," p. 3.

41   Ibid., p. 8.

42   Piper, *Buildings and Prospects*, p. 12.

43   Cullen, "Prairie Planning," p. 34.

44   Cullen, *Townscape*, p. 13 (emphasis added)

45   Savage, *Renewing Class Analysis*; Savage et al., "Ordinary, Ambivalent and Defensive."

46   Cullen, *Townscape*, pp. 10, 14.

47   John Van Maanen, *Tales of the Field: On Writing Ethnography* (Chicago, IL: University of Chicago Press, 1988).

48   Sharp, *Town and Townscape*, p. 3.

49   Ibid., p. 6.

50   Nairn, "Outrage," p. 372.

51   Douglas J. Porteous, *Environmental Aesthetics: Ideas, Politics and Planning* (London: Routledge, 1996), p. 153.

52   Betjeman, *First and Last Loves*, p. 1.

53   Ibid., pp. 1–2.

54   Ibid., p. 3.

55   Betjeman, *First and Last Loves*.

56   Savage, *Renewing Class Analysis*; Savage et al., "Ordinary, Ambivalent and Defensive."

Bibliography

Aalto, Alvar (1958) "Instead of an Article," *Arkkitehti-Arkitekten*, reprinted in Göran Schildt, *Alvar Aalto Sketches* (Cambridge, MA: MIT Press, 1985), p. 160.

Albert, R. S. (1980) "Family Positions and the Attainment of Eminence," *Gifted Child Quarterly*, 24: 87–95.

Albrecht, Donald (1986) *Designing Dreams: Modern Architecture in the Movies* (London: Thames and Hudson).

Ames, Kenneth (1978) "Meaning in Artifacts: Hall Furnishings in Victorian America," *Journal of Interdisciplinary History*, 9: 19–46.

Anon (1996) "Drop City: A Model Hippie Commune," *The Lay of the Land* (spring) (http://www.clui.org/clui_4_1/lotl/lotlsp96/drop.html).

Apollonio, Umbro (ed.) (1973) *Futurist Manifestos* (London: Thames and Hudson).

Arnold, Dana (ed.) (1998) *The Georgian Country House: Architecture, Landscape and Society* (Stroud, Gloucestershire: Sutton).

Bachelard, Gaston (1934) *Le nouvel ésprit scientifique* (Paris: Presses Universitaires de France, 1934), trans. A. Goldhammer, *The New Scientific Spirit* (Boston: Beacon Press, 1984).

— (1938) *Le psychanalyse du feu* (Paris: Gallimard), trans. A. C. M. Ross, *The Psychoanalysis of Fire* (London: Quartet, 1987).

— (1958) *La poetique de l'espace* (Paris: Presses Universitaires de France), trans. M. Jolas, *The Poetics of Space* (Boston: Beacon Press, 1969).

Balint, Michael (1968) *The Basic Fault: Therapeutic Aspects of Regression* (London: Tavistock).

Ballantyne, Andrew (1997) *Architecture, Landscape and Liberty* (Cambridge: Cambridge University Press).

— (ed.) (2002) *What is Architecture?* (London: Routledge).

Bamford, James (1982) *The Puzzle Palace: America's National Security Agency and its Special Relationship with Britain's GCHQ* (Harmondsworth: Penguin; repr. with new afterword, 1983).

Banham, Reyner (1960) *Theory and Design in the First Machine Age* (London: Architectural Press).

— (1966) *The New Brutalism* (London: Architectural Press).

— (1981) *Design by Choice*, ed. Penny Sparke (London: Academy Editions).

— (1984) *The Architecture of the Well-tempered Environment* (London: Architectural Press).

Barnett, Anthony and Scruton, Roger (eds) (1998) *Town and Country* (London: Jonathan Cape).

Bataille, Georges (1955) *Manet*, trans. Austryn Wainhouse and James Emmons, *Manet: Biographical and Critical Survey* (Lausanne: Skiva).

— (1967) *La Part maudite* (Paris: Les Éditions de Minuit); also *L'Histoire de l'érotisme* and *La Souveraineté* in Georges Bataille, *Oeuvres complètes* vol. 8 (Paris: Gallimard, 1976), trans. R. Hurley, *The Accursed Share, volumes 1, 2 and 3*, 2 vols (New York: Zone, 1988, 1991). Note: the English translation is published in two volumes; the title of volume 2 is *The Accursed Share, volumes 2 and 3*.

— (1970–88) *Oeuvres complètes*, 12 vols (Paris: Gallimard).

— (1985) *Visions of Excess: Selected Writings, 1927–1939*, trans., ed. and intro. Allan Stoekl (Minneapolis, MN: University of Minnesota Press).

— (1990) *Hegel, Death and Sacrifice*, trans. Jonathan Strauss, *Yale French Studies*, 78: 18.

— (1992) "Architecture," trans. Dominic Faccini, *October*, 60: 26.

Baucom, Ian (1999) *Out of Place: Englishness, Empire and the Locations of Identity* (Princeton, NJ: Princeton University Press).

Bergson, Henri (1907) *L'évolution creatrice* (Paris: Presses Universitaires de France), trans. A. Mitchell, *Creative Evolution* (London: Macmillan, 1911).

Berman, Marshall (1982) *All that is Solid Melts into Air* (New York: Simon and Schuster).

Betjeman, John (1952) *First and Last Loves* (London: John Murray).

Betsky, Aaron (1997) *Queer Space* (New York: William Morrow).

Bois, Yve-Alain and Krauss, Rosalind E. (1997) *Formless: A User's Guide* (New York: Zone).

Bookchin, Murray (1971) "Towards a Liberatory Technology," in *Post-scarcity Anarchism* (London: Wildwood House, 1974).

Bourdieu, Pierre (1979) *La Distinction: critique sociale du jugement* (Paris: Les Éditions de Minuit), trans. R. Nice, *Distinction: A Social Critique of the Judgement of Taste* (London: Routledge and Kegan Paul, 1984).

— (1989) "Social Space and Symbolic Power," *Sociological Theory*, 7 (1): 14–25.

Bowdoin, Birdaline (1913) "Children's Rooms," *Good Housekeeping* (April): 157–8.

Bowlby, J. (1960) "Grief and Mourning in Infancy and Early Childhood," *Psychoanalytical Study of the Child*, 15: 9–52.

Boyle, G. and Harper, P. (eds) (1976) *Radical Technology* (London: Wildwood House).

Brace, C. (1999) "Finding England Everywhere: Regional Identity and the Construction of National Identity, 1890–1940," *Ecumene*, 6 (11): 103.

Branden, Barbara (1986) *The Passion of Ayn Rand* (New York: Doubleday).

Brandom, Robert B. (ed.) (2000) *Rorty and his Critics* (Oxford: Blackwell).

Branzi, Andrea (1984) *The Hot House: Italian New Wave Design* (London: Thames and Hudson).

Brook, Chris (ed.) (1997) *K Foundation Burn a Million Quid* (London: Ellipsis).

Brooks, H. Allen (1972) *The Prairie School: Frank Lloyd Wright and his Midwest Contemporaries* (Toronto: University of Toronto Press).

Bruere, Martha Bensley (1914) "The House that Jill Built," *Good Housekeeping*, April: 509–13.

Bürger, Peter (1974) *Theorie der Avantgarde*, trans. M. Shaw, *Theory of the Avant-Garde* (Minneapolis, MN: University of Minnesota Press, 1984).

Burrows, W. (1987) *Deep Black: Space Espionage and National Security* (New York: Random House).

Butti, Ken and Perlin, John (1980) *A Golden Thread* (New York: Van Nostrand Reinhold).

Campbell, Duncan (1984) *The Unsinkable Aircraft Carrier: American Military Power in Britain* (London: Michael Joseph).

— (1988) "They've Got it Taped," *New Statesman* (August, 12): 10–12.

— (1999) *Development of Surveillance Technology and Risk of Abuse of Economic Information* (An Appraisal of Technologies of Political Control), vol. 2/5. Directorate General for Research, Directorate A, The STOA Programme (Luxembourg: European Parliament).

— and Melvern, Linda (1980) "America's Big Ear on Europe," *New Statesman* (July, 18): 10–14.

Carpelan, Bo (1987) *Room Without Walls* (London: Forest Books).

Carson, Rachel (1962) *Silent Spring* (Harmondsworth: Penguin).

Casanova, Maria (ed.) (1993) *Gordon Matta-Clark* (Valencia: IVAM Centro Julio Gonzàlez).

Childs, John (1998) *The Military Use of Land: A History of the Defence Estate* (Bern: Peter Lang).

Clark, E. (ed.) (1998) *Sibelius: The Forest's Mighty God* (London: Sibelius Society).

Clarke, David B. (ed.) (1997) *The Cinematic City* (New York: Routledge).

Cleveland, Rose (1888) "Introduction," *The Social Mirror: A Complete Treatise of the Laws, Rules, and Usages that Govern our Most Refined Homes and Social Circles* (St Louis, MO: L. W. Dickerson).

Coates, Nigel (1983) "Narrative Break-up," *The Discourse of Events* (London: Architectural Association).

Cobb, Edith (1993) *The Ecology of Imagination in Childhood* (Dallas: Spring).

Colomina, Beatriz and Ockman, Joan (eds) (1988) *Architectureproduction: Revisions* no. 2 (New York: Princeton Architectural Press).

Commoner, Barry (1972) *The Closing Circle: Nature, Man and Technology* (New York: Alfred A. Knopf).

Corner, John and Harvey, Sylvia (eds) (1991) *Enterprise and Heritage: Crosscurrents of National Culture* (London: Routledge).

Cosgrove, Denis (1985) *Social Formation and Symbolic Landscape* (Totowa, NJ: Barnes and Noble).

— and Daniels, Stephen (eds) (1988) *The Iconography of Landscape* (Cambridge: Cambridge University Press).

Cram, Ralph A. (1885) "The Decoration of City Houses: Second Part – The Entrance Hall," *The Decorator and Furnisher*, 7 (December): 90.

— (1886) "The Decoration of City Houses: Part Three – The Dining Room," *The Decorator and Furnisher*, 7 (February): 150.

Crinson, Mark and Lubbock, Jules (1994) *Architecture, Art or Profession? Three Hundred Years of Architectural Education in Britain* (Manchester: Manchester University Press).

Cromley, Elizabeth (1990) *Alone Together: New York's Early Apartments* (Ithaca, NY: Cornell University Press).

Cullen, Gordon (1953) "Prairie Planning in the New Towns," *Architectural Review* (July): 33.

— (1961) *Townscape* (London: Architectural Press).

Daniels, Stephen (1993) *Fields of Vision: Landscape Imagery and National Identity in England and the United States* (Cambridge: Polity Press).

Den Uyl, Douglas J. and Rasmussen, Douglas B. (eds) (1984) *The Philosophic Thought of Ayn Rand* (Urbana, IL: University of Illinois Press).

Derrida, Jacques and Thévenin, Paule (1998) *The Secret Art of Antonin Artaud*, trans. Mary Ann Caws (Cambridge, MA: MIT Press).

Dessauce, Marc (ed.) (1999) *The Inflatable Moment: Pneumatics and Protest in '68* (New York: Princeton Architectural Press).

Dickson, David (1974) *Alternative Technology and the Politics of Technical Change* (Glasgow: Fontana/Collins).

Dickstein, Morris (ed.) (1998) *The Revival of Pragmatism: New Essays on Social Thought, Law, and Culture* (Durham, NC: Duke University Press).

Didi-Huberman, Georges (1994) "Pensée par image, pensée dialectique, pensée altérante: L'enfance de l'art selon Georges Bataille," *Les Cahiers du Musée Nationale d'Art Moderne* (Winter): 4–29.

Dodds, Klaus (1998) "Enframing the Falklands: Identity, Landscape, and the 1982 South Atlantic War," *Environment and Planning D: Society and Space*, 16: 733–56.

Dostoevsky, Fyodor (1864) *Notes from Underground*, trans. J. Coulson (Harmondsworth: Penguin, 1964).

Duke, Simon (1987) *US Defence Bases in the United Kingdom: A Matter for Joint Decision?* (London: Macmillan).

Dunham-Jones, Ellen (1998) "The Generation of '68 – Today: Bernard Tschumi, Rem Koolhaas and the Institutionalization of Critique," *Proceedings of the 86th ACSA Annual Meeting and Technology Conference* (New York: Association of Collegiate Schools of Architecture), pp. 527–33.

Eastlake, Charles (1869) *Hints on Household Taste in Furniture, Upholstery and Other Details* (London: Longmans, Green).

Ehrenzweig, Anton (1967) *The Hidden Order of Art* (London: Weidenfeld and Nicolson).

Eisenstadt, J. M. (1978) "Parental Loss and Genius," *American Psychologist*, 33: 211–23.

Ellin, Nan (1996) *Postmodern Urbanism* (New York: Princeton Architectural Press).

Eriksen, E. (1964) *Insight and Responsibility* (New York: Norton).

Evans, Robin (1982) *The Fabrication of Virtue* (Cambridge: Cambridge University Press).

Farmer, Ben and Louw, Hentie (1993) *The Routledge Companion to Architectural Thought* (London: Routledge).

Fenichel, Otto (1947) *The Psychoanalytical Theory of Neurosis* (London: Routledge and Kegan Paul).

Fisher, C., Paul, C., and Paul, I. H. (1959) "The Effects of Subliminal Visual Stimulation etc.," *Journal of American Psychoanalytical* Assignments, 7: 38–54.

Fishman, Robert (1977) *Urban Utopias in the Twentieth Century: Ebenezer Howard, Frank Lloyd Wright, and Le Corbusier* (New York: Basic Books).

Foucault, Michel (1975) *Surveiller et punir: naissance de la prison* (Paris: Gallimard), trans. A. Sheridan, *Discipline and Punish: The Birth of the Prison* (New York: Vintage, 1977).

— (1980) *Power/Knowledge: Selected Interviews and Other Writings, 1972–77*, ed. Colin Gordon (New York: Pantheon).

Freud, Sigmund (1953–74) *The Standard Edition of the Complete Psychological Works of Sigmund Freud*, ed. James Strachey, 24 vols (London: Hogarth Press), reprinted in paperback with minor changes as *The Pelican Freud Library*, and subsequently as *The Penguin Freud Library* (Harmondsworth: Penguin).

Friedman, Alice (1998) *Women and the Making of the Modern House* (New York: Harry Abrams).

Fuller, Richard Buckminster (1970) *The Buckminster Fuller Reader*, ed. J. Meller (London: Jonathan Cape).

Geertz, Clifford (1973) *The Interpretation of Cultures* (London: Hutchinson).

Gerson, J. and Birchard, B. (eds) (1991) *The Sun Never Sets: Confronting the Network of Foreign US Military Bases* (Boston, MA: South End Press/American Friends Service Committee).

Giedion, Sigfried (1941) *Space, Time and Architecture: The Growth of a New Tradition* (Cambridge, MA: Harvard University Press; 4th edn, 1963, 5th edn, 1967).

Gill, Peter (1994) *Policing Politics: Security Intelligence Agencies and the Liberal Democratic State* (London: Frank Cass).

Gold, John R. (1997) *The Experience of Modernism: Modern Architects and the Future City, 1928–1953* (London: Spon)

Goodwin, F. K. and Jamison, K. R. (1990) *Manic-depressive Illness* (Oxford: Oxford University Press).

Gowan, James (ed.) (1975) *A Continuing Experiment: Learning and Teaching at the Architectural Association* (London: Architectural Press).

Grogan, Bradley (1999) "Curb Appeal," *Urban Land*, 58 (March): 70–83.

Gropius, Walter (1935) *The New Architecture and the Bauhaus*, trans. P. M. Shand (London: Faber and Faber; paperback edn, Cambridge, MA: MIT Press, 1965).

Grover, Kathryn (ed.) *Dining in America* (Amherst, MA: University of Massachusetts Press).

Gruffudd, Pyrs (1990) *Reach for the Sky: The Air and English Cultural Nationalism*. Department of Geography Working Paper no. 7, University of Nottingham.

Hall, Peter (1988) *Cities of Tomorrow* (Oxford: Blackwell).

Hardy, Denis (1991) *From Garden Cities to New Towns* (London: Spon).

Hart, Clive and Stevenson, Kay Gilliland (1995) *Heaven and the Flesh: Imagery of Desire from the Renaissance to the Rococo* (Cambridge: Cambridge University Press).

Hastings, H. D. C. (1944) "Exterior Furnishings or Sharawaggi: The Art of Making an Urban Landscape," *Architectural Review* (January): 8.

Hays, K. Michael (ed.) (1998a) *Architecture Theory since 1968* (Cambridge, MA: MIT Press).

— (ed.) (1998b) *Oppositions Reader* (New York: Princeton Architectural Press).

Heffernan, M. (1995) "For Ever England: The Western Front and the Politics of Remembrance in Britain," *Ecumene*, 2: 293–323.

Heidegger, Martin (1971) *Poetry, Language, Thought*, ed. and trans. A. Hofstadter (New York: Harper and Row).

Herrick, Christine Terhune (1911) "First Principles, a Department for Young Housekeepers," *Woman's Home Companion* (March): 47.

Hollier, Denis (1997) *Absent without Leave: French Literature under the Threat of War*, trans. Catherine Porter (Cambridge, MA: Harvard University Press).

Hudson, K. (1978) *Food, Clothes and Shelter* (London: John Baker).

Hughes, Jonathan and Sadler, Simon (eds) (2000) *Non-plan: Essays on Freedom, Participation and Change in Modern Architecture and Urbanism* (Oxford: Architectural Press).

Hugo, Victor (1862) *Les misérables*, trans. N. Denny, *Les Misérables* (Harmondsworth: Penguin, 1982).

Husserl, Edmund (1954) *Die Krisis der europäischen Wissenschaften und die transzendentale Phänomenologie: Eine Einleitung in die phänomenologische*

Philosophie, trans. D. Carr, *The Crisis of European Sciences and Transcendental Phenomenology* (Evanston, IL: Northwestern University Press, 1970).

Illingworth, R. S. (1969) *Lessons from Childhood* (London: Livingstone).

Jacobs, J. M. (1996) *Edge of Empire: Postcolonialism and the City* (London: Routledge).

Janis, I. L. (ed.) (1969) *Personality: Dynamics, Development and Assessment* (New York: Harcourt, Brace and World).

Johnson, Byron A. (1978) "Probate Inventory: A Guide to Nineteenth-century Material Culture," *Curator*, 21 (3) (September): 188–90.

Jones, S. R. (1936) *English Village Homes* (London: Batsford).

Kärkkäinen, M. (ed.) (1992) *Functionalism: Utopia or the Way Forward. Proceedings of the 5th International Alvar Aalto Symposium* (Jyväskylä: Alvar Aalto Symposium Committee).

Kernberg, O. F. (1974) "Further Contributions to the Narcissistic Personalities," *International Journal of Psychoanalysis*, 18: 51–2.

Kirschner, Suzanne R. (1996) *The Religious and Romantic Origins of Psychoanalysis: Individuation and Integration in Post-Freudian Theory* (Cambridge: Cambridge University Press).

Knorr-Cetina, K. and Cicourel, A. V. (eds) (1981) *Advances in Social Theory and Methodology* (London: Routledge and Kegan Paul).

Koolhaas, Rem (1978) *Delirious New York* (London: Thames and Hudson).

Kostka, Alexandre, Wohlfarth, Irving, and Buddensieg, Tilmann (1999) *Nietzsche and "An Architecture of our Minds"* (Los Angeles: Getty Research Institute).

Lahti, L. (2001) *Alvar Aalto: Ex Intimo* (Helsinki: Rakennustieto).

Laing, R. D. (1969) *The Divided Self* (Harmondsworth: Penguin).

Lakey, Charles D. (1875) *Lakey's Village and Country Houses* (New York: American Builder).

Langer, Suzanne K. (1942) *Philosophy in a New Key: A Study in the Symbolism of Reason, Rite and Art* (reprinted Cambridge, MA: Harvard University Press, 1993).

Latour, Bruno (1999) *Pandora's Hope: Essays in the Reality of Science Studies* (Cambridge, MA: Harvard University Press).

Le Corbusier (1923) *Vers une architecture* (Paris: Crès), trans. F. Etchells, *Towards a New Architecture* (London: Architectural Press, 1987).

Lee, Pamela (2000) *Object to be Destroyed: The Work of Gordon Matta-Clark* (Cambridge, MA: MIT Press).

Lefebvre, Henri (1991) *La Production de l'espace* (Paris), trans. D. Nicholson-Smith, *The Production of Space* (Oxford: Blackwell).

— (1996) *Writings on Cities*, ed. and trans. Eleonore Kofman and Elizabeth Lebas (Oxford: Blackwell).

Levas, S. (1972) *Jean Sibelius: A Personal Portrait* (Helsinki: WSOY).

Ley, D. (1983) *A Social Geography of the City* (New York: Harper and Row).

Lorand, Ruth (ed.) (2002) *Television: Aesthetic Reflections* (New York: Peter Lang).

McEwan, Indra K. (1992) *Socrates Ancestor* (Cambridge, MA: MIT Press).

Marinetti, F. T. (1909) "The Founding and Manifesto of Futurism," trans. R. W. Flint, in *Marinetti: Selected Writings* (New York: Farrar, Strauss and Giroux, 1971).

Maroni, M., Morawska, L., and Bofinger, N. (eds) (1995) *Indoor Air: An Integrated Approach* (Oxford: Elsevier Science).

Massey, Doreen (1994) *Space, Place and Gender* (Cambridge: Polity Press).

Matless, David (1990) "Definitions of England, 1928–89: Preservation, Modernism and the Nature of the Nation," *Built Environment*, 16 (3): 179–91.

— (1998) *Landscape and Englishness* (London: Reaktion Books).

May, Rollo (1976) *The Courage to Create* (London: Collins).

Meacham, Standish (1999) *Regaining Paradise: Englishness and the Early Garden-City Movement* (New Haven, CT: Yale University Press).

Meadows, Donella H., et al. (1972) *Limits to Growth* (London: Earth Island).

Menin, Sarah (2001) "Relating the Past: The Creativity of Sibelius and Aalto," *Ptah: Alvar Aalto Foundation Journal of Architecture Design and Art*, 1: 32–44.

Milbank, John (1996) "Stories of Sacrifice," *Modern Theology*, 12: 27–56.

Miller, Alice (1989) *The Drama of Being a Child: The Search for the True Self* (London: Virago).

Miller, T. (n.d.) "Roots of the Communal Revival, 1962–1966," *The Farm* website (http://www.thefarm.org/lifestyle/root1/html).

Milner, M. (1950) *On Not Being Able to Paint* (London: Heinemann Educational).

Morris, M. (1997) "Gardens 'For Ever England': Landscape, Identity and the First World War Cemeteries on the Western Front," *Ecumene*, 4: 410–34.

Mumford, Eric (2000) *The CIAM Discourse on Urbanism, 1928–1960* (Cambridge, MA: MIT Press).

Muthesius, Hermann (1904) *The English House*, trans. J. Seligman (London: Lockwood Staples, 1979).

Nairn, Ian (1955) "Outrage," *Architectural Review* (June): 372.

Nayak, Anoop (1999) "White English Ethnicities: Racism, Anti-racism and Student Perspectives," *Race, Ethnicity and Education*, 2 (2): 177–202.

Nesbitt, Kate (ed.) (1996) *Theorizing a New Agenda for Architecture: An Anthology of Architectural Theory, 1965–1995* (New York: Princeton Architectural Press).

Neuman, Dietrich (ed.) (1996) *Film Architecture: Set Designs from Metropolis to Blade Runner* (Munich and New York: Prestel).

Nietzsche, Friedrich (1878) *Menschliches Allzumenschliches*, trans. R. J. Hollingdale, *Human All Too Human* (Cambridge: Cambridge University Press, 1986).

— (1882) *Die fröliche Wissenschaft*, trans. W. Kaufmann, *The Gay Science* (New York: Vintage, 1974).

— (1889) *Götzen-Dämmerung*, trans. R. J. Hollingdale, *Twilight of the Idols* (Harmondsworth: Penguin, 1968).

Nixon Hopkins, Una, "The House of Efficiency," *Good Housekeeping* (April 1914): 513.

Noever, Peter (ed.) (1993) *The End of Architecture? Documents and Manifestos* (Munich: Prestel).

Ochse, R. E. (1990) *Before the Gates of Excellence: The Determinants of Creative Genius* (Cambridge: Cambridge University Press).

Ockman, Joan, and Eigen, Edward (eds) (1993) *Architecture Culture 1943–1968: A Documentary Anthology* (New York: Columbia Books of Architecture/Rizzoli).

O'Hare, David (1981) *Psychology and the Arts* (Sussex: Harvester).

Oliver, Paul (ed.) (1976a) *Shelter in Africa* (London: Barrie and Jenkins).

— (ed.) (1976b) *Shelter and Society* (London: Barrie and Jenkins).

Pawley, Martin (1975) *Garbage Housing* (London: Architectural Press).

— (1990) *Theory and Design in the Second Machine Age* (Oxford: Blackwell).

— and Tschumi, Bernard (1971) "The Beaux-Arts since '68," *Architectural Design* (September): 553–66.

Pearson, David (1994) *Earth to Spirit* (London: Gaia Books).

Perrett, Antoinette Rehmann (1911) "Model Bedrooms," *Good Housekeeping* (June): 728–32.

Pevsner, Nikolaus (1936) *Pioneers of the Modern Movement* (London: Faber and Faber).

Phillips, Adam (1988) *Winnicott* (London: Fontana).

Pierpont, Claudia Roth (1995) "Twilight of the Goddess," *The New Yorker* (24 July): 70–81.

Piper, John (1948) *Buildings and Prospects* (London: Architectural Press).

Popper, Karl (1957) *The Poverty of Historicism* (London: Routledge and Kegan Paul).

Porteous, Douglas J. (1996) *Environmental Aesthetics: Ideas, Politics and Planning* (London: Routledge).

Prizeman, John (1975) *Your House: The Outside View* (London: Hutchinson).

Pugin, Augustus W. N. (1836) *Contrasts: or, A Parallel Between the Noble Edifices of the Middle Ages and Corresponding Buildings of the Present Day* (London).

— (1841) *The True Principles of Christian or Pointed Architecture* (London).

Rand, Ayn (1936) *We the Living* (New York: Macmillan).

— (1943) *The Fountainhead* (New York: Bobbs-Merrill).

— (1957) *Atlas Shrugged* (New York: Random House).

— (1964) *The Virtue of Selfishness: A New Concept of Egoism* (New York: New American Library).

Reber, A. S., (1985) *Dictionary of Psychology* (Harmondsworth: Penguin).

Richards, J. M. (1980) *Memoirs of an Unjust Fella* (London: Weidenfeld and Nicolson).

Richelson, Jeffrey (1999a) *America's Space Sentinels: DSP Satellites and National Security* (Kansas: University Press of Kansas).

— (1999b) *The US Intelligence Community*, 4th edn (Boulder, CO: Westview Press).

— and Ball, Desmond (1985) *The Ties that Bind: Intelligence Cooperation between the UKUSA Countries* (London: Allen and Unwin).

Robbins, David (ed.) (1990) *The Independent Group: Postwar Britain and the Aesthetics of Plenty* (Cambridge, MA: MIT Press).

Robertson, James (1958) *Young Children in Hospital* (London: Tavistock).

Rogers, Richard and Power, Anne (2000) *Cities for a Small Country* (London: Faber).

Rorty, Richard (1980) *Philosophy and the Mirror of Nature* (Oxford: Blackwell).

— (1989) *Contingency, Irony, and Solidarity* (Cambridge: Cambridge University Press).

Ruskin, John (1903–12) *The Works of John Ruskin*, ed. E. T. Cook and A. Wedderburn, 39 vols (London: George Allen).

Rykwert, Joseph (1996) *The Dancing Column* (Cambridge, MA: MIT Press).

Sack, Robert D. (1986) *Human Territoriality: Its Theory and History* (Cambridge: Cambridge University Press).

Sadler, Simon (1998) *The Situationist City* (Cambridge, MA: MIT Press).

Saint, Andrew (1983) *The Image of the Architect* (New Haven, CT: Yale University Press).

Salmon, Frank (2000) *Building on Ruins* (London: Ashgate).

Samuel, Raphael (1988) *Patriotism: The Making and Unmaking of British Identity* (London: Routledge).

Sanders, Joel (ed.) (1996) *Stud: Architectures of Masculinity* (New York: Princeton Architectural Press).

Sanders, William S. (ed.) (1996) *Reflections on Architectural Practices in the Nineties* (New York: Princeton Architectural Press).

Savage, Mike (2000) *Renewing Class Analysis* (Oxford: Blackwell).

—, Bagnall, Gaynor, and Longhurst, Brian (2001) "Ordinary, Ambivalent and Defensive: Class Identities in the Northwest of England," *Sociology*, 35 (4) (2001): 875–92.

Schildt, Göran (1984) *Alvar Aalto: The Early Years* (London: Rizzoli).

— (1985) *Alvar Aalto Sketches* (Cambridge, MA: MIT Press).

— (1986) *Alvar Aalto: The Decisive Years* (New York: Rizzoli).

— (1991) *Alvar Aalto: The Mature Years* (New York: Rizzoli).

— (1995) *Lånade vingar: Ungdomsminnen* (Helsinki: Söderström).

— (1998) *Alvar Aalto: In his own Words* (New York: Rizzoli).

Sclare, Donald (1980) *Beaux Arts Estates: The Architecture of Long Island* (New York: Viking).

Scully, Vincent J. (1955) *The Shingle Style, Architectural Theory and Design from Richardson to the Origins of Wright* (New Haven, CT: Yale University Press).

Serres, Michel (1987) *Statues: Le second livre des fondations* (Paris: Bourin).

Seymour, E. L. D. (1916) "Inexpensive House for Farmer or Tenant," *Country Life in America* (October): 78–9.

Sharp, Thomas (1948) *Oxford Replanned* (London: John Murray).

— (1968) *Town and Townscape* (London: John Murray).

Shelley, Percy Bysshe (1821) "A Defence of Poetry," in *Shelley: Selected Poetry and Prose*, ed. Alasdair D. F. Macrae (London: Routledge, 1991): 204–33.

Simon, Roger (1991) *Gramsci's Political Thought: An Introduction*, rev. edn (London: Lawrence and Wishart).

Smith, Oliver P. (1854) *The Domestic Architect* (Buffalo, NY; facsimile edn Watkins Glen, NY: The American Life Foundation, 1978).

Somol, R. E. (ed.) (1997) *Autonomy and Ideology: Positioning and Avant-garde in America* (New York: Monacelli Press).

Soltow, Lee (1993) "Wealth and Income Distribution," in *Encyclopedia of American Social History*, ed. Mary Kupiec Cayton, Elliott J. Gorn, and Peter W. Williams, vol. 2 (New York: Charles Scribner's Sons).

Steadman, Philip (1975) *Energy, Environment and Building* (Cambridge: Cambridge University Press).

Storr, Anthony (1988) *The School of Genius* (London: Andre Deutsch).

— (1991) *The Dynamics of Creation* (Harmondsworth: Penguin).

Sullivan, Louis (1947) *Kindergarten Chats and Other Writings*, ed. Isabella Athey (New York: Wittenborn, Schulz).

Sutherland, John (2002) "Can You See the Precog Turning?: Spielberg, Philip K. Dick and the Commodification of Paranoia," *The Times Literary Supplement* (July 12): 8–19.

Tarasti, E. (1991) "Signs of Anxiety or the Problem of the Semiotic Subject," *Acta Semiotica Fennica*, 2: 51–7.

Tawaststjerna, Erik (1997) *Sibelius, vol. 3, 1914–1957* (London: Faber and Faber).

Taylor, Richard and Christie, Ian (eds) (1988) *The Film Factory: Russian and Soviet Cinema in Documents 1896–1939* (London: Routledge and Kegan Paul).

Thackeray, William Makepeace (1899) "May Gambols; or, Titmarsh on the Picture Galleries," in *Ballads and Miscellanies* (London: Smith Elder).

Thayer, Richard (1994) *Gray World, Green Heart: Technology, Nature and Sustainability in the Landscape* (New York: John Wiley).

Thorburn, John M. (1925) *Art and the Unconscious* (London: K. Paul, Trench, Trubner and Co.).

Tiles, Mary (1984) *Bachelard: Science and Objectivity* (Cambridge: Cambridge University Press).

Tivers, Jacqueline (1999) "'The Home of the British Army': The Iconic Construction of Military Defence Landscapes," *Landscape Research*, 24 (3): 303–19.

Trollope, Anthony (1855) *The Warden* (London).

Tschumi, Bernard (1994) *Architecture and Disjunction* (Cambridge, MA: MIT Press).

— (1997) *Architecture in/of Motion* (Rotterdam: NAi Publishers).

Tuan, Yi-Fu (1979) *Landscapes of Fear* (New York: Pantheon).

Upton, Dell and Vlach, John Michael (eds) (1986) *Common Places* (Athens, GA: University of Georgia Press).

Vale, Lawrence (2000) *From the Puritans to the Projects: Public Housing and Public Neighbors* (Cambridge, MA: Harvard University Press).

Van Maanen, John (1988) *Tales of the Field: On Writing Ethnography* (Chicago: University of Chicago Press).

Veblen, Thorstein (1899) *The Theory of the Leisure Class* (New York: Dover, 1994).

Venturi, Robert (1966) *Complexity and Contradiction in Architecture* (New York: Museum of Modern Art).

—, Scott Brown, Denise, and Izenour, Steven (1977) *Learning from Las Vegas* (Cambridge, MA: MIT Press).

Vernon, Magdalen D. (1962) *The Psychology of Perception* (Harmondsworth: Penguin).

Vitruvius (1914) *The Ten Books on Architecture*, trans. M. H. Morgan (reprinted New York: Dover).

Walker, John A. (1993) *Art and Artists on Screen* (Manchester: Manchester University Press).

Watkin, David (1977) *Morality and Architecture* (Oxford: Oxford University Press); 2nd edn: *Morality and Architecture Revisited* (London: John Murray, 2001).

Weisberg, Robert W. (1993) *Creativity: Beyond the Myth of Genius* (New York: W. H. Freeman).

Welter, Volker M. (2002) *Biopolis: Patrick Geddes and the City of Life* (Cambridge, MA: MIT Press).

Wentworth, Ann (1911) "Modern Bedsteads," *House Beautiful* (November).

Whyte, Iain Boyd (1985) *The Crystal Chain Letters* (Cambridge, MA: MIT Press).

Williams, Raymond (1973) *The Country and the City* (New York: Oxford University Press).

Wilson, Colin St John (1995) *The Other Tradition of Modern Architecture: The Uncompleted Project* (London: Academy Editions).

Winnicott, D. W. (1948) "Fear of Breakdown," reprinted as *International Review of Psycho-Analysis*, 1 (1973).

— (1958) *Collected Papers: Through Paediatrics to Psycho-analysis* (London: Tavistock).

— (1963) "Psychoanalytical Studies of the Personality," *International Journal of Psycho-Analysis*, 34: 43.

— (1964) *The Child, the Family and the Outside World* (Harmondsworth: Penguin).

— (1965) *Maturational Processes and the Facilitating Environment* (London: The Hogarth Press/The Institute of Psycho-Analysis).

— (1971) *Playing and Reality* (Harmondsworth: Penguin).

— (1987) *Home is Where We Start From: Essays by a Psychoanalyst* (Harmondsworth: Penguin).

Woodfield, Richard (ed.) (2001) *Framing Formalism: Riegl's Work* (New York: Gordon and Breach).

Woodward, Rachel (1998) "'It's a Man's Life!': Soldiers, Masculinity and the Countryside," *Gender, Place and Culture*, 5 (3): 277–300.

Wright, Patrick (1985) *On Living in an Old Country* (London: Verso).

— (1996) *The Village that Died for England: The Strange Story of Tyneham* (London: Vintage).

Wright, Steve (1998) *An Appraisal of the Technologies of Political Control: Interim STOA Report* (PE 166.499), Directorate General for Research, Directorate A, The STOA Programme (Luxembourg: European Parliament).

Youngblood, Denise J. (1985) *Soviet Cinema in the Silent Era, 1918–1935* (Ann Arbor, MI: UMI Research Press).

— (1992) *Movies for the Masses: Popular Cinema and Soviet Society in the 1920s* (Cambridge: Cambridge University Press).

Index

Page numbers in *italic* refer to illustrations.